THE STAY-AT-HOME SURVIVAL GUIDE

Melissa Stanton

THE STAY-AT-HOME
SURVIVAL
GUIDE

Field-tested strategies for staying

smart, sane, and connected

while caring for
your kids

SEAL PRESS

The Stay-at-Home Survival Guide
Field-tested strategies for staying smart, sane, and connected while caring for your kids

Copyright © 2008 by Melissa Stanton

Published by
Seal Press
A Member of Perseus Books Group
1700 Fourth Street
Berkeley, California

Library of Congress Cataloging-in-Publication Data

Stanton, Melissa.
The stay-at-home survival guide : field-tested strategies for staying smart, sane and connected while caring for your kids / Melissa Stanton.

p. cm.
ISBN-13: 978-1-58005-247-4
ISBN-10: 1-58005-247-9
1. Stay-at-home mothers—United States. 2. Motherhood—United States. 3. Parenting—Psychological aspects—United States. I. Title.

HQ759.46S83 2008
306.874'30973—dc22
2007049500

Cover design by Gerilyn Attebery
Interior design by Megan Cooney
Printed in the United States of America
Distributed by Publishers Group West

9 8 7 6 5 4

For my husband and children, of course.

CONTENTS

Why is Stay-at-Home Motherhood Something to *Survive?*

Surely, for some women, being a Stay-at-Home mother is an entirely magnificent, totally blissful, always fulfilling, happily-ever-after dream come true.

This book isn't for those women.

Instead, *The Stay-at-Home Survival Guide* is for all the other women out there who are doing the 24/7, hands-on work of raising children by being full-time Stay-at-Home moms—be they brand new mothers or veterans—and who, from time to time, struggle with the challenges of this kind of in-the-trenches motherhood.

The Guide is for women like me (a Stay-at-Home mother for more than six years) and, I suspect, like you, for whom motherhood and round-the-clock parenting often have as many downs as ups. As with any job (and full-time, Stay-at-Home parenting *is* a job), we have moments of feeling overwhelmed, overworked, unappreciated, and under-compensated. And all that's before the 9:00 AM start of the traditional workday.

Stay-at-Home motherhood is certainly not something a woman needs to survive in the same way one survives disease or trauma or

1

disaster or extreme hardship. Still, the constant demands that come from being the sole adult charged with the care of little minds and bodies (and the surroundings in which they exist) call for a daily routine that many Stay-at-Home moms need both skill and fortitude to survive.

The work involved in full-time parenting is often harder than many women imagined it would be. The initial relief from the pressures of paid employment—or of juggling work *and* family—can be quickly replaced by the demands of our new Stay-at-Home reality, identity, resulting insecurities, and lifestyle complexities. Over time, you realize that you work as many, if not more, hours than you did at a "real" job. And even though as a Stay-at-Home mom you're never without something to do, the day can drag, and entire weeks can feel empty of adult company or personal fulfillment. Then, in the rare instance you get to mingle among grownups without kids clinging to you, someone asks you what you do, and you struggle between saying, "I'm a Stay-at-Home mom . . ." or "Well, I used to be . . ." or some tortured combination thereof. It can make you want to cry.

For a woman who, before motherhood, had a job she enjoyed, experienced career success, lived independently, and had an active social life, setting all that aside for Stay-at-Home motherhood can be a mixed blessing. It's wonderful for a mother to be able to devote herself to the full-time care of her family—without the distractions, stresses, and demands of an office or workplace. It's wonderful for a child to be raised under the constant care of a parent instead of a nanny, sitter, au pair, daycare staff, or afterschool program—or any of the other childcare solutions that parents need to piece together in order to earn an income. In a nation where two incomes are often essential to a family's well-being, and where single parents need a job in order to pay and keep up with the bills, Stay-at-Home mothers are often told how *lucky* they are "not to work."

I know I'm lucky that my family has been able to live securely for several years with only one income. But I'm also a woman who had a significant career as a magazine editor in New York. I once held senior positions at *People* and *LIFE* magazines. I have a master's degree. I have professional skills I want to use, but they've been put on the back burner. Putting those parts of me aside to fill sippy cups and push swings hasn't always been easy on my sense of self.

Women become Stay-at-Home moms because they choose to. They also become Stay-at-Home moms because circumstances require it—such as when quality childcare options aren't available, or too much of the household's income goes toward the cost of daycare, or both parents' jobs are so demanding that neither is home much for the kids. In many cases, the "choice" isn't much of a choice. The reasons women leave the workforce to be Stay-at-Home moms generally boil down to logistics and love.

This book won't go into the details of why the women quoted in these pages have left the workforce to be home with their children. That's the past (and is a topic worthy of an entire book in itself). *The Stay-at-Home Survival Guide* is for the present and the future. It's for the gals—us *lucky* gals—whom many consider to be living the dream or, say some critics, are living in a dream world oblivious to our dependency. (More on that later.)

No matter how firm our Stay-at-Home convictions, there are times—*many, many* times—when Stay-at-Home mothers don't feel lucky at all. Stay-at-Home motherhood is many great things, but it is also exhausting, difficult, uninspiring, isolating, mind-numbing, monotonous, depressing, frightening, self-esteem robbing, and never-ending. In that sense, for a woman to endure the demands of being a full-time Stay-at-Home mom, she'd best have great strength of body, mind, and soul. In other words, she'd best have strong survival skills.

Stay-at-Home mothers come in many varieties. I've met women who are blissfully happy being the 24/7 caregivers (and, in the case of those who home-school, educators) of their children. They are living their dream. The most memorable merry mom I've met was a very pleasant mother of three, a former tennis pro I had invited to join a neighborhood playgroup that would include her youngest and my twins, who were then two.

"I've never been in a playgroup," she responded. "What is it?" This was a mother of three children under age five.

"It's a playdate for kids, but all the moms are there," I explained. "You usually get together once a week and rotate among different houses."

"That sounds nice," she said. "We've never really had kids here or played at other people's houses."

Huh? How had this woman survived all these years? I asked her what she and her children did all day.

"We play, we read books. We have a lot of books," she said.

"Doesn't it make you crazy? Being home alone all day with your kids?" I asked.

"No, not at all," she declared earnestly. "I love playing with my kids."

I've met others like her, but just a handful. These gals are probably exceptional mothers, but they are likely far from the Stay-at-Home mom norm.

In her 1963 manifesto *The Feminine Mystique,* Smith College–grad turned Stay-at-Home mom Betty Friedan wrote about "the problem that has no name," which was the description given by the author for the feelings of sadness and anxiety her Stay-at-Home peers could not shake. Middle-class wives and mothers of Friedan's era were essentially prevented from using their education, intelligence, and professional skills in the workplace. Many employers held that marriage, and certainly motherhood, required a woman to resign her post.

While married women with children are allowed to stay in the workforce today, many can't, due to the realities involved in juggling the demands of work and the needs of a family. And while highly educated women are accused of "opting out" of the workforce to be mommies, many are actually forced or squeezed out for trying to be both an employee and an involved parent. Even if the precise reasons for staying home are different from those experienced by our mothers and grandmothers, the feelings that result can be the same.

Unlike many other books on the subject, *The Stay-at-Home Survival Guide* will not sugarcoat, sentimentalize, or reduce to slapstick the realities of Stay-at-Home motherhood. For those of us who have good days and bad, who sometimes absolutely adore and appreciate being home with our kids and sometimes can't stand it, parenting books in which the author and interviewees gush about their love of being a mom and surrendering to motherhood just don't jibe with all the realities. Ditto the books that joke about the sleepless nights and messy minivans and days without showering—but, alas, each quip or complaint is couched by an "I wouldn't change it for the world" sentiment. For the woman whose every mothering moment isn't a greeting card moment, such rosy pictures can actually be demoralizing: *I don't like playing peek-a-boo and going to the park every day. I don't like being at the beck and call of someone else's moods and needs. Sometimes I don't want to be around my kids. I must be a terrible mom.*

You're not a terrible mom. You're a typical mom.

A couple other notes about the book:

- I am not a commentator, expert, or outsider looking in. (I am *so* in.) And although I do my fair share of naval-gazing in these pages, this book is not about me—my story is a tiny piece of the picture of Stay-at-Home motherhood. As a whole, *The Stay-at-Home Survival Guide* is about capturing the voices, observations, and experiences of women from a variety of locations and backgrounds who are Stay-at-Home mothers. The intent is to learn from fellow Stay-at-Home moms, identify with them, and be supported by them. The reality checks and affirmations of being a Stay-at-Home mom will come from the shared experiences of these women.

- While hiring a full-time nanny or au pair is a fantastic survival technique for a Stay-at-Home mom, this book is for women who can't, or don't want to, take that option (unless required to do so for medical reasons or some other emergency situation). While *The Stay-at-Home Survival Guide* does talk about ways to find a sitter and occasional help, it does not offer any tips on hiring regular domestic staff, such as a full-time nanny, au pair, or housekeeper.

If there's one thing I hope women will learn from this book, it's that *it is okay to sometimes not love being a Stay-at-Home mom.* Women often fear that admitting as much is tantamount to saying to the world and themselves that we regret not being part of the paid workforce. The reality is, sometimes, some of us do regret leaving careers, or wish for something more. That's normal. That's healthy. It doesn't mean we don't love our children. It doesn't mean we'd make a different choice if we had a do-over. It definitely doesn't mean we're bad mothers, or that we're not doing a good job. Few people love their job every minute of the day. The same goes for the job of being a Stay-at-Home mom.

So hang in there! Even though you may be alone in your house right now with *[fill in the applicable number]* child(ren) crying, hanging on you, and demanding your immediate attention, you are not alone. Even though you may feel you're flying a solo mission, you aren't, especially when it comes to your conflicted feelings: 10:00 AM: "Being a Stay-at-Home mother is *great!*" 11:00 AM: "Being a Stay-at-Home mother *sucks!*" Noon: "Being a Stay-at-Home mother is *[fill in an adjective here]!*"

Sound familiar? The personal narratives, reporting, professional advice, and resources contained in *The Stay-at-Home Survival Guide* will hopefully help you "survive" this rewarding *and* challenging time of your life.

Perhaps the best thing about this book is that it doesn't require a big commitment on your part. Believe me, I know you're busy and that getting undisturbed, uninterrupted time to sit with a book and read it straight through is likely a fantasy. That's no problem: *The Guide* was designed to be read in pieces—a chapter, or even a sidebar or page at a time. You can pick it up for five minutes here and there, between Mommy & Me classes, or during your toddler's afternoon nap. And if you fall asleep in the middle of a paragraph, well, good for you! Unlike your children, this Support-Group-in-a-Book will patiently await your attention.

—*Melissa Stanton*

P.S. If you're an expectant, first-time mom who's planning to stay home, please don't let anything said here or elsewhere in this book freak you out. You'll be fine. You'll love your new life with your baby. Just keep *The Stay-at-Home Survival Guide* handy, in case things get tough.

From the Author

I know what you're thinking: *If this woman is a full-time Stay-at-Home mom with no help, how did she have time to write this book?*

It's an excellent question.

Every book is written a word, a sentence, a paragraph at a time. But this book was *literally* written a word, a sentence, a paragraph at a time, often while sitting in my kitchen, stationed in front of my laptop while my three children—a then eight-year-old boy and four-year-old twin girls—played, watched TV, and entertained themselves in the adjacent family room. I wrote while being interrupted at three-minute intervals to fill sippy cups, serve snacks, make meals, help with homework, set up paints, clean spilled paints, tie shoes, and mediate disputes. The process taught me to tune out my surroundings and make the most of small bits of time.

For a while, I secured the help of my twelve-year-old neighbor, Lauren, during which time she'd play with the kids for a couple of hours while I'd attempt to work behind a locked bedroom door. Other times, when I could recruit a college student to baby-sit, I'd escape to the library, a Starbucks or, sometimes, my car, parked out of view of the house. I disappeared on weekends to write, when my husband could take charge of the kids. I wrote during the two hours in the mornings the girls were at preschool. Mostly, I worked the vampire shift, often first sitting down to write at 8:30 PM and going until 1:00 AM most nights, sometimes 3:00 AM. I was able to work at night because most of the interviewing for the book was done by emailed questions to sources and an emailed survey sent to interested Stay-at-Home moms. In many ways, I couldn't have written this book without Anderson Cooper, Jon Stewart, Stephen Colbert, David Letterman, and Conan O'Brien. Those late-night TV gentleman kept me company and kept me awake.

I've been asked to explain why I didn't just hire a sitter to watch the kids while I worked. The not-so-short answer is threefold.

First, it isn't easy to find a part-time, temporary daytime sitter to manage three kids who attend three different, distant schools. As I live in a rural area, I spend most of my day on the road, shuttling children. During the time I was writing the book, there were many days I put one hundred miles on my car just driving my trio to and from schools and one child's speech therapy appointments. As I discuss on page 48, it's hard enough for a mom to safely operate a vehicle containing frequently uncooperative passengers; for me, trusting someone else to safely do so didn't seem worth the risk. (Although I might be jaded, because when I *did* place an ad for an occasional sitter, the gal who responded missed our appointment because she got into a car accident on the way to my house. I kid you not, that's what she told me.) A second reason was the cost of a sitter or, in my case, a sitter-chauffeur. The expense would have likely exceeded the money I was paid for this book.

Granted, both obstacles could have been overcome by not being a cheap worrywart. But I strongly felt that since I was writing a book about and for 24/7 Stay-at-Home moms who have no regular childcare help, I needed to continue to live the 24/7 Stay-at-Home mom life I'd been living. I believe it would have been disingenuous of me to write this book while my kids were in the care of a nanny. Hence, my days and evenings were spent in kid-care mode, my late nights occupied by writing. I became used to the schedule, and even though the book is done, I've kept up the pace by taking on other flexible writing and editing projects. (Thank God for email and the Internet.) In an odd way, the routine actually keeps me motivated and energized.

However, on the mornings after those really late nights spent working on the book, I'd often catnap in the back of my minivan after waking at 7:00 AM and leaving my house an hour later to drive my girls to preschool about twenty miles away. (By the way, as I discuss on page 105, I recommend minivan napping *only* if you have tinted side and rear windows.)

The Survey, and Other Details

Since few Stay-at-Home mothers, myself included, have the time or freedom to hang on the phone or meet in person for in-depth adult conversation, most of the interviews for this book were conducted by email and via a forty-question survey completed by "qualifying" Stay-at-Home moms.

For the purposes of this book, a qualifying Stay-at-Home mom was defined as a woman who is the full-time, hands-on caregiver of her children. She does not have a nanny or a significant amount of hired childcare help. (Although two such moms did send me a completed survey, and their views were of use.) The woman could not be engaged in the full- or part-time workforce, other than for whatever paid work she might manage to do while the kids are in school, are asleep, or can be in the care of her partner. (Work of this type is often taken on to keep skills current, to remain active, or to stay sane. Such efforts rarely provide more than pocket change.)

The survey was distributed nationwide via my friends, former colleagues, acquaintances, mother-related clubs, websites, and chat rooms. More than sixty women responded to the survey in detail.

Several dozen others contributed via emails and during encounters at school events, social gatherings, and children's activities, as well as in waiting rooms and at playgrounds.

Although information about economic status and household income was not specifically requested, I know from the responses and from time spent with many of the women that there is a socioeconomic mix among the respondents. (Perhaps as much of an economic mix as there can be when dealing with families who are able to live on one income.)

The women who responded to the survey represent urban dwellers (Chicago, Seattle, Manhattan) as well as rural residents (Jennifer from Wyoming, among others). The pricey suburbs of Boston, New York, San Francisco, and Washington D.C. are represented, as are communities in places such as New Hampshire, Ohio, Georgia, and upstate New York, which aren't clustered around traditional skyscraper cities. I know that some of the women have big houses, a few have vacation homes, others live in apartments, and at least one mother of three has to schlep dirty clothes to the Laundromat. One woman, who is now very comfortable, was once homeless and spent a summer living out of her car while working and caring for her two toddlers. Although some of the women you'll meet in *The Guide* are married to highly paid doctors, lawyers, investment bankers, or corporate executives, others are living on more moderate incomes, including from military or other government jobs, or on the fluctuating earnings of a business owner or self-employed spouse. The women themselves have a range of backgrounds, from upper-level executives who walked away from six-figure salaries to school teachers or office assistants, for whom it didn't make sense financially or logistically to keep working after having a child or children.

The mothers who appear in the book are identified by their first names only, along with some information about their Stay-at-Home lives: age, number of children, former career. In a few cases, women asked that a pseudonym be used, or for the privacy of others I've assigned one. Basic details about many of the women can be found on page 379 in a section called "The Moms You Met."

TWO NOTES ABOUT TERMINOLOGY

"Am I" or "Was I"? When I refer to the work a woman did before staying home with her children, I use the word "former," as in a "former sales rep" or a "former attorney." I do this to make clear that the woman is a Stay-at-Home mom and is no longer working as a teacher, physician, etc. The reality is, as pointed out by Jen, a lawyer, women who leave the workforce to care for kids don't necessarily lose their abilities or licensing to perform in the occupation that was once their livelihood. "I am still an attorney," says Jen. "I'm just not working as an attorney right now."

Who's "working"? Unfortunately, the English lexicon uses the term "working mother" to describe a woman who has a paid job and also has children. Hence, if a woman has children but doesn't have a paid job, the language implies that she doesn't work. Stay-at-Home mothers *are* working mothers. They work as mothers. So to avoid demeaning myself and my Stay-at-Home peers, and to avoid having to use the construction "working mothers" or "so-called working mothers," I refer to mothers who work at paid jobs as "employed mothers."

INTRODUCTION

Walking Away from Having It All

For fifteen years, I climbed the corporate ladder of magazine publishing, working my way up from an entry-level fact-checker to a senior editor at one of the nation's most popular and profitable magazines. In my career I earned more money than I ever imagined I would. I interacted with newsmakers and celebrities. ("I gotta go, George Clooney is on the other line." Really!) I managed sizeable staffs. I had large offices with windows. And after I had a child, I even negotiated a one-year unpaid maternity leave and then a four-day work week.

But it all came at a price. To get to work in Manhattan, I commuted by car, two trains, and a subway, often more than ninety minutes each way. I never had a nine-to-five day, and I was commonly at the office until after 9:00 PM. When I did leave at a normal hour, I worked on the train or logged into the office from home. While I was at work, my son was cared for by a nanny, whom he stayed with for up to twelve hours a day, until either my husband or I arrived home. Many days, I saw my child awake for less than an hour. He cried when I left in the morning. I spent my days stressed out, worrying about home while I was at work, about work when I was at home.

Yet I went to work, because we needed the money, and also because I had invested so much effort for so many years to get to the level I was at. I had a job people both in and out of my business coveted, and most of the time I really enjoyed my colleagues and my work. I also worked because I felt I had to. Growing up, I'd seen my mother and other women struggle through failed marriages, their economic well-being rising and falling accordingly. No way, I decided early on, would I be economically dependent upon a man. Once I had advanced in my career, I felt a responsibility to my company and to my bosses for allowing me the opportunities I had. I also felt I had a duty to my younger female colleagues, many of whom said I gave them hope that they too could have a family and a high-level career.

In the fall of 2001, everything changed. The stress caused by my juggling act was building. My biological clock was ticking toward a second pregnancy. My nanny, who now had a child of her own, was finding her work schedule with us tiring. And my immediate future promised even more pressure. Staffing at my office had been reduced, so those of us who remained were taking on extra work. My husband, who had been precariously employed by two struggling dotcoms during the prior two years, had just accepted a lucrative job out of the New York area. As a result, he would be living in another city during the work week, leaving me to be a weekday single mom with a demanding job far from our child and home. After the events of 9/11, which my World Trade Center–bound spouse witnessed and ran from when the towers fell, my anxiety about my balancing act increased, until I woke one morning and decided I could no longer stand the way I was living. I decided I needed to change my life—live a different way, work a different way. So I quit my job.

As someone who has always worried about having enough money, who from adolescence saved and tried to prepare against the unexpected, purposely forsaking my career was a move I never imagined. I did envision someday not working the way I was, but I always thought it would be something forced upon me, like in a layoff. A year before I quit, a colleague left her staff job to pursue family-friendlier freelance work, telling me she was no longer letting her fear of the future control her present. It was (and is) good advice. I followed it.

The initial transition from being a career-woman-with-child to a mother-who-worked-when-she-could wasn't as traumatic as I had imagined. I realized that while I wasn't financially dependent upon my husband, I was fully dependent upon my childcare provider. And whenever that arrangement would go awry, as it frequently did, my life would fall apart. By marrying me, my husband had made a commitment to stick with me. My nanny had made no such promise.

The tougher adjustment was in figuring out where I fit in. Like many employed moms, I rose through the corporate ranks. I can manage large-scale projects, and I am able to succeed as either an employee or a boss. But I no longer do any of those things. For a long time, I felt different from most of my Stay-at-Home mom friends, several of whom didn't like their jobs or had long aspired to be an at-home wife and mother. Over time I began to meet more and more women who, like me, were thankful to be home yet sometimes mourned what was left behind.

Perhaps hardest to shake still is the feeling that I've failed in not being able to "have it all." In quitting, have I added fuel to the fire stoked by those who believe women can't have a career and family? Have I put my family and myself at financial risk? Will I end up as a woman who has nothing fulfilling going on in her own life, while her friends who stuck it out will have both a career and children?

Maybe. But I'm trying to look on the bright side. For the most part, I'm not stressed to the hilt anymore. And I don't have aching guilt over whether or not I'm doing right by my family—which, since putting my career on hold, has grown to include twin girls. I like to think that I'm living according to a healthier, female- and family-friendly model. I did one thing for fifteen years. Now I'm a home-based mother and occasional freelance writer and editor. (And, like many at-home moms, I am a dutiful volunteer.)

Once my children are in school all day, I hope to do something else. Why do I have to be one thing all of my life? Why does anyone? Maybe the traditional progress of career—work tirelessly on one path until you get laid off, retire, or die—isn't conducive to women. Maybe women need to follow a different path. I know, for now, I do. Many of the women you'll meet in this book feel the same way. Perhaps you do too.

VOICES

You will notice as you read through *The Stay-at-Home Survival Guide* that the many smart and capable women interviewed and surveyed for this book have a lot to say. Most often, the observations and experiences of these women have been incorporated into *The Guide's* running narrative. But sometimes they just need to be heard directly, like here:

WHAT'S GREAT ABOUT BEING A STAY-AT-HOME MOM?

"There are those snippets of time when your children are so cute, or loving, or teachable or vulnerable—moments you would have missed if you weren't home full-time. I also don't think anyone could love my children like I do. If they drive me crazy, how would someone who didn't have a vested interest in their lives treat them when they misbehave?

—Sarah B.

"To be honest, it's somewhat refreshing to be out of the career track. My successes are now defined by moments of love and quality time, not deadlines."

—Megan

"I was a nanny and a childcare provider in different environments for years, and I quickly realized that if I ever had children, I would want to be home with them. So much happens in those first five years, so many little moments that often nannies are the only ones to witness."
—Jennifer

"I was five months pregnant and working in midtown Manhattan on 9/11. I had been planning on returning to work after a maternity leave—we had a great live-in nanny and I made a good salary—but after that day, none of that mattered, and my decision was a no-brainer. My days, even the crappy ones, are so much more meaningful today because I'm a part of things that I will never have the chance to go back to. I can go back to work. I can go back to New York. I can go back to working in finance, but I can never go back to my children's childhoods."
—Erin Z.

"I love that I have the bond I do with my girls. I absolutely believe it wouldn't be the same if I worked outside the home. I also love the security they have in knowing a parent is with them all the time. Other benefits include being part of my community in a way I'd never been before, being outdoors and enjoying nature more, and all the hugs and kisses any human being has a right to enjoy."
—Gerri

"The stress in our house is less. I manage the household needs— groceries, laundry, the lawn—during the day, so as a family we have the evenings and weekends to spend together with few 'honey-do' lists."
—Pat

"Being able to cherish the baby-ness and toddler-ness of my girls and not have the stress and constraints of daycare and commuter trains. I love being able to live in the moment and not worry about time ticking away."
—Aoife

"After working in corporate America and seeing dysfunctional adults wreaking havoc on their direct reports, colleagues, and even bosses, I think it's so important to spend time with the next generation, as I'm doing with my kids, and care for them so they'll eventually contribute positively to society."

—Sheriene

"Staying at home is intellectually interesting. I have a PhD in animal behavior, and my child is turning out to be an amazing subject!"

—Anne

WHAT'S NOT SO GREAT ABOUT BEING A STAY-AT-HOME MOM?

"I feel I have to constantly convince those who don't stay home, and myself occasionally, that what I'm doing is beneficial and worthwhile, not only for my children, but for me. Being a Stay-at-Home mom can be hard on the ego."

—Sarah B.

"I've had many days when I think to myself, 'I went through all that schooling, and all I do is clean up poop!' I often feel as though people think I have all the time in the world to devote to 'mom' things that they, as busy 'working' people, don't have time to do. My husband will walk by a pile of laundry for days and not touch it except to pick out what he needs. I resent that."

—Jen

"I always knew I would stay home with my children, and I thought it would be nice to leave behind the corporate bullshit, but I had no idea being at home with two children would be ten times more depleting."

—Joni

"I don't enjoy feeding my kids because they are picky, eat like birds, and make a huge mess—at least three times a day. It gets old."

—Kara

"It's been the best choice for my family, but there are days I think a desk job would be a lot easier than being home with a one- and four-year-old."

—Diane A.

"I long for the ability to run an errand without strapping and unstrapping three kids into and out of car seats."

—Annabel

"It's hard not having anyone say what a great job I'm doing. While my husband does say it about once a month, other than that, there's not a whole lot of appreciation around here for what I do."

—Liz H.

"I miss being able to leave in a moment's notice, without preparing a bag to bring along, as well as being able to concentrate on a given task uninterrupted. I also miss sitting down for a meal and not having to jump up a dozen times for the kids."

—Megan

"I hate that some men and a lot of working moms don't think what I do is valuable. The importance of childcare and the impact of childcare workers, including Stay-at-Home moms, just isn't appreciated and valued as much as stereotypically male pursuits. But what's more powerful than molding the future?"

—Heather

The Best of Times, the Worst of Times

There are so many incredible things about being a full-time Stay-at-Home mother, and a goal of this book is to fully acknowledge and celebrate the good stuff.

At a time when most American families need two incomes to get by, and even the youngest children are influenced by the desires and demons of society at large, it is a gift for a child to be cared for at home, by a loving parent. As a mom, it's reassuring not to be dependent upon a nanny or daycare provider to take care of your brood. It's a relief not to worry about home when you're at work and about work when you're at home. It's comforting to know first-hand how your kids are doing during the day, and to know you are providing your child with the love and security too many children in the world grow to adulthood without. Heck, we're even lucky that we were able to make an informed decision about whether or not we would stay home, and that a mother today has the *option* of either staying home to care for her children, staying in the paid workforce, or taking on a bit of both. (Lest we forget, only a generation or two ago, women in the United States had neither societal support or the full legal rights and protections to pursue many options other than marriage and homemaking.)

At the same time, life as a 24/7 Stay-at-Home mom is much like the opening line of *A Tale of Two Cities*, in which Charles Dickens writes, "It was the best of times, it was the worst of times." We've covered some of what's best about being a Stay-at-Home mom; this is what falls on the worst spectrum: Caring for small children is physically tiring and emotionally exhausting. Being out of the paid workforce can make a Stay-at-Home parent financially dependent and vulnerable. The daily grind of caregiving and housekeeping easily wears down even the most devoted mom. All of these experiences, and so much more, are addressed in these pages.

With *The Guide*, you'll hear from experts, me (not an expert by any means), and scores of women who are going through or have gone through what you're experiencing right now or may soon. We'll talk about *everything*—past, present, future, kids, friends, money, marriage, mistakes made, lessons learned, loneliness, socializing, work, new opportunities, future goals, sex (and a lack thereof), sleep (and a lack thereof)—and then some. What you surely know—and if you don't yet, you will—is that Stay-at-Home motherhood is filled with great days and rotten days, and lots of in-between or both days. The best way to enjoy the good and endure the bad is to have great skills and a super support system in your, for the time being, diaper bag.

THE GOOD MOTHER

Aside from the practical challenges of physically caring for children full time, a stressor for many of us—and one that shouldn't come with the territory—is that our society sends notoriously mixed messages to women, particularly in regard to motherhood: "If a woman isn't going to stay home and care for her kids, why did she have them?" we're scolded, followed by statements asserting, "Women who stay home with their children put their families at financial risk." Although females now outnumber males as college undergrads and can reach for the highest rungs of professional success, women in the workforce still need to play the game as played by men; support for families is conspicuously lacking. If a woman wants a child or children *and* needs or wants to also pursue a career, it's essentially up to her to figure out a way to combine the two.

When I left my job in 2001, I did so with trepidation and sadness, but also with the belief that I was doing the right thing by my child, my marriage and—by not juggling so many balls in the air—by me. For my first five years as a Stay-at-Home mom, I lived in a whirlwind that included two years of a commuter marriage, a difficult twin pregnancy, weekday single parenting of a four-year-old and two newborns, a relocation out of state, two house moves, and a renovation. When I finally emerged from my fog, it was to a chorus of writers and social commentators telling me—and countless women like me—that the work we were doing was not only bad for us, it was bad for womanhood at large.

In *Get to Work: A Manifesto for Women of the World,* retired Brandeis University professor Linda R. Hirshman is unwavering in her view that educated women should not leave the workforce. "Bounding home is not good for women, and it's not good for the society," she writes. "The women aren't using their capacities fully; their so-called free choice makes them unfree dependents on their husbands. Whether they leave the workplace altogether or just cut back their commitment, their talent and education are lost from the public world to the private world of laundry and kissing boo-boos." (Hirshman does allow that women needn't forsake their ability to be mothers, and she recognizes that having multiple children can make it hard to also hold down a job. As such, she proposes that women go on a "reproductive strike" and, like her, have only one child.)

In *The Feminine Mistake: Are We Giving Up Too Much?* Leslie Bennetts, a contributing editor at *Vanity Fair* magazine, argues that women who leave the workforce to care for their kids are putting themselves in a potentially terrible situation. It's "too risky," writes the journalist, a mother of two, "to count on anyone else to support you over the long haul."

I don't fully disagree with either author, or the others who've been weighing in on the "work–family debate." Yes, women leaving, or not fully participating, in the workforce has negative repercussions for society at large. Yes, the work of a mother and homemaker can be mind-numbing. Yes, being financially dependent on a man is terribly risky. In this book, Stay-at-Home moms acknowledge all of those things. They talk about the drudgery, they talk about the risk, and they talk about the leap of faith they often make in order to take that risk. The truth is, every work–family choice any woman makes—to work for pay, to not work for pay, to have children, to not have children—has a consequence, and, hopefully, a benefit.

What doesn't help in the discussion is the vitriol and the condescension that comes from those who have a platform from which to make grand pronouncements, like this one Bennetts made while promoting her book: "Among full-time homemakers, [the] overdeveloped capacity for denial is often accompanied by a highly combative sense of indignation about views that challenge their own. In recent years, Stay-at-Home moms have gone on the offensive, demanding that their choices be respected and attacking those who question them."

Who's attacking whom? The truth is, the pendulum swings back and forth: Some years, employed mothers are vilified. Other years, they're praised. Some years, Stay-at-Home moms are the heroes; other years they're the ignorant losers. Each "side," instead of working to support the other (which would be beneficial to all women, and our daughters), gets defensive about choosing either to care for their own children and rely on someone else for financial support, or provide their own financial support but rely on someone else to care for their children.

Neither choice is perfect. And often, the "choice" isn't really a choice. Bills need to be paid, so a parent (or both) go to work. Children need hands-on care, so someone stays home to provide it. Rather than working to level the playing field by making it possible for women and men to both partake in parenting and domestic matters without workforce penalties or societal stigma, politicians and clergy and employers and regular ol' folks focus on the behavior of mothers—or, for that matter, the behavior of *all* women of child-bearing age. Motherhood is too often treated as a spectator sport, with women on the field as its fiercest competitors. It's destructive to us all when either side takes the hit.

I'M NO CAROL BRADY

In *Mommy Wars: Stay-at-Home and Career Moms Face Off on Their Choices, Their Lives, Their Families,* Leslie Morgan Steiner, a *Washington Post* advertising executive and work–family blogger, presents first-person essays by female writers from the "working" and "Stay-at-Home" points of view. In a *Post* article adapted from her 2006 book, Steiner makes her viewpoint clear, saying "I have to work. I wouldn't be myself if I didn't. My job (most days) makes me feel energized, important, successful—a happy mom to my kids." Then, tossing a bone to the other side with a hugely backhanded compliment, Steiner offers that she's "envious of the trust Stay-at-Home moms seem to have in their husbands and in life, a breezy Carol Brady confidence that they will always be taken care of."

I read that article while sitting in the cramped waiting room of a speech therapist's office. I was there with several other mothers who, like me, make the twice-weekly trek so her severely speech-delayed child can partake in a thirty-minute, one-on-one therapy session. Most of us have to drive long distances to be there, and several of us have to drag their child's siblings along as well. As I watched each woman attempt to occupy her children while flipping through a magazine she never actually got to read, I commented to one gal, a mother of four, about the effort each of us had to put into getting our child to such a short therapy appointment. "Tell me about it," she agreed. "To get out the door of my house, I have to find and put on five pairs of shoes, including mine. That involves rounding up ten individual, correctly matched, shoes. That can be harder than it sounds." (And, as any mother who has tried to get out of the house with kids knows, the prep work for actually exiting the home needs to begin long before you have to leave.)

The women in that room were hardworking and tired.

As soon as I got home, I dashed off an email to the *Washington Post*, which printed my edited comments a few days later. (For clarity, I've reinserted some of what the newspaper cut.)

> Having been a "working mom" who is now a Stay-at-Home mom, I can relate to many of Leslie Morgan Steiner's observations. But the only path Steiner understands is the one she's been fortunate enough to take.
>
> Many similarly educated and ambitious women don't have the flexible high-level careers, commutes and child-care options that make Steiner's juggling act possible. I didn't have those family-friendly elements; nor did my husband. So I let go of the career ladder. I now work a sixteen-hour-plus day caring for three children age seven and younger, with no help. I get no sick days or vacations. I don't feel I have, as Steiner says Stay-at-Home moms do, "a breezy Carol Brady confidence that [I] will always be taken care of." For someone who is so "taken care of," I do an enormous amount of work and caretaking.

During my more than six years as a Stay-at-Home mom, even though I've struggled with the requirements and limitations of my new life, I had at least felt somewhat noble in my decision to make caring for and raising my children my full-time job. As Jacqueline Kennedy Onassis famously said, "If you bungle raising your children, I don't think whatever else you do well matters very much."

The repeated anti–Stay-at-Home nattering has made me question my choice. But at the same time, it has made me appreciate the value, intelligence, and resiliency of Stay-at-Home moms.

As a woman many would consider to have "opted out" of the workforce, I also appreciate the observation made by Columbia University labor historian Alice Kessler-Harris, who is quoted in a *Columbia Journalism Review* article titled "The Opt-Out Myth." The term is a myth, and misleading, says Kessler-Harris, who instead looks at mothers leaving the workforce "as redistributing household labor to adequately take care of one's family."

Exactly. When you have children, physically caring for and raising them is a necessary job, not a fallback position because you don't want to "work." (And even if your decision to stay home did have something to do with not liking your career or job, it's unlikely you believed being a Stay-at-Home mom would be a casual, continuously glorious walk in the park.) In a household, the work that needs to be performed has to be taken on by the adults who are available or, if they can't or choose not to do the specific tasks, by hired help. That's one reason the "opt-out" language is unfair: Both jobs—earning an income and caring for children when you have them—are required, not optional, responsibilities. Women don't "opt-out" of careers because it's easier to bake cookies and change diapers. But as is true of people in the workforce who enjoy and get satisfaction out of their jobs, many women love being Stay-at-Home moms because, despite the trade-offs and hardships, they enjoy and get satisfaction out of the job.

"I [love] not feeling like I'm giving 50 percent at work, as a mom, and as a wife," explains survey respondent Beth, a Dartmouth

MBA and pension plan asset manager turned Stay-at-Home mother of two. Cindy, a former attorney and also a mom of two, says, "I enjoy knowing my kids are being cared for by someone who loves them—me." Jen, another attorney at home with two children adds, "I feel fortunate that I can be here and not have to worry about, or be envious of, what my children are doing with their sitter."

The huge truth that's often lost in the motherhood debate is that children don't care for and raise themselves. But much of the pontificating on both sides of the aisle fails to address that reality. Those who acknowledge that, for financial reasons, women *need* to work, and those who advocate that women *should* work, haven't been successful in creating a support system to accommodate the needs of employed women with children. Those advocating that women should give birth, regardless of their desire to have a child or their ability to care for one, fail to support all that happens after that child arrives in the delivery room. Both sides tell women what they *should* do. But when it comes to actually caring for children, parents (and often only mothers) are essentially on their own.

In lieu of perfect solutions, a woman needs to do what's best for herself and the children she has committed to raising. Whatever the choice, it's important to recognize that just as one woman doesn't forsake her love for her children by going to work, another doesn't lose her intelligence, talents, capabilities, and ambition by leaving the workforce to provide the full-time, hands-on care required for her kids.

I keep on my refrigerator a letter published in *The New York Times* in 2006 about the "opt-out" debate. In it, physician Amy B. Tuteur argues that many educated women, having tried to meet the demands of both career and family, "have concluded that there is simply no way to do both jobs well at once." She articulated for me, better than I ever had at the time, my decision about leaving my career for home.

Who Cares for Katie Couric's Kids?

A great mystery surrounding the "smart moms work" arguments are the details about who cares for the kids. How are these über-women able to manage demanding careers and children? How much time do they actually spend with their kids? I'm not judging. I would just like to know the complete picture.

When I was an editor at *People,* I cringed whenever a writer or source gushed about a famous actress or celebrity being a "devoted" mom. It's an empty statement, and one that's hard to reconcile when we see a superstar celebrity, who happens to have children, making movies, posing for fashion shoots, attending parties, appearing on talk shows, traveling the world. While I don't question the love any globetrotting star has for her children, someone is behind the scenes caring for her children while the "devoted" mom is out making millions by being so fabulous. Because there's little transparency about exactly how super successful, celebrated women with children do it all, real-life moms look (and often feel) like a bunch of slackers. For us merely mortal "devoted" moms, children are life- and figure-altering forces.

Like Hollywood stars, jet-setting female journalists appear magical in how they can spend days away from home, often in war zones, tackling serious news and complex issues when they have children at home. I specify female journalists because, unlike their male counterparts, female news celebrities often achieve additional star power through their motherhood status. (Think Katie Couric, a widowed mom of two, and Soledad O'Brien, a mother of four, including twins.) Like many of the don't-stay-home proponents, the public presentation of successful women with children glosses over the practical details of parenthood. For example, accompanying its review of Leslie Bennetts's book, *The Feminine Mistake, People* magazine, my former employer, included a picture of the author's very attractive high school–age son and daughter. In a brief interview with Bennetts, the magazine states, "Your kids don't look scarred." That comment is followed by Bennetts declaring, "Research shows children whose moms work are better socialized—and more likely to do housework themselves!"

Why not ask the author of a book about the risks of women leaving the workforce *how* she was able to have a hard-charging career while also raising such great kids? That information, rather than the assertions that appeared, would have been useful to women who want or need to do the same. For the record: Bennetts had a nanny (who is one of the people she dedicates her book to) and often worked from home.

Professional writers and commentators with media access sometimes act oblivious to the fact that most people can't perform lucrative, flexible, often home-based work. A similarly narrow worldview can also come from women and men lucky enough to have a family-friendly corporate career. An executive I know specializes in work–family matters for her employer. After she had a child, she was allowed to work four days, one from home, yet still receive a full salary because she logged forty hours a week. When I explained that I took a pay cut for my four-day week or lamented my troubles juggling work and family, she'd offer such platitudes as: "Why don't you get in earlier, so you can leave earlier?" Or, "If you work four ten-hour days, you won't need to work a fifth." It was as if, having been blessed to work in an intentionally family-friendly job, she couldn't fully understand that most executive-level people don't work a set shift and punch out for the week at forty hours, or that business meetings often begin at 4:00 PM and end an hour later with marching orders of work to complete in the office before the day is done.

Sometimes the ability to really, *really* have it all depends on each woman's personal definition of having it all. Does it mean work *or* family, work *and* family, work *then* family? Sometimes "having it all" hinges on the ability to subcontract the hands-on care of children, and to have enough money to do so. For others, "having it all" involves an amazingly flexible job. For some people, like us, it may mean needing, choosing, or wanting to step out of the workforce, for a while, or even forever, to manage one or more really important, make-or-break projects called [*fill in the name(s) of your child(ren) here*].

TWO

A Day in the Life

Following is the actual text of a late-night email I received from Jessa, a Stay-at-Home mother of two preschoolers:

> Everyone celebrates motherhood, but we mothers feel guilty for not loving every second of motherhood, and no one really wants to hear us say we actually do not like it all the time. How blasphemous, huh??!!! Just today I was playing with my kids outside to stay sane, and I was thinking how fricking *bored* I was. How much I love them to death but how *bored* I was playing on the swings, bikes, etc.

Jessa and I crossed paths as volunteers for a local mothers' organization. While working on the club's newsletter, she and I casually emailed moments of maternal malaise back and forth. Knowing that Jessa and other moms like her exist helps me in my daily life as a full-time Stay-at-Home mom. It's comforting to know that despite truly loving my children and having chosen to devote prime years of my adult life to staying home to care for them, there are women who, like me, sometimes get "fricking *bored*" entertaining a child on the playground. It's reassuring to know that there are other women to whom an impatient child's whine of "Mommy, Mommy" can be as nerve-wracking as fingernails scraping across a chalkboard.

I also think it can be reassuring for new mothers to hear comments from new moms such as Jennifer D., a survey respondent who left a management career at a Big Four accounting firm to care for her child. "I feel like I'm supposed to love every minute of being with my son," she says. "But sometimes I just want time to myself that isn't for him or my husband."

Like many women with colicky babies or hard-to-handle children, Stay-at-Home mom Molly, a former project manager, felt she was the only person who could tolerate caring for her high-maintenance infant, who's now two-and-a-half years old. "My son has been a handful from day one," she says. "I spent many sleepless days and nights wondering how a daycare worker would handle his incessant crying and no sleeping. Motherhood is the hardest job I've ever had. I think 'work' would be like a vacation. Sometimes I dream about it, in that respect, just to get a mental break."

Such sentiments, which most of us have at some time, don't make us bad mothers. They do make us human, and real. Unfortunately, the reality of motherhood often conflicts with the version depicted by parenting guides and advertisements in which mothers are euphoric (in some cases almost *orgasmic*) simply from cradling their infants to their breasts, or pushing toddlers on a swing. Those warm, fuzzy moments do occur, but not every minute of the day.

"Many moms are ashamed to feel negative about their situation, because they made this choice and they love their children," says Laura, a Stay-at-Home mom of two preschoolers who was once a linguist in the U.S. Army. "But it's hard to never have an uninterrupted conversation. Between napping needs, eating needs, and behavioral issues, it's hard to go anywhere on a regular basis for any amount of time. And even when you do get out, your kids are with you, and they want and need your attention."

And then there's the monotony and routine.

"Many days I live the movie *Groundhog Day*," says Cindy, one of several moms who compared her life to the 1993 film in which Bill Murray keeps reliving the same day. A lawyer and mother of two, Cindy has been a Stay-at-Home parent for seven years. "It's the same day, over and over," she observes. "It's also the ultimate catch-22. I adore my children, but my twelve-hour-plus days with them are brutal. I find it hard to be around *anyone* for more than twelve hours a day. I wind up yelling a lot more than I would like to admit."

Several moms, me included, yell a lot more than we'd like to admit. My own mother, who had three children, was a screamer, and I vowed never to become the hysteric I remember her to be. I was great with my son, but when the twins arrived and I too became a mother of three, the screamer in me emerged. I feel terrible about it. But knowing that other moms sometimes lose it too helps me not feel like a total monster. "I need to work on my patience," admits Amy, a mother of two. "Sometimes I snap at my kids, and you can just see it in their eyes when it's not deserved."

It really does take an enormous amount of love and self-control to not scream at (or run screaming from) a little creature that doesn't let you out of its sight, insists on being carried, barks orders, covers you with gross fluids, and routinely cries, shrieks, and kicks. As Anne, a biologist expecting her second child, points out: "Providing the scaffolding for a child's life is not glamorous."

I keep a clipping in my wallet from an article about parenting in which Scott Smith, a Maryland-based psychologist, is quoted as saying, "It takes a special kind of person to be a Stay-at-Home parent. You have to be calm, nurturing, warm, expressive, and patient." I showed that article to my husband. He read the clip, then looked at me and said, "Wow, that's not you at all." (For the record, I protest: I believe I am nurturing, warm, *and* expressive.)

Raising children to adulthood requires a variety of skills, and those of us (female or male, at home or employed) who do the job are better at some aspects of it than others. Raising children to adulthood is work. And for a Stay-at-Home mom, it's work done for hours on end. But by looking at Stay-at-Home motherhood as a job (and, dare we say it, a job more important than most "real" occupations people are paid to do), women can cut themselves some slack for their occasional negativity and frustration. We can love and enjoy our children while acknowledging we do not love and enjoy every minute of every day spent devoted to their care.

WORKING FIVE TO NINE

A typical day for a Stay-at-Home mom—including her "on duty" hours and her opportunities for interaction with other adults— varies greatly, depending on the number of children she has, their ages, her family's finances, her home, and the woman herself. One of the ironies of Stay-at-Home motherhood is that although you have many peers, and your neighborhood may be filled with women just like you, you work alone and, as a result, you spend much of your day alone (save for the company of children).

Caring for and cleaning up after kids puts everything else—housekeeping, cooking, personal hygiene—at the bottom of the to-do list. Women with newborns literally work around the clock. Moms with older babies often wake up at or before dawn, and while that child probably naps during the day, he doesn't go down for the night until after dusk. It's quite common for a mother to start her day at 5:00 AM and not be done with kids and household tasks until 9:00 PM or later. Mothers of very young children often don't get out of the house, or even out of their pajamas, for what feels like weeks, because they have to plan their days around naps and feedings.

As a mom to three young children, my day typically starts at seven and ends at midnight, even when I'm not writing a book. Once the kids are all down by nine, I'm up for several hours doing the banking, paperwork, and emails; getting life in order for the next day; maybe reading or watching a TV program; spending time with my husband; or simply enjoying the late-night quiet of my home. Because my day is spent in the service of three children who attend three different, very distant schools, I can no longer commit to playdates or join other moms for daytime kid outings. If a woman has several children, it's likely she has been accompanied by a child every minute of that seventeen-hour day. It's also likely she hasn't eaten well (mac and cheese, anyone?) or sat down (other than while driving).

Lots of moms, not wanting to spend an entire day stuck in the house, keep themselves and their preschoolers busy with playground visits, playdates, mother–child classes, library story times, or walks in the mall. I knew a mother of three who was so insistent that her kids not nap during the day—lest they stay awake beyond their eight o'clock bedtime—that she ran her brood ragged from morning til night.

Busyness, however, doesn't negate boredom. Because mother-hood can lend itself to being busy but bored, some women get through the day by turning basic tasks into major undertakings, just to have something involved and mildly interesting to do. When you're trying to kill or fill time, errands can become major events. Baking and decorating cupcakes become the day's achievement. Planning a first birthday party becomes as involved as planning a surprise bridal shower. Or, women lower the bar of their expecta-tions: A day in which the beds get made and the sink is clean is considered full and successful.

For women who survive the baby and preschool years and re-main Stay-at-Home moms, there is a payoff. These moms, whose kids are now in school all day, can finally meet a pal for lunch or get involved in daytime activities. Working from home or very part-time may also be an option. But come three o'clock, they're back on duty for bus pickups, sports practice, dinner, homework, orthodontist appointments, and overall hands-on parenting and supervision.

Why You Didn't Vacuum (or Take a Shower)

The next time you wonder why you ran around all day but got nothing done, here's what likely happened:

Little children have short attention spans: There's a reason activities at nursery school are planned for ten- or fifteen-minute blocks of time. Preschoolers typically can't stick to a particular activity for much longer. The same happens at home. You set your child up with crayons and paper, which occupies her until she gets thirsty, or the crayon she is using breaks, or she gets frustrated that she can't draw a cat. There's very little a small child can do on his or her own that will provide a mom with the amount of time needed to actually get something of substance done.

Some children need constant supervision: It's amazing how much trouble a toddler can get into when a grown-up isn't looking. One of my daughters is a human tornado. She'll go into her dresser to get a shirt but empty the entire drawer. She stops up toilets by using too much paper. I have a friend whose two-year-old is such an escape artist he snuck out of the house, hopped into a motorized kiddie car that was kept in the garage, and drove himself to a friend's house two blocks away.

Siblings: When a mother has more than one child, much of her day is spent catering to one child or another, mediating disputes, or even having to protect the kids from each other.

You're worn out: By 9:00 AM you've been at work for several hours, even though the official workday for most employed persons is just starting. Enough said.

THE STAGES OF STAY-AT-HOME PARENTING

Although Stay-at-Home moms often don't have free time in common with each other, there's a great commonality to the cycle of their typical day, depending on which phase of motherhood they're in. I think of the phases as follows:

- Phase 1: Stay-at-Home Mom to Stay-at-Home Children
  This includes moms of newborns, babies, toddlers, and preschoolers.

- Phase 2: Stay-at-Home Mom to Stay-at-Home and School-Age Children
  One or more of the above coupled with at least one full-day student.

- Phase 3: Stay-at-Home Mom to School-Age Children
  All kids are in school, all day!

Each phase is difficult and wonderful in its own way. For example, I'm in Phase 2 right now. And while I miss the coziness of Phase 1 (its napping, cuddly babies), I don't miss the isolation and the constant carrying, diaper changing, and child-proofing. Like many Phase 1 and Phase 2 moms, I fantasize about the relative freedom that comes in Phase 3. As Jessa wrote me: "I hope you have a special chapter for Stay-at-Homes who parent kids under the age of five. It has to be a whole different ballgame staying at home if your kids are away at school for seven hours a day, right?"

Phase 1: Stay-at-Home Mom to Stay-at-Home Children

A typical day for Whitney, a mother of a two-and-a-half-year-old and three-month-old, is spent mostly at home and is dictated by meals, breastfeeding, diaper changes, and naps (for the kids, not her). As her son is a nursing infant, she works nights as well.

"I wake up at 6:00 or 7:00 AM, change my daughter's diaper and feed her breakfast, during which time my son wakes up and I need to change and breastfeed him. I play with both children until I either put my son down for his morning nap or, if the weather is good, try to get him to sleep in the sling so I can take my daughter out for some fresh air.

"We're back in the house for lunch. We eat. I change diapers again, breastfeed, and then attempt to put both children down for a nap. If I'm lucky, this works, and I get some time to myself. That usually doesn't happen. By the time my son finally naps, my daughter is about to wake up. I change her and make her a snack. If I didn't get out of the house that morning, I'll try to get us all to a park. Otherwise, we'll stay home and play inside so my son can have at least one or two good naps at home.

"I get somewhat of a break when my husband comes home. We prepare dinner together. Then I start the bedtime routine for my son while my husband and daughter play. He does her bedtime. We try to get both kids to bed between seven and eight."

Phase 1 is the boot camp of parenting, especially during the first year as a first-time mother, when parenthood is a new, grueling, frightening, but exciting experience. Making it through feels like a real achievement. Sore nipples? Done that. Colicky baby? Been there. Sleepless nights? Lived through 'em. Mommy & Me classes? Aced each one! Like a good marine, some women reenlist and move on to the second child. When both little ones are home with mom all day, motherhood is a bit like trench warfare: You're in the midst of the action, most all of which takes place within arm's reach. The next theater of operation? The advancing and ever-shifting front lines.

Phase 2: Stay-at-Home Mom to Stay-at-Home and School-Age Children

A typical day for Deb, a mother of three—ages seven, four, and sixteen months—involves short spurts at home or at various destinations and a lot of getting kids into and out of the car.

"I'm awakened around 5:45 AM, either by my sixteen-month-old or by my husband getting ready for work. He leaves at 6:30. I pack lunches, make the beds, empty the dishwasher—all the incredibly mundane tasks I never thought would take up so much of my time and thoughts—and get my seven-year-old off to school by 8:30. I'm then home with my four-year-old and the baby. I drive my middle child to school at 12:30, all the while praying the baby won't fall asleep in the car and waste her nap for the day. If the baby naps at home, I try to exercise, straighten the house, pay bills, or make phone calls.

"After I get my daughter from elementary school at 2:30, the three of us pick up my son from preschool. We come home, and I make what seems like endless snacks. This is my least favorite time of the day. I try to get dinner ready, but everyone is fussy. My husband gets home around 6:30, and we eat, clean up, get the kids ready for bed, and read to them. We are finally finished around nine, and we're exhausted. I'm typically in bed by ten or ten-thirty."

Deb has a hectic day. But get a load of Heather's. She's a thirty-year-old mother of three, ages six, four, and two:

"I'm up by 5:30 AM to make my husband's breakfast and pack a lunch for my four-year-old and a school snack for my six-year-old. I take a shower, get dressed, and make breakfast for myself and the children. By 8:30 we leave to get my four-year-old to preschool by 9:00. We sometimes stay and visit for a while. I'm usually home by 10:30 and making lunch for my youngest and oldest, because we leave in an hour for kindergarten. I then have ninety minutes with just my two-year-old. We run errands, or I clean the house, before it's time to get my four-year-old. At 3:15 I'm at the school to get my six-year-old. We come home. The kids and I eat dinner. I give them a bath, read one story each, and then a chapter book to get them into bed between 7:30 and 8:30 PM. I then tidy up until my husband comes home and has dinner. I'm learning Dreamweaver to help him with his website, so I sometimes work on that from whenever I get the kids to bed until around 11:30 PM. If I have laundry, I usually stay up until it's all folded.

"Also, each week I have to go grocery shopping and do at least twelve loads of laundry in a community laundry facility with just two washers and dryers. I trade carpool to preschool once a week with another mom, so I try to do the laundry that day, since to get it done, I have to be home for five hours straight. I usually go from my apartment to the machines every forty minutes to add extra quarters and change the loads. I also make an effort to squeeze in soccer and gymnastics classes for the kids, a weekly knitting playgroup (moms knit, kids play) and a hiking playgroup."

Defensive Driving

Before we move on to Phase 3, it's critical to mention an aspect of Stay-at-Home parenting that most all Phase 1 and Phase 2 moms share, and that is the logistical challenge involved in going anywhere. Strollers, car seats, infant carriers, backpacks, and diaper bags are among the many pieces of equipment a mother needs in order to get herself and her children out of the house. While urban moms struggle with getting kids into and out of taxis, up and down train station staircases, and through busy sidewalks and streets, suburban and rural mothers have to overcome the difficulty of driving alone with children in the car.

Because of car seat laws, infants ride in the backseat, facing to the rear of the vehicle. (It's as if babies are relegated to that safe spot in order to protect them from their own and other mothers trying to drive while twisting a right arm backward toward a baby's face.) Having a crying child out of reach while you're driving is a nightmare scenario for every mother. Even when no one fusses, a mom knows she's on borrowed time until the demands start to spill forth from her passengers.

I'm always impressed by the ability of mothers to drive safely while being bombarded by such distractions, which, depending on one's bundles of joy, may be more of a driving hazard than talking on a cell phone or having downed a glass of wine. Like school bus drivers, mothers operate high-powered vehicles under demanding driving conditions. Considering all that's stacked against us, women with children are excellent drivers.

When my kids fuss in the backseat and demand my assistance or intervention, I often shout back, "I'm not an octopus! I have two arms, not eight! I need at least one arm for driving the car, and the other can't reach you! Cut it out!" While they wish I were an octopus, I actually wish I was Helen Parr, aka Elastigirl, the stretchable, long-limbed mom in the movie *The Incredibles.*

But, as the saying goes, this too shall pass. A time will come when your car won't be crammed full of car seats, and your children will be able to manage their own seatbelts. And a time will come when each baby-turned-toddler-turned-preschooler matures enough to spend most of his or her day unattached to a hands-on caregiver. When this occurs, many a Stay-at-Home mom stands at the proverbial fork in the road, faced with the choice between (using the generally accepted turns of phrase) "going back to work" or continuing to "stay home." Since continuing to stay home to care for a family *is* work, this fork really represents a choice between choosing to reenter the paid workforce or continuing to work as a Stay-at-Home mom, albeit with different hours and fewer physical demands than before.

Phase 3: Stay-at-Home Mom to School-Age Children

Lyn, a mother of three—ages eight, ten, and twelve—describes her schedule as varying depending on the time of year—the different "seasons," which she characterizes as "normal life, the volunteering season, and summer."

"Most days start at about 5:30 AM, with packing lunches, making breakfast, dealing with school papers, and getting my head together for the day. I wake the kids; get them fed, dressed, packed, and off to the school bus. I then start doing all the typical household tasks: paying bills, grocery shopping, errands, housekeeping, waiting for repair people, and so on. It's nothing earth shattering, but the more time I have, it seems, the more tasks I have. The kids get home around 3:30 PM, and the rest of the day is spent managing their needs and getting them to various sports practices. My husband and I both coach sports, so it can be days before he and I have time together to even have a conversation. Summer has the same family responsibilities as the rest of the year, but without the pressure of school, it's somehow more relaxed. I have friends who dread the day school ends, because their kids are home all day every day. I look forward to it.

"When my youngest entered kindergarten, I did think about going back to work. But then I took on a large volunteer project at the kids' school that lasted for nearly four years and involved hours of computer work, phone calls, and meetings. It was like having a real job, except it carried none of the sympathetic benefits earned from having had a hard day at the office."

Survival Tips from a Professional Nanny

Latonya Nicholas has worked as a full-time nanny for more than a decade, during which time she also attended night school to become a registered nurse. Although not yet a mother herself, Latonya has more experience as a Stay-at-Home caregiver and mom than most mothers. She has cared for newborns and school-age children, often at the same time, while typically working an eleven- or twelve-hour day. Following are her tips for surviving a day home alone with little children.

HAVE CHILDREN FOLLOW A ROUTINE

Example:

1. Wake up
2. Make your bed
3. Brush your teeth, wash, get dressed
4. Eat breakfast
5. Have a little fun-time (playing a game, working on a project, or watching a favorite show)
6. Get out the door for school, an activity, or camp

KIDS WILL DO WHAT YOU WANT, SO LONG AS IT'S FUN

So, let them assist you in:

- making meals
- unloading the dishwasher
- folding clothes
- watering plants
- setting the table
- dusting
- sweeping the floor

It may take more time to complete the task, and the job won't be done perfectly, but the point is to have fun, keep the kids busy, and teach them to do such chores themselves.

SCHEDULE PLAYDATES

Playdates should include fun activities and snacks. One-on-one playdates are best. Start with a one-hour get-together if it's your first time having that friend over. Depending on the age of the child, you might want the mother to stay, to be with her child and so you get to spend time with another adult. While you can prepare games and activities for the kids to do, also allow them to play on their own. Children need to learn how to share and solve problems without adult intervention.

TRY TO FIND FRIENDS (FOR YOU) WHO HAVE SIMILAR SCHEDULES

If you do, you can:

- take turns with drop-off and pickup from school
- have brunch together
- schedule playdates with your kids, so you can visit with each other
- join forces to take your respective children on a field trip or outing

TO DEAL WITH MISBEHAVING CHILDREN

- Identify the problem: Is the child tired, not feeling well, hungry, or truly being mean and cranky?
- Assess the problem: Talk to the child about it, try to solve it or talk it through.
- If the misbehavior continues, consider a timeout or take away a favorite toy. (Make sure the punishment is age appropriate.)
- When all else fails, make sure the child is okay and in a safe place—and then *ignore* him or her. Kids pretty much act on your reactions. If you don't show you're upset, the child will eventually tire of fighting a losing battle.
- When the child decides to behave, acknowledge the good behavior. Thank her for acting better than she did before. Show her that behaving is better than misbehaving, and reward her for it. (The reward can be an actual treat or just a hug and a high five.) Children love to be rewarded and will try more often to behave than misbehave.

WHY KIDS OFTEN BEHAVE BETTER FOR SITTERS, TEACHERS, AND OTHER ADULTS THAN THEY DO FOR THEIR PARENTS

- With parents, children know what buttons to push and how far they can go. Many parents threaten punishments for

misbehavior but don't follow through. A sitter, teacher, relative, or other adult may be more likely to actually do what she says she'll do if the child doesn't shape up.
- Also, children like when other people tell their parents they were good.

TO NOT GO WACKY BEING HOME ALL DAY WITH KIDS

Try to talk to other adults everyday. As a nanny, I often need to chat with another nanny who has been through and understands a situation I'm dealing with. It helps a lot. It's also great to be part of a support team, to have people you help and who you can call on to help you.

IS BEING A FULL-TIME NANNY AS HARD AS BEING A STAY-AT-HOME MOM?

Yes, because I do exactly what a Stay-at-Home mom does all day. No, because I don't start and end my day with children, and when I'm not working, I can have entire days without having to care for children. My job is hard, but if I had my own kids, it would be so much harder.

THE HOLY GRAIL

All the kids are in school, *all day!* In many ways, these Stay-at-Home women are living the dream shared by mothers who stay home with small children *and* those who work outside the home. The envy can be palatable, as I experienced during an email go-around between several women in a club I belong to.

One gal, a Stay-at-Home mom, wrote asking if anyone wanted to join her at a midweek, midday movie. To be inclusive, she made the offer to everyone. Many of the Stay-at-Home moms with school-age children answered with an enthusiastic yes. I declined, explaining that I'm tied to my kids by day until my coming out party in September 2008 (when my twins begin full-day kindergarten). The employed women responded to the matinee invite with comments along the lines of "It must be nice" and "I have to *work* for a living," inspiring meow moments among very good and supportive friends.

Some Phase 3 moms are busy with volunteer work so intense they essentially have part-time jobs. Some are busy with errands and household tasks that can't be done once their older children arrive home and need help with homework, need to be driven to and fro, and need to be supervised. (Babies and toddlers are hard, but tweens and teens bring their own special challenges.) I do know women who are lonely being home much of the day. I also know some who are bored and would like to work but can't find a job—or one worth taking—that has the flexibility they still need. For others, the hours they get to spend on their own just somehow fill up: Getting ready to go to the store. Going to the store. Shopping in the store. Traveling home from the store. Putting the groceries away. All of those steps provide some women with several hours of needed activity.

Conversely, when you're a mom with all of your kids at home, or in preschool very part-time, a supermarket run becomes something you do as quickly as you can, during your two hours of non-kid time or before your preschoolers have a meltdown. When you're crazy busy with small children, it's hard to empathize with people who seem to have all the time in the world.

For those of us who don't yet have (or may return to the work-force before getting) five, six, or seven daytime hours *on our own,* the idea of such freedom is like nirvana, heaven on Earth, the elusive Holy Grail. Imagine being able to get to the projects around the house you haven't been able to do! Imagine being able to work part-time, exercise, volunteer, see friends, veg out, do errands without kids in tow! Imagine being able to do all those things . . . at least until 3:00 PM, when you're back on the mother clock.

When you're a Stay-at-Home mom to small children, your days are filled with lots of good moments and bad (hopefully more of the former than the latter). Since little ones have wills and needs of their own, unblemished days are rare. As a new mom juggling feedings and nap schedules, you think you'll never leave your house again. As a mom to multiple children of varying ages, you may be on the road so much, shuttling kids between schools and activities, you long to return to that housebound era. And once the kids are big enough to be in school all day, you may actually miss having them underfoot. Like many jobs, Stay-at-Home motherhood can seem monotonous day after day. Unlike many jobs, however, it changes greatly over the years.

Survival Tips from the Front Lines

Kelly O'Brien of Annapolis is a Stay-at-Home mother of two preschoolers. She is also a PhD who, in her pre-mom life, was a human factors engineer working with the U.S. military to determine what soldiers needed their weapons and equipment to do. (Among her credits are the cockpit controls in the Apache longbow helicopter.)

Following are her (battle)field-tested parenting strategies:

Formula: Since baby formula is strictly regulated, and all brands are virtually the same nutritionally, you can save a lot of money by purchasing a store brand (such as from Target or Costco) instead of a brand-name formula.

Taking a shower: If you have a separate soaking tub and shower stall in your bathroom, put your crawling baby, a no-slip mat, and some toys in your bathtub to contain your child while you shower. (If you think your babe might turn on the water, either remove the faucet handles or cover them with a childproofing device.)

Don't lose mittens: Sew a mitten to each end of a shoelace so the pair is connected by a string. Take your child's coat and thread one mitten through the opening of one sleeve, and then weave it out from the opening of the other sleeve. (So the string will nestle between your child's back and the inside of the coat.) Leave the mitten-ribbon in place for the season.

Child-Proofing: Stretch a hair scrunchy across cabinet knobs to keep very little children out. To keep toddlers from getting into the trash, put small trash receptacles up high and out of reach, such as on tabletops or on top of the toilet tank.

Craft containers: Empty baby-wipe containers are great for storing crayons, markers, and other art supplies.

Dual supplies: If you live in a two-story home, duplicate your most-used toiletries (toothbrush, toothpaste, sunscreen, lipstick) in the downstairs powder room so you don't have to keep climbing the stairs carrying an infant. Do this for diapers and changes of kid clothes as well.

Toy clutter: Store random baby toys in laundry baskets. They're safe, portable, and useful once the kids get bigger and the toys change—and, of course, for laundry.

Eat in peace: While you eat dinner, occupy your already-fed toddler by letting him or her gnaw on an empty cake-style ice cream cone in a high chair. If you're really daring and don't mind some mess, let your toddler "fingerpaint" on his high chair tray with whipped cream or ketchup.

OTHER MOMS SUGGEST:

Get fresh air: Since cooped-up mothers and kids tend to get cranky, sometimes the best (and only) thing you can do is to change the scenery by simply going outside. "I can remember one winter day when it was about 10 degrees out," recalls survey respondent Nancy. "But I was determined to get us out of the house. It took me thirty minutes to bundle-up my baby and toddler in order to walk around my condo complex just to get some fresh air. I then spent the next thirty minutes unbundling them. The walk outside was the highlight of our day."

Healthy eats: Mary, who is home with two preschoolers, suggests that moms prepare vegetables first when making dinner. "That way, when children complain they're starving, you can give them a bowl of veggies to snack on," she says. "It makes for a less stressful dinner, since the kids have already had their vegetables." She also advises bringing vegetables as play-ground and pool snacks: "Kids are less picky eaters when they're really hungry."

Snip in a clip: Mother of two Andrea believes that every mom is well-served by keeping a pair of small scissors in her purse. "I find a use for them almost every day," she says. "My favorite was when my kids were first trying to drink from fast food cups using straws. They always struggled and tipped the drink because the straw was too tall. I would pull out my scissors and shorten the straw." Other uses: Removing irritating clothing tags, cutting a balloon string that's been knotted on to a child's wrist, opening a snack package, and clipping gum out of a ponytail.

Port-a-Potty: Keep a plastic potty, plastic grocery bags, tissue or toilet paper, and wipes in your car for times your trained toddler needs to go but can't wait for you to find a real bathroom. A one-piece, molded potty is best so you can dump the "contents" along the side of the road and clean the potty with water or a baby wipe. For number-two events, place a plastic grocery bag in the potty so the mess (including the toilet paper) can be contained in the bag, tied up, and tossed in a trash can. Boys have the added advantage of being able to pee in the bushes or directly into an empty, plastic beverage bottle. (Little boys love the bottle option. Just make sure you don't lose the cap!)

Staying connected: When your kids are old enough to venture out a bit on their own—such as to school or a friend's house—you can provide them with a cell phone that you've programmed so only certain numbers can be called or received. Having a phone can be useful if a child gets off at the wrong school bus stop, or if a parent is running late for pick-up and needs to tell the child what to do. Some cell phones even come with kid-tracking GPS systems. On a similar but less technical note, Liz R., a mother of

► three active boys, advises that a parent's name and phone numbers be noted on or inside a child's bicycle helmet, backpack, coat, or sports uniform. "That way, if you're not right there, you can be reached if your child is hurt," she says.

Several Kids, Special Needs,
but Still Just One You

It's 5:00 PM on a Wednesday. We've been back in the house for less than a half-hour after school pickups and karate, but my eight-year-old son is already arguing with one of his four-year-old twin sisters over whose turn it is to sit on the sought-after red chair. As I mediate the chair debate, I'm clearing snacks and drinks from the kitchen counter while attempting to wash watercolors off of my other daughter.

Channeling Goldie Hawn from her *Laugh–In* days, my own golden-haired girl has decorated most every surface of her exposed skin with purple and green paint. Before I can scoop her into the sink for a wipe-down, I have to empty the dishwasher to make room for the dirties awaiting their turn. I'm also ready to keel over from the stench of the hamster cage, which I *planned* to clean after doing the dishes and starting dinner and getting my son to begin his homework . . . until my painted lady made her debut.

During times like these, I look at the chaos of my kitchen and the children who are fighting me, each other, and the order of my home, and I wonder, as the Talking Heads asked, *How did I get here?* What I wouldn't give to go back in time ten years, when 5:00 PM would find me in my Manhattan office, working at a job I enjoyed, and later, when I felt like it, heading home to an evening alone with my husband, or maybe out with friends. At the same time on any given weekday in my present reality, I don't want to be in the company of my bickering, havoc-wreaking, relentlessly needy children.

But as the day turns to night and the harried activity begins to wane, I can describe to my husband, with a laugh, our daughter's experimentation with body art and her exhibitionist second act, when she shed her clothing and ran naked through the house as her siblings screamed in delight. When I tried to dress her, she took hold of my face, declared "No, Mommy," and gave me a big kiss on the lips.

When there's finally calm in my kitchen, and I start sorting through the paperwork that generates from and for a family of five, I can talk to my other daughter about how amazing she was in her karate class that day. I can enjoy her smile and the enthusiasm she can't contain about finally being able to play a team sport like her big brother does. "I'm still so excited about soccer," she tells me, nearly a week after her first Saturday-morning practice. My dark-haired daughter never holds back her emotions. While her bad moods are horrors, her good ones can be truly grand.

Once the girls are in bed, I can have one-on-one time with my son, the way I did before his sisters arrived. When he asks, "Mommy, will you cuddle with me tonight?" I try to say yes. I know that in a year or so, he won't even want me within arm's reach. When I describe the changes to come, my son assures me, with complete sincerity, "That won't happen, Mommy. You can cuddle with me until I leave for college."

Would I ever trade the life I have with my children? Of course not. Just don't ask me on a weekday afternoon.

As a mother of three, two of whom are twins, one of which has some special needs, my day revolves around constant demands, minicrises, and someone always having a need that (they believe) must be immediately met. We can all picture the idealized image of motherhood, either from a TV commercial or our own pre-kid fantasies, wherein one complacent child quietly colors while his mother sits at his side smiling and sipping a mug of herbal tea. That's not me, nor—if you have more than one child—do I expect it's you.

THE MORE THE MERRIER—AND THE BUSIER

You've surely heard the saying, or a variation of it: "Having two kids is twice as hard as having one, but having three kids isn't twice as hard as two."

I disagree. Three is hard, if for no other reason than mothers have two hands, not three. I now realize how easy it was to have just one child. I stayed home with my son for his entire first year. Although I had many moments of boredom and tiredness, I also learned so much about him and myself. It truly was fascinating to see how my son changed week by week. It felt like a real accomplishment when the two of us made it to his one-month birthday, his two-month birthday, and so on. Everything about the experience was new, and often challenging. I am so thankful I was able to be part of every minute of that first year. My only sadness is that my son doesn't remember any of the wonderful things we did together when he was my only child. His memories of me are more likely to be of a too-busy, often overwhelmed woman stressed out by three children.

I love my girls, but since they weren't the first, their infancy wasn't as fascinating as my son's. Because they're twins, and I was without help most of the time, caring for them was constant, frequently terrifying, work. Unlike with my son, I didn't have time to cradle a baby for hours in my arms while she slept. And because the girls have always been with me, I don't have the absence-makes-the-heart-grow-fonder moments I had with my son when I went back to my magazine job just before he turned one.

A 2007 study concluded that first-born children, or those raised as the oldest child, score higher on IQ tests than the siblings that come after. Parental attention, not genetics, was offered as a possible cause, since parents of one child have more time and energy to devote to that child's social and intellectual development. The study was criticized for its small survey pool (Norwegian men) and insignificant conclusions (the IQ spread typically differed by only three points between the eldest and second child). Still, it's not hard to image that birth order does have some impact.

As the oldest of three, I know I had time to be special to my parents and grandparents. Conversely, as the eldest child of divorced parents, I was also handed a lot of responsibility earlier than most kids. My husband, who is the third of five, is differently affected by having been one of a crowd. While he had the benefit of lots of playmates at the ready, he didn't get a ton of one-on-one parental attention. It wasn't possible: His dad worked six days a week, and his Stay-at-Home mom gave birth to five children in seven years.

That's a tough routine for a young couple. Parents, particularly mothers, just can't give as much to consecutive children as they can to the first, and perhaps to whomever ultimately gets to be the baby or has the most pressing needs (due to medical issues). That's a reality, not an insult. Nor does it mean a parent loves later children any less.

Still, moms of many often feel bad. "I always have a lot of guilt. I wasn't able to devote a lot of time to my first child when the twins came," says Florida, whose second and third sons arrived almost a year to the day after her first son's birth. "I just try to tell myself I'm doing the best I can."

Deb, also a mother of three, says: "I feel like I'm pulled in so many different directions and I can't give enough to any of the kids. I also feel like my entire day is made up of schlepping children to various places. Someone always needs me."

On the other hand, Liz R. feels three children (all of hers are boys) is exactly the right number for her and her husband. "I see people with four and just know that would be too much for me. And somehow thinking of having two seems like it wouldn't be as much fun," she says. "Three does make it hard. There's no longer an easy way to have a lot of one-on-one time. On the weekends, you have to work out coverage with your spouse to get every boy to his sports or activities. During the week, it means each child is dragged to a sibling's event, which I think is actually healthy. It teaches children that life is about compromise and not always about them."

When she becomes outnumbered by her subordinates, a Stay-at-Home woman adds the title of department head or manager (or army captain) to her mom duties. As Liz R. notes: "With three or more, you and your husband go from a man-to-man to a zone defense." For the good of all, including herself, a Stay-at-Home mother needs to be a benevolent dictator; in other words, someone who is loving but *in charge*. However, if you've ever tried it, being a dictator isn't easy, especially when the opposition has identified your weak spots and knows how to wear you down, or even topple your regime.

We've established that three is tough. But Laura P. doesn't find the day any easier with two girls, ages five and two. "We are always juggling the nap schedule of my younger daughter with the hours of my oldest daughter's preschool and activities," she says. "No one gets my full attention. And because I'm never alone, I feel distracted and selfish trying to fit my things into the day—exercising, not playing with them but emailing and cooking, things I used to do when my older one napped."

Adds Erin Z.: "I find two children barely manageable, and I have incredible respect for my friends with three, four, and even five. I like having one adult per child. I think if we were outnumbered there would be total anarchy."

Interestingly, the survey respondents who have four or more children actually came across as less overwhelmed than the moms with fewer kids. "Having four children and one on the way defines who I am," says Colleen. "I have surrendered to being a Stay-at-Home mom and would not change a thing." I know two Stay-at-Home moms with six kids apiece. Both are very religious (Mormon and evangelical Christian) and have lots of energy, but each admits that she relies on her spouse, friends, extended family, and older children to help keep it all together. As Sharon, whose kids range in age from thirteen to three, told me, "If my mother didn't live with us and help me with the children, I *would* be insane."

For many families, the headcount is what determines whether a woman will stay home. The cost of quality childcare for multiple children—whether they arrive individually or in bulk—is restrictive, even prohibitive, as are the logistics of having to get children of differing ages to different schools and activities. Making daycare or after-school arrangements for one child is hard enough. With every additional little one, the challenge and the costs escalate. While mom staying home solves the overall childcare problem, the day-in, day-out of being outnumbered by kids can be particularly rough on the woman herself.

"Before I had children, I inadvertently offended an old friend when she had a second child," explains Sandra, a former trial attorney, now a mom to a twelve- and ten-year-old. "I said, 'Wow, one is an indulgence, two is a lifestyle!' Years later, she told me I was right. Two is a lot more work than twice one. Not only are you managing two kids, you're managing the dynamic between them, not to mention the logistics of having to go in two directions at once, because, if they're like mine, they have different interests and activities."

Having several children can also put a screeching halt to a woman's ability to spend time with other moms or participate in playgroups. Mothers with just one child might not welcome a home invasion by your three-, four- or more-some. And it's hard to spend time with friends, or make new ones, when you're trying to wrangle several children (such as at a playground) and your schedule doesn't jibe with that of other women in your same situation.

"It was so easy to get together for coffee and talk when we all just had infants or even young toddlers," recalls Deb, whose children are ages seven, four, and sixteen months. "It gets more difficult, and even more isolating, when the kids get older and you have more of them. In the times you do get together, it's rare that you can spend quality time talking with friends. With two kids, I made a point to get out of the house every day. I find this more difficult with my third, because much of my day is spent getting the two others to and from school and just managing a house that has three kids living in it."

Does it sound as if we ladies doth protest too much? It may, especially to someone who hasn't had to "work the merry-go-round," as mother of three Nicki puts it. "You just wait for the next child to come around, which is usually in five seconds." Do we seem as if we have regrets, or are trying to warn moms behind us from boosting their baby counts? That's not the intent. Acknowledging the difficulty of the work doesn't mean we don't want to do the work, or that others should avoid the same path. Like life in general, having several children brings both great joy and great demands. If anything, the message is: Know what you're getting into, and know, despite what you or your spouse or others around you may believe, your work as a Stay-at-Home mom will get much harder, at least initially.

"After the first year, having two children is definitely better than one," notes Gerri. "The girls play with each other, which translates into less demands on me for entertainment. I also find that the three of us make a very good team. We have fun together."

I enjoy each of my three children individually. And I especially enjoy when my husband and I spend time together as a family with all three kids. However, I often don't enjoy being one adult managing three children on my own. A couple of years ago, a friend of mine, a mother of two, was having baby angst and began debating whether or not to try for a third. One day, we took all five of our children to the zoo. It was a disaster, largely due to the needs and demands of my trio. Soon after, I sent her a note saying, "When you consider three, remember me, and keep that I.U.D!" (She has.)

The Numbers Game

An unscientific assessment of the headcount impact on a Stay-at-Home mom, based on the experiences of the women who helped create *The Guide*:

Having **one child** is wonderful *and* hard, because it's totally new and so intense.

Two kids are tough on a mom during the first few years, particularly if the children are close in age. But the two parents/two kids ratio is nice, and the duo may even give mom a break. Says Liz H., of Seattle: "Life is much better with two than one. At least they can occupy each other and I don't have to be the 'entertainment committee' all by myself!"

Having **three children** seems to make for the most overwhelming scenario for Stay-at-Home moms—and the spousal or partner relationship. The parents are now outnumbered, and the kids are often at three very different stages of development—and, as a result, have different schedules. Many of the most crazed moms are those who have one child in elementary school, one in preschool, and an infant who needs a morning and afternoon nap. In such cases, a Stay-at-Home mom may be home for only short stretches at a time, with the bulk of her day spent getting into and out of the car.

Once the headcount hits **four or more,** the Stay-at-Home mom has likely become a real pro. The older kids can help with the younger ones. By this time, the mother often knows how to do everything for everyone at once. It's also probable that couples with four or more kids either *really* wanted to have that many children or were nonplussed if it happened. One survey mom, a former teacher, has five children and would gladly have another if her husband would sign on. She and her spouse each come from large families, both of which live nearby and are available to help. Most days, this mother is racing around to get everyone fed and where they need to be, but there's nothing she'd rather do.

MOTHERS OF MULTIPLES

Having a baby changes everything. Having more than one baby at a time changes it tons more. In my younger days, when I thought about having children, I always envisioned myself with two. My husband wanted at least three. For years I'd tell him, "The only way you're getting three kids out of me is if we have twins." God was on his side.

Nowadays, twins are commonplace. Triplets aren't even so unusual. Although many people think that multiple births among older moms are always due to fertility treatments, as I learned at age thirty-seven, the older you are, the wackier your ovulation can be. But whether it's chance, a medical boost, or age that gives you multiples, what is uniformly true is that it truly does "take a village"—as the proverb goes—"to raise a child." This is especially true when the multiples arrive into a family that already has children. When a woman in my neighborhood with three children gave birth to a set of triplets (resulting in her having *six* children under age six), my own retired mother and other "villagers" came to her aid. Financially, hiring help wasn't an option. So for a long time, this mom's big outing of the day was to walk alone to the corner to meet her kindergartener's bus, and she could only do that if a volunteer was at her house with the remaining brood.

The word "confinement" once referred to a period of time before and after a birth, during which a woman would not be seen in public. She was essentially confined to her home, so as not to reveal her swollen midsection or nursing breasts. I felt I was in a forced confinement for several months before and after my twins were born. During the pregnancy, my petite frame could barely support the weight of my erupting belly, which ultimately contained two full-term babies, weighing in at seven pounds, six ounces each. Afterward, it just wasn't possible to be a still-recovering woman out and about and managing a preschooler and two infants. In many ways I was like a cow or sow penned with her offspring. During the pregnancy and for seven months afterward, my husband and I were living in different cities during the week. On my lucky days, a visitor popped by to give me a break or bring me a meal. For mothers of multiples, being a Stay-at-Home mom is often a literal description.

If you have or are expecting twins (or more) and don't already know other mothers of multiples, do try to meet some. When I discovered I was pregnant with the girls, I called two mothers of twins I knew only as acquaintances. These women were enormously helpful in directing me to an obstetrician who specialized in multiple gestation and high-risk pregnancies, and they were fonts of knowledge about which twin-specific baby products work or don't.

While women who have never had twins (or more) may say things like, "Oh, I wish I had twins" or "Having twins is easier than having two close together," women who have been through a multiples pregnancy and delivery, and who have cared for two or more newborns at once, know the drill. They understand why you don't go to the playground without help. They understand why you can't "just get a babysitter." (Reason: Even experienced moms are intimidated by caring for two babies at once; you can't simply hand two infants to the sixteen-year-old next door.)

One Christmas season, I received a wonderful gift from a woman I met when I first moved to Maryland. Lora and I had occasionally chatted at the neighborhood pool and at school functions. Like me, her first child was followed by twins. Since her children were now in school during the day, she offered to stay with my one-year-olds for two mornings so I could do my holiday shopping. I accepted her offer, with full confidence that she could handle anything my twins threw her way.

WHICH ONE OF YOU HAD CHICKEN POX?
KEEPING TRACK OF MEDICAL MATTERS AND MILESTONES

When you're a new, first-time mom, you're sure you'll remember every wonderful thing about your child: His first smile. Her first tooth. His first word. Her first step. You do remember those things, until additional children arrive. Then the milestones, the illnesses, the cute stories all mix together, and you can't answer even the simplest inquiries, such as, "Mommy, how old was I when I started to walk?" Mothers have different solutions for keeping track of such important information.

I have a spiralbound journal for each child in which I record shots, illnesses, milestones, and achievements. Separately, I have a school memories book (an album with pages and pockets) in which I paste the kids' school photos and store their report cards. My former neighbor, a mother of four, had a filing cabinet with files and folders on each child. Many moms use keepsake boxes. Anything special goes in the box. (And if the woman doesn't have time to organize and scrapbook the contents, that box can someday be handed to an adult child by a downsizing parent.) Rose Kennedy, the matriarch of the Kennedy family and a mother of nine, recorded all medical information about her children on cards she kept filed in a recipe box. Finding a system that works for you, and using it, will enable you to keep useful information at your fingertips—and alleviate any guilt you may have from being a busy mother of several children.

Another mom tradition that wanes with the arrival of each new child is scrapbooking. My son has an overstuffed scrapbook filled with photos and notes and other keepsakes of his first year of life. When I made the book, I was pretty impressed with myself. Then I attended a scrapbooking party hosted by a friend who had started to sell scrapbooking supplies. Compared to Pam's scrapbook, and those of her party regulars, my scrapbook looked as if it was made by my year-old son instead of for him. I bought a bunch of supplies from Pam and vowed to improve the scrapbook, but then I went back to work, and then I had twins.

Not only haven't I improved my son's scrapbook, I haven't made books for my girls. At nearly five years old, they have one keepsake box each. My son's keepsake box was overflowing by his first birthday. During my efforts at documenting our first child's first year, my husband said he hoped I planned to do the same for any future children. I have on my Future Projects To-Do List, which I will work through once all my children are in school full-day: *Make scrapbooks for the girls.* I'm careful not to bring out my son's scrapbook when the twins are around.

My friend Karen, a mother of three whose first-born is the same age as my son, decided early on not to even start down the scrapbooking path. "Why set myself up for failure?" she said, in explaining why she wouldn't join me at Pam's scrapbooking party.

The women who successfully scrapbook, create albums, or otherwise document the details of their children's lives are also creating a portfolio of their own invaluable accomplishments. Many scrapbookers find the hobby an enjoyable, creative task from which they can appreciate the fruits of their labor.

"When my children were very young, my special alone time was in the evenings when my husband worked nights," says Debbie, a mother of three. "I made a scrapbook for each child with photos from birth to one year, and no matter how hard the day was, when I looked at those cute pictures, I only remembered the good things about my baby. The photos made me feel good about motherhood, and the work was a great stress reliever that made me love my child even more."

But if the actual creation of such a personal archive will cause you more stress than satisfaction, you're probably better off following Karen's lead (and not even starting down memory lane) than mine—which, having chronicled the first child, means I'm playing catch-up for the other two.

A SPECIAL WORD ABOUT SPECIAL NEEDS

My twins are so unalike that we refer to them as the "anti-twins." In addition to one being dark-haired with brown eyes, and the other being a blue-eyed blonde, they are at the opposite ends of the "normal" range within the developmental spectrum. The dark-haired girl is eighteen months ahead of where she should be developmentally; her sister is eighteen months behind. So in some ways, my twins are three years apart.

Much of my day is oriented around the needs of the twin who is speech delayed. She attends a special preschool far from our home, and twice a week I take her to individual speech therapy, which also involves a long drive. Because of logistics, the kids and I spend a lot of time in the car, shuttling between schools, therapy, and my son's also distant school bus stop. By day's end, we're wiped out and cranky. For me, it's tiresome dealing with the whining and weepiness of a child who's not fully able to explain what she wants, and it's hard having to accommodate everyone's schedule around the specific educational and therapeutic services she receives. But compared to other women I encounter daily, my child's disability and my routine aren't so bad.

Because my daughter receives early-intervention and special-education services, many Stay-at-Home mothers in my world have a child with special needs. The term is a catchall phrase that includes autism, behavioral and learning problems, developmental delays, Down's syndrome, Asperger's syndrome, cancer, brain injuries, leukemia, epilepsy, severe allergies, ADHD (attention deficit hyperactivity disorder), and birth defects. The conditions typically require extensive physical, educational, and occupational therapies, and also medical intervention. Because of the time and unique care required, a child's special needs are often what leads a mother to stay home or, if she's already home, causes her to remain there.

While the Stay-at-Home moms of "typically developing" children go to playgrounds and Mommy & Me classes, have play-dates, and compare notes about preschools, mothers with special needs children are more often than not juggling doctor visits and therapy appointments, and comparing information about insurance coverage, service providers, treatment methods, experts and theories, adaptive equipment, dietary protocols, and Individualized Education Plans (IEPs) for schooling. Caring for a child with special needs can be a full-time job in and of itself for a Stay-at-Home mom, many of whom become experts in, and effective advocates for, their child and the condition he or she has.

I've been assured that my daughter will eventually catch up with her peers, and I have seen great strides in her abilities. But as a mom, I feel guilty at every turn: For not focusing more on her speech development, for letting her needs distract me from spending time with the other kids, for losing my temper because I'm pulled at all day.

Many moms of special needs children don't receive assurances that give them hope, and their children don't have conditions they'll eventually grow out of. A woman I used to sit near in a therapy waiting room has two severely autistic sons. She knows she'll likely be their primary caregiver for the rest of her life. Although she's a Stay-at-Home mom, she works full-time as a care provider, therapist, and representative for her children, and she is a constant advocate for more research into autism and the needs of families like hers. Another mother I know with an autistic preschooler has created a specialized classroom in her home and has become trained in an educational curriculum that has been successfully used with children like her son.

Other Stay-at-Home moms with special needs kids spend much of their time nursing their children through surgeries, therapies, and chemotherapy treatments, or educating and caring for a child using methods recommended for the condition at hand, be it Asperger's, dyslexia, or the now common ADHD. In each situation, parental and often family accommodations need to be made. Just as I take my young daughter to a special preschool and services far from our home, other moms regularly retrieve an older child from an elementary or middle school early or during recess to take the student to and from a therapy appointment. Although survey respondent Barbara's son is in fourth grade, he has social and learning difficulties that still require her significant involvement. "It's necessary that a parent be nearby for emotional support and day-to-day things like homework," she reports. As a result, after several years as a Stay-at-Home mom, Barbara returned to the workforce as a part-time Realtor in her suburban New Jersey town, as opposed to going back into the type of full-time, Manhattan-based, corporate-finance job she held in the past.

The stress and demands caused by having a child with medical or developmental challenges can also challenge a parent's contentment ("I didn't sign up for this") and a couple's marriage, with the result that one parent (often the mother) is essentially left to handle the child's needs alone. Sometimes a parent checks out entirely, requiring the other to work (for an income and health insurance) while single-handedly raising a special-needs child.

It's impossible for this book to adequately address the uniqueness of being a Stay-at-Home mom with a special needs child. But a woman with such responsibilities and challenges should look especially to the chapters about avoiding loneliness (page 285), finding childcare help (page 315), making friends (page 259), and securing time for herself (page 243).

I've found that in my situation, it has been enormously helpful to spend time, even in passing, with other moms whose children have speech delays. These women have taught me about how to access the services my daughter needs. And when I'm around those women or other moms of special needs kids, I know I won't be asked why one of my twins is so different from the other (no one knows) or required to explain that child's immature behavior (lots of clinging and crying), or have to justify why I don't just hire someone (as has been suggested) to drive her to her many destinations.

A mother I often cross paths with has one child, a son who suffered brain damage at birth, resulting in severe disabilities. She takes him to five therapists a week and does constant battle with insurance companies and public school administrators. "Lots of people don't or can't understand the magnitude of what you're up against," she told me. "So you just have get over your sadness and fear and do what's necessary for your child's needs. If you don't, no one else will."

YOUR EMPLOYMENT CONTRACT

Children aren't small forever, and leaving the workforce for home doesn't have to be forever. But for a woman committed to being home until her child is in elementary school, one's stint as a Stay-at-Home mom will require a minimum of five years. With each child added to the family, or a child born with special needs, the commitment extends one or several years, or maybe doesn't end. Before she knows it, a woman can be out of the paid workforce for a decade or more.

I'm stunned that I've been a Stay-at-Home mom for more than six years. When I chose to leave my magazine career in New York, I did so because the decision was right, and necessary, for that moment. At the time I didn't do the math about how many years I'd be out of the paid workforce if I had other children and cared for them on my own until they were all old enough for full-day school. In fact, it wasn't until my son entered first grade that I did the precise calculations about when the girls would follow suit. When I did, I learned that due to my twins' autumn birthday and the age cut-off in my county's school system, the girls would be home with me for an extra year. I had intentionally spaced my first and second pregnancies, not wanting to be overwhelmed by having two very small children. (Ha! The best laid plans.) I truly didn't think about what such spacing would mean on the other end, how I would be stretching the expanse of years during which I'd either be a Stay-at-Home or an employed mom with very little children. Many women go the other route, by having their children close together and, as a result, bunching the collective preschool years into a shorter period of time.

Unlike Stay-at-Home moms, few people in the paid workforce these days remain at the same job for years upon years. And although our young client-base does age (and chances are good that since our parents are also aging, we may be helping to care for them as well), our overall job responsibilities and compensation remain the same. Oftentimes, however, we are the ones who change. A woman who may have positively marked the fifth anniversary of her Stay-at-Home career might not feel as fortunate or self-fulfilled upon her twelfth. Or she might. My best friend from high school and I were pregnant at the same time with children who are now preschoolers. But while I was still in my early Stay-at-Home years, she was already a veteran who, with an eleven- and nine-year-old, had made it to "the other side": those coveted-by-many years when a Stay-at-Home mom can actually have time to herself while her kids are at school. Starting anew was a conscious choice on Ann's part, even though she knew she would be reenlisting for another half-dozen years, either at home or by figuring out childcare for a small child. "Our family just didn't feel complete," she explained.

Eventual college tuitions and wedding planning aside, family size and children's needs have an impact on a Stay-at-Home mom's at-home career, which, depending on her choices and circumstances, can be either very short ("You're weaned. I gotta catch a train!") or extremely long lived ("I can't believe my baby has finished college, is moving out, and getting married!").

Survival Tips for Leaving Your House

It's challenging enough for a new mom to go out and about with a baby. Have you packed enough diapers? Clothing? Bottles? Going out with two or more small children—or, in some cases, a special needs child—can be so intimidating, a mom may not even try. Looking back, I was on-the-go and mobile with my first. Comparatively, when the twins arrived, I felt like the babies, my four-year-old, and I were under house arrest. Over time, however, we did manage to make a few public appearances. Some strategies:

Hire a young helper: Often, all you need is an extra pair of hands and speedy feet. And those appendages can belong to a teenager, or even a preteen neighbor. Such a mother's helper can help push a stroller, carry a bag, and chase after a toddler or two while you're busy nursing a baby. (See page 325 for more about recruiting young helpers.)

Go out with another mom: Partner up so you can help one another. For instance, one mom can stay with the babies while the other takes the preschoolers to the bathroom.

Scope out the exits: Try to find a playground or play area that's fenced, with only one way in (and out), then stand guard at the gate.

Supersize it: Many supermarkets and big-box stores now have carts that can safely seat multiple children, including infants. Identify these stores so you can shop when you need to and also get the gang out of the house.

▶

Use color coding: If you're going someplace where you'll have to keep track of your little ones while they mix and mingle among other children, dress yours in matching clothes, or at least the same colors. Doing so will help you spot your children quickly and reduce the number of panic moments you have when trying to locate and count kids.

Deputize: I'm an oldest child, and I know the pros and cons of burdening a first born with too much responsibly. But when you have several children, your oldest is sometimes the only assistant you have. My son helps keep his sisters entertained, he holds their hands when we have to cross streets, he alerts me when one of them wiggles out of her car seat, and he shadows one while I stick with the other.

Label your kids: If it makes you feel better when you're out on your own with multiple children, you can label your kids with their names, your name, and cell phone number. This can be done by sewing labels into their clothing, putting name tags on their jackets (think ski-lift tickets), or by having them wear accessories such as bracelets or necklaces featuring the contact information. (The last option only works if your child won't remove the jewelry.) Another way to be prepared in case of lost children is for you to carry recent photos of your kids in your wallet, so you can show fellow searchers who you're looking for, or prove that a found child is yours. Some companies make actual ID cards for children, complete with a photo, fingerprint, vital stats, and contact information. These cards are usually kept in a parent's wallet, but if duplicates are ordered, one can be held by the parent or a caregiver and another placed in the child's backpack.

Ask for help: Store clerks, other moms who are out and about, even passersby will help you watch or locate a child or carry a stroller up a flight of stairs. Sometimes folks will see your need, other times all you need to do is ask.

Jack(ie)-of-All-Trades

According to a 2007 assessment by Salary.com, the domestic labor of a woman who stays home to care for her children is worth an impressive $138,095 a year. (That's a three-percent raise from the $134,121 "earned" the year before.) By the way, that salary is compensation for a 91.6-hour work week, which—at more than twice the standard forty-hour workweek—is the average amount of time a Stay-at-Home mother spends "on the job."

Employed mothers "earn" $85,939 a year for their domestic duties, which they take care of piecemeal both from work and especially at night once they return home. While Stay-at-Home moms don't work outside the home, like employed mothers they too keep working long after the traditional workday is done.

The work Stay-at-Home moms do is not only hard, but sometimes literally thankless, as survey respondent Heather, a Stay-at-Home mother of three, writes:

> Every day you pick up toys, but more toys are everywhere by the time you're done. You clean the house, and it gets messy right away. You make breakfast, then lunch, then

dinner, every day. You do the laundry and fold it, and two days later you have to do it again. Your work never ends, but so many people think you have it easy. When I worked, not only was I paid for what I did, which is pretty reinforcing in and of itself, but the people I worked with respected me and appreciated what I did. Now if the house isn't clean or the laundry isn't done or we have pasta for dinner, someone will complain. But if the house is spotless and the laundry is put away and I've made a nice dinner, no one says anything. Also, unless you have enough money to stay home and have a babysitter, staying home is a twenty-four-hour job with no breaks.

Generally, when a house with a woman at home needs to be cleaned, it's the woman who does the cleaning—or attempts to—while caring for children. Since that can be hard to do by day, with little hands and feet messing whatever has just been wiped or put away, women often clean and tidy after their kids go to bed. Also on the homemaker's to-do list: holiday shopping, sending birthday cards to relatives, doctor's appointments, pet care, waiting for the cable company, kid homework, basic household maintenance, auto care, and more. Granted, such tasks are easier for the Stay-at-Home person to manage than for an employed person stuck at the office. But the fantasy image of Stay-at-Home motherhood is that the moms have a lot of time on their hands. And some do, once their kids are in school full-day. Some of those women even complain of being bored. (See Chapter Thirteen about struggles with boredom, which can stem from being busy, but with uninteresting tasks, or being bored because you feel you have nothing to do.)

As Marilyn Yalom, a women's studies professor and author of *A History of the Wife,* writes, "Obligations to home, family, and the community always seem to expand into the hours one tries to sequester for oneself, perhaps because homemaking is, by nature, always open to the unpredictable—a sick child, a broken washing machine, storm damage to the roof. Moreover, without the extra income of a second wage earner, housewives often have to sacrifice material rewards in order to stay at home."

While twentieth- and twenty-first-century homemakers certainly have it much easier than their predecessors did (no one really appreciates how wonderful dishwashers, microwaves, and vacuum cleaners are), Yalom found that when comparing the 1920s and the 1960s, modern conveniences did not lessen the amount of time women devoted to housework. Instead, "Higher standards of household cleanliness and personal attractiveness, promoted by TV, the women's magazines, domestic advice literature, and consumer ads gave homemakers more to do and more to worry about."

Also, although actively employed women now comprise an estimated 46 percent of the U.S. workforce, many aspects of daily life are still based on the traditional model of a man going to work and a woman staying home. The school day still ends by or around 3:00 PM, and schools close for more than two months in the summer. Except for rare exceptions, deliveries, home-repair services, and medical appointments must occur during the typical workday. Delivery services and home-repair technicians often call the night before, with a "window" of time in which they'll arrive. While such short, and vague, notice is absolutely dreadful for employed people, it often isn't much better for Stay-at-Home moms, who have to shuttle children to schools or appointments or meet them at bus stops at precise times.

Blast from the Past

"To keep a house and grounds in good order, purchase every article for daily use, keep the wardrobes of half a dozen human beings in proper trim, take the children to dentists, shoemakers, and different schools, or find teachers at home, altogether made sufficient work to help keep one brain busy, as well as all the hands I could impress into the service. Then, too, the novelty of housekeeping had passed away, and much that was once attractive in domestic life was now irksome."

—Elizabeth Cady Stanton

So wrote the pioneering suffragette in her autobiography, published in 1898. The language may sound stilted to our ears, but the mothering day Stanton (no relation) describes could have been yesterday. Her sentiments are the same as many of us share today, on the playground or via email or chat rooms or blogs.

The fact that medical professionals don't as a matter of course have evening and weekend hours has always confounded me. Doctors only want to treat patients who have health insurance. The primary way to have health insurance in this country is by having a job. Yet if an employee has to keep taking time off to go to the doctor, or to take a spouse or children to the doctor, that can put an employee's job at risk. The difficulty of getting to a doctor can, in fact, put Stay-at-Home moms with small children at health risk. Among the reasons women neglect getting a mammogram or pap smear is that they don't have someone to care for their kids while they spend hours sitting in a medical office waiting for a five-minute audience with the physician. Recently, I spent $80 on babysitting just so I could go to the dentist in the morning, and then head out again in the afternoon for a routine mammogram.

Just like at a paid job, women who work as Stay-at-Home moms have a hard time getting time off from work to handle personal matters.

THE JOBS YOU REALLY DO . . .

Human Resources Administrator, President, Executive Vice President, Chief Executive Officer, Chief Financial Officer, Chief Operating Officer. Do these titles sound impressive? They are, and each of these corporate titles is synonymous with the responsibilities and work involved in being a Stay-at-Home mom.

"I try to think of myself as the president and CEO of my family, and I try to excel in that role," says Beth, a Dartmouth MBA in suburban Boston who managed a pension plan and is now home with a one- and two-year-old. Tracy, a business manager turned Stay-at-Home mother of a two-year-old and a newborn, describes herself as a "Vice President, Domestic Affairs." Scott, an author and former colleague of mine, upon hearing about this book, emailed to offer his wife's input. "Lisa is home with our four," he wrote. "We consider her our Director of Human Development."

Packaged Facts, which publishes consumer marketing data, issued a paper in 2006 declaring "New Market Research Reveals Stay-at-Home Mom as Family CEO." The report says that compared to Baby Boomer women, "Gen X and Gen Y" homemakers "have put careers on hold—or at least on pause, sometimes freelancing or consulting after hours—in order to participate in every facet of their young children's lives. . . . They are big on spirituality and values, and health and nutrition, and have translated their years of business experience into a kind of corporate savvy for the home."

Many Stay-at-Home women do think of the work they do at home in terms of a corporate hierarchy and the titles and tasks such a structure represents. Doing so is a way of showing that running a household well requires organizational skills, creativity, and intelligence. Some commentators make fun of such descriptions, as if Stay-at-Home moms are trying to pretend to be something more than "just" housewives. They also say describing domestic pursuits by using business terminology is simply a way for marketers and parenting magazines to kiss up to a constituency each needs but, according to Leslie Bennetts, author of *The Feminine Mistake,* actually considers to be "somewhat dimwitted second-class citizens who aren't really up to the task of dealing with reality."

As hard as it can be to deal with life's big-picture issues when you're busy every minute of the day caring for children, Stay-at-Home moms must deal with reality and the outside world—more so than many working folks are required to during the course of their business day. And at the same time, the employers, service providers and policy makers of the "outside world" also need to deal with the realities faced by families, and the societal benefits of having children properly cared for and raised to be productive citizens of the world. Children need to be tended by someone. If it's not smart for women, or anyone, to be out of the paid workforce, who will take care of the children society continues to produce?

The recent arguments against Stay-at-Home motherhood seem to be saying it's better for smart men and women to work and, if they're going to also have children, leave the care of any offspring to daycare centers or, perhaps, the less intelligent or less affluent adults who are willing to work as babysitters. (Continuing that line of thinking, if adults shouldn't leave or reduce their roles in the workforce, does it mean that paid childcare providers should either not have children or else bring their children to work?)

HELP WANTED: STAY-AT-HOME WIFE AND MOTHER

In the aforementioned calculations estimating that the work of a Stay-at-Home mother is worth an annual average salary of $134,800, Salary.com included the following jobs.

Housekeeper .... 22.1 hours per week
Daycare Provider 15.7
Cook 13.6
Computer Operator 9.1
Laundry Machine Operator 6.7
Janitor 6.3
Facilities Manager 5.8
Chief Executive Officer 4.2
Van Driver 4.2
Psychologist 3.9

All Jobs Combined .... **91.6 hours per week**

Absolutely, Stay-at-Home mothers should earn at least six figures, but the website's calculations don't include or fully explain the details of all the jobs a Stay-at-Home mom actually does. Following is a sampling of the HELP WANTED ads that would have to be placed to really encompass all the tasks at hand.

Nanny: Patient, loving woman who requires neither sleep nor adult interaction needed to care for child(ren) 24/7/365. Other duties include all those listed following this ad.

Housekeeper: Responsibilities include cleaning and tidying a family home several times daily. Must be willing to work nights, weekends, and overtime and find joy in cleaning and tidying the same areas over and over again.

Chauffeur: Driver needed to transport child(ren) to all activities beyond the domicile, including, but not limited to, school, sports, medical appointments, therapies, entertainment venues, and social events. Applicant must be skilled in defensive-driving tactics and able to drive safely, regardless of passenger behavior. Having extra-long arms is useful in this position but not essential.

Chef: Passable cooking and meal-preparation skills needed for short-order establishment serving three full meals and filling dozens of beverage and snack orders per customer per day, for both sit-down dining and carryout. The chef is also responsible for procuring and restocking supplies, serving meals, all dishwashing, as well as the full cleaning of both the kitchen and multiple dining areas.

Teacher/Coach: Instructor wanted for child(ren) ages newborn to adult for lessons in academic, athletic, social, and life skills.

Position involves both one-on-one instruction and classes of mixed-age pupils.

Psychologist: Compassionate, wise, and patient person needed to listen to the problems and concerns of household members. Pediatric and couples-counseling experience recommended.

Accountant/Money Manager: Financially competent person needed to record account receivables, supervise cash flow, track and pay invoices, and manage savings and investment funds.

Building Superintendent/General Contractor: Manager sought to keep domicile in working order by arranging for trade technicians (plumbers, electricians, etc.) to both fix and maintain household systems and appliances.

Handyman: Skilled individual needed to perform small household repairs on an as-needed basis.

Executive Secretary: Organized person sought to handle all correspondence and interaction between the household and the outside world. Position involves extensive filing and record-keeping.

Rights Advocate: Protector and supporter required to represent and/or speak for household members either unable or unwilling to do so for themselves.

Wardrobe Manager/Dresser: Fashion- and bargain-saavy person needed to acquire, alter, organize, and maintain clothing and footwear for all members of a household, for all seasons. Other duties include ensuring that appropriate clothing is worn by all household members. Wrestling skills are helpful but can be developed.

Launderer: Help needed for all aspects of the cleaning and maintenance of various wardrobe collections.

Entertainer: Positive, upbeat person sought to keep household members happy. Applicant must possess diverse talents and be able to work with a variety of audiences in a variety of situations. Costumes are acceptable attire.

Sex Worker: Attractive, enthusiastic woman needed, immediately. Creativity and experience required. (Though not too much experience.)

Maybe you should update your résumé. . . .

HOUSEKEEPING HELP
(OR, LOWERING YOUR STANDARDS)

"I love being a Stay-at-Home mom, but I hate being a housewife!" says Erin Z., a New Jersey mother of two, expressing a sentiment shared by so many of us.

Jennifer, a former nanny and new mom, describes the condition of a house containing children in the following, quite accurate, way: "Adding a child to the home environment is like throwing everything up in the air each morning and hoping you have time to catch it as it all comes back down."

Before I had kids, when I went to the office every day, I used a cleaning service for a while, which, in retrospect, makes no sense. My husband and I were working full-time, so the house didn't really get messy. We didn't need a cleaning service, at least not as compared to when the children started arriving. Although I kept the service when I was home on maternity leave with my son, doing so wasn't as helpful as I thought it would be. When a baby naps twice a day, it's hard to arrange a good time for a cleaning crew to come in. I also found I wound up tidying the house and putting away personal items before the cleaners arrived, making more work for myself. I then found it very odd to be in the house, trying to stay out of the way, while other people cleaned my family's mess.

The Household Chores (S)Hit List

According to *The Guide's* survey respondents, the housekeeping tasks that most sap our enthusiasm are:

Emptying the dishwasher and/or folding laundry: Several women said the same thing, simply: "I hate emptying the dishwasher." "I hate folding laundry." The connecting theme: Both involve dirty things becoming clean and then needing to be put away.

The constant picking up/cleaning up: "It makes me feel like a hamster running in its wheel," says Laura. "No matter how much you do, you're going to end up in the same place you started."

Preparing meals and snacks: Writes Lyn: "Before having kids, I enjoyed cooking. I'm not sure now that what I do even qualifies as cooking. It's more like putting food on plates that will not be rejected by the person you put it in front of. There *is* a direct correlation between how much work is involved in making a meal and how much your children will hate it!"

When I left my job for good, I stopped the cleaning service. We needed to economize, and I didn't see the use in hiring folks to clean once every two weeks when I still had to clean in between cleanings (and now that I have three kids, clean at the end of each day).

Guilt also factors in: "I hate cleaning the house," says Sarah G., a Virginia mom of two school-age children. "But I don't feel justified in hiring someone when I'm here to do it."

Many Stay-at-Home moms swear by having a cleaning service come to their homes, usually every other week. Even though the house gets messy on a daily basis, and they need to clean between "deep" cleanings, several report feeling a sense of relief in knowing that at least once in a while, their house will get a thorough scrubbing. As Tracy points out: "It's really hard to find the time or energy to 'clean' after picking up all day." Adds Heather: "Finally this year we have enough money to hire a housecleaner. It's a miracle to have a clean slate once a week, and to have one day per week when I can entirely focus on the kids." A few years ago, a neighbor told me it wasn't until her two children were in school full-day that she decided to hire housekeeping help, which she did in part to rescue her diminishing self-esteem. "I was starting to feel as if my husband and kids got to go off and interact with the world, and experience new things," said Kathie, "while I was stayed home to clean up the mess they'd left behind."

Several women noted that since they're now home, their spouses no longer pitch in with any cleaning, unless specifically asked (or begged) to do so. Unhelpful or busy partners often lead to a gal hiring a cleaning service to come in once every week or two.

If hiring out isn't an option, and a Stay-at-Home mom is truly overwhelmed by all that needs to be done to keep ahead of the kids and the house, it's time she talk to her partner about sharing the load. One way to look at the situation: He works for pay, likely in a place that is cleaned and maintained by someone else and isn't occupied round-the-clock. You work in a busy place that is used 24/7, yet you are expected to keep it clean and in order all by yourself. It's not unreasonable to ask that some of the burden be shared.

HOUSEWORK FOR HIM

While the partner of a Stay-at-Home mom can't be expected to take care of things around the house while he's at work earning money to support his family, no man in this day and age should be allowed to claim he "doesn't know how to . . . *[fill in the blank]*"— do laundry, empty the dishwasher, shop for groceries, cook a meal, or change a diaper or even a light bulb. (True story: One woman interviewed for this book, who shall remain nameless here, revealed that due to her now being home full-time, her husband believes it's her job to replace any burnt-out light bulbs. His changing a bulb, she says, "is him doing a favor" for her.)

While weekends are open times for all sorts of chore sharing, employed partners who aren't bringing work home or getting home super late *can* help with the following weekday chores:

- **Kid care:** Dinner, bathing, story time, tuck-in, occasional nighttime feedings.

- **Loading and emptying the dishwasher:** It's better to do this before going to bed, so the next day starts with a clean slate.

- **Laundry:** Clothes can be washed and dried by day or in the evening, but once the kids are down, the folding and sorting can be done by one or both partners while having a conversation or watching TV.

- **Mopping, vacuuming, and dusting:** While one person entertains the kids, the other can tackle a room that needs cleaning.

- **Grocery shopping:** Stores are open late. He can stop by the supermarket on the way home from work, or she can set out on her own once he's home to stay with the kids. Whoever does the shopping benefits from an extra set of adult hands at home to help unload and put away the groceries.

TIME- AND ENERGY-SAVING TIDYING TIPS

We stay home to be with our children, not so we can have the pleasure of mopping floors and changing bed linens. But let's admit that stuff is unavoidable, and at least make it go as fast and easy as possible. As the best nanny ever once said, "Just a spoon full of sugar . . ."

Clean as you go, rather than all at once: Hence, scrub the toilet when you're in the bathroom anyway, or dust a room a day.

Don't even bother tidying until your kids go to bed: Unless you want to clean up the same toys and messes repeatedly during the same twelve hours, wait until they're asleep.

Make a Top 10 list: Guests are arriving, and you're overwhelmed by how much needs to be done to get your house in order. Survey respondent Mary suggests that you "pick ten things that will make an impact on guests, and do those things before they arrive." For instance, vacuum, clean the bathrooms, make the beds, take out the stinky garbage, put toys away. The unfolded laundry and piles of unopened mail on your master to-do list can be hidden in a closet during the visit.

Be careful about the toys you allow into your house: When you shop for your children, or accept gifts for them, pay attention to the *little pieces*. In all likelihood, you'll be the one having to pick up the toys and their tiny parts, or you'll be the one having to ride herd on your kids to pick up the toys and all their tiny parts. (Children's meals from fast-food restaurants are notorious contributors to crappy toy clutter.) Also, simple can be better, says Sandra, a mom of two preteens: "My kids played with the garish, ugly, noisy toys other people brought into our home—once or twice. The toys they played with again and again were the old classics: blocks, sticks, and, of course, the boxes that other things came in. We recently got a piece of furniture delivered in an enormous box. My children, who are twelve and ten, and the neighbors, thirteen and fifteen years old, went *crazy* over the box! After a month, I finally got rid of the ratty thing, and they all complained. A fantastically crafted, utterly realistic, molded toy can only be what it is. But blocks, sticks, or boxes can be anything."

Limit the toys: A parent doesn't need to be a scrooge in order to keep a child's toy collection from becoming ridiculous and over-whelming. You just need to be practical. If you have a birthday party for a one-year-old, does your child really need to be indulged with a gift from every guest? As the host, you can ask that guests instead make a donation to a children's charity, or buy a gift that you'll deliver to a program for needy children. Sometimes it's the parents of small children who get caught up in receiving presents: a baby shower gift, a new baby gift, a christening or other religious gift, Valentine's Day, Easter, Halloween, Christmas or Hanukkah or Kwanza . . . . (Have you ever met a mom who has a six-month birthday party? I have.) Most toddlers and preschoolers are thrilled with one or two items. Too many gifts become overwhelming.

Teach your kids to clean up after themselves: Success here varies greatly. Toddlers can do it, with help (or singing: *"Clean up, clean up, everybody clean up."*) Older children can clean and tidy, they just need to know they're required to do so. It's essential that children be taught to clean up after themselves, and sometimes others, so they have the skills for their own futures—and because Stay-at-Home moms aren't maids! Besides, cleaning can be made into something fun, at which kids can excel. "I recently let my five-year-old son do some vacuuming," notes Leslie, a mother of two. "He loved it. It made him feel grown-up. Kids are given toy brooms and vacuums to play with. Why not let them do the real thing?"

Don't bother making the beds: This is a tip from my husband and son, both of whom think making a bed every morning is unnecessary since the bed will just get unmade again at night. The only time they will concede to making a bed is when it's time to change the sheets or in order to tidy when guests are visiting. I admit to being hardcore about the importance of bed-making, so this advice is especially tough for me to follow, but even I'm learning to let these things go. And when the rumpled sheets are really driving me nuts, I do a quick pull of the top blanket so it's at least neat—or I close the door to the bedroom.

Lighten up: So long as your house isn't unsanitary, or falling into disrepair from neglect, it's okay not to have a pristine, Martha Stewart–worthy home. In fact, when there's more than one child in the house, it can be near impossible to maintain a pristine environment, unless you have a household staff. "I'm a believer that, when your children are young, it's better for your house to be a little messy so you can use the time you would have spent cleaning to instead be with your kids," says Jill, a New Hampshire mom of two preschoolers.

Sweep the mess into a corner: Rather than having to stoop over and crawl around the floor to pick up scattered toys, Laura M., a mother of two, recommends keeping a broom handy for the sole purpose of sweeping toys into piles. The Matchbox cars, Fisher-Price people, and puzzle pieces can be swept, scooped, and dumped into a bin, and then cleaned, sorted, and put away.

THE OTHER FAST FOOD

Cooking for children can often involve a lot of effort for little satisfaction. It's also hard to make a meal while fending off children lest they get too near to a sharp knife or pot of boiling water. Kids often won't eat what's served, or they eat just a few bites. Couples rarely get to relax over the meal, much less eat any of it hot. Then, moments after preparing the meal, it's time to clean up the mess. As eating is essential to human survival, and especially to growing children, we have to feed our young ones, even if we don't always enjoy doing it. The following are some helpful strategies related to the Other Fast Food—not food you get through the drive-thru, but food you can procure and prepare quickly:

Shop for groceries online: Depending on where you live, your local supermarket can deliver your order, based on the selections you make from its website. You can even issue standing orders, requesting that milk and diapers be delivered every Friday, for example. If you don't want to cook, you can order prepared entrees. Most stores have a minimum order amount and a small service fee. Still, you'll likely save money by not succumbing to the impulse buys that happen at the store. (Think of all the money you spend when you go to the store *just* for a gallon of milk.) Another (big) benefit is not having to drag the kids into the store. Sometimes a supermarket run can be a fun outing and a way to fill time. Sometimes it's not.

Visiting chefs: Culinary professionals—often Stay-at-Home moms themselves—can be hired to come to your home and prepare one or two weeks' worth of meals that can be stored in your freezer. (Or they can cook in their own kitchens and deliver the meals to you.) While the service may seem geared toward employed people, it can be useful for a household with a Stay-at-Home mom, especially if the mom has just come home from the hospital with a new baby or is otherwise under the weather—or if she's simply too busy caring for kids to cook.

Meal prep kitchens: A current franchise trend—run under the brands Super Suppers, My Girlfriend's Kitchen, My Neighbor's Kitchen, Let's Eat, and others—meal prep kitchens are storefront businesses where a person can put together all of the raw ingredients for one entree or a dozen. The benefit is that all the shopping and prep work has been done for you, leaving you to make an appointment to go in and assemble the recipes, putting your nearly finished entree into a plastic bag or disposable oven pan for freezing, and later, cooking, in your home. The result is like having a homemade frozen dinner, but for someone who doesn't cook well, or doesn't have the time to cook, meal prep kitchens provide a way to prepare and serve up a fancy chicken Marsala. While each four-serving meal generally costs around $20, time and money is saved by not having to buy the ingredients at a grocery store.

Be your own meal prep kitchen: For a very short time, I spent a few Saturdays working for a friend at a meal prep franchise. (I figured it would be a fun way to get out of the house and make some pocket change.) While the recipes are tasty, and not having to shop and chop is a big timesaver, for some of the menu items, the prep work is so easy, anyone could do the same at home. For instance: A chicken parmesan platter amounts to little more than placing frozen, boneless chicken breasts in an aluminum pan, spreading on some jarred tomato sauce, and sprinkling shredded mozzarella and parmesan cheeses over the top. The concoction is covered and frozen, then popped unthawed into the oven. With a little shopping forethought (and adequate freezer space), a person can whip up several future meals in a few minutes. Other prepare-ahead solutions: Fresh vegetables (such as broccoli) can be cut and bagged for use later in the week. Rice can be cooked, cooled, put in a plastic bag, frozen, and then reheated in the microwave. One mother of two keeps peanut butter and jelly sandwiches in the freezer for use as school lunches. Put in a backpack in the morning, the sandwich is defrosted and ready to eat by lunch. As with many foods, there's a similar, prepared product on the market, but the do-it-yourself option is far more affordable.

Cook on weekends: Every old-world grandma knows you spend a day making your sauce or stock for use throughout the week. Many favorite recipes take time to prepare, so cooking on weekends means that you or your partner can prepare a fridge or freezer full of food while the other watches the kids. Or you can cook together, and take turns addressing the children's needs—or when possible, allow the kids to help.

Crock-Pot it: Because slow cookers are designed to take it slow, you can put frozen or thawed meat in the pot in the morning, cover it with a homemade or store-bought gravy, plug in the cooker, and leave it alone for the day. Slow cookers are good for making beef stews, pot roasts, pork tenderloins, potted chicken, chili, and soups. Unlike pressure cookers, which can be a bit scary, a slow cooker is simple and safe. Supply yourself with a Crock-Pot and a cookbook, and you'll be able to make home-cooked, hot meals every night of the week.

Eat healthy, not fancy: Again, life changes once you have children. While you may know how to whip up a mean soufflé, you really only have time to whip up some mashed potatoes. (And even in that case, maybe only the instant kind.) When kids are small, the goal is to get everyone fed and properly nourished. To do the latter often requires such cooking trickery as adding protein powder to pancake or cake mixes or pureeing vegetables and adding them (and their nutrients) to pizza sauce. There's time enough later in life for experimenting with new gourmet recipes and enjoying five-course, sit-down meals.

STAY-AT-HOME SURVIVAL GEAR:
DON'T LEAVE, OR STAY HOME, WITHOUT IT

Being a Stay-at-Home mom sometimes means you are so *at home* you don't get out of the house to replenish needed supplies. Other times, it can mean you and the kids are hardly home at all. No matter how old your brood is, there are certain must-haves that can get you through any day spent entirely in or out of the house.

Cheerios: All members of a household can eat, enjoy, and obtain nutrition and sustenance from a bowl of Cheerios (with or without the milk), and if you're on the go, it's an easily portable snack that does a great job of taking the edge off a cranky kid's hunger. In many ways, it's the universal food. Cheerios (or a generic knock-off) are perfect for toothless babes, preschoolers, big kids, teens, husbands, or the family dog, cat, hamster, bird, or fish. (Guess what my critters eat when I've run out of their specified pet food and can't get to the store?)

UHT shelf-stable milk: This product is a major find for families that drink milk. Sold under various brand names, the ultra-pasteurized milk needs no refrigeration until it's opened. That means you can keep fresh milk handy in your car, stroller, or diaper bag and not have to worry about refrigeration. The milk, which is commonly used in countries without readily available refrigeration, typically comes in one-quart aseptic cartons or in a six-pack of individual serving boxes (like a juice box). While it costs more than normal milk (about $2 a quart versus $1.60), a household can load up on the stuff and keep a milk reserve on hand in the pantry. (The cartons do have expiration dates, which are usually several months out.) Because my family of five goes through a gallon of milk a day, I try to keep at least two cartons on hand for our "we're out of milk!" emergencies. The milk tastes a little sweeter than regular milk, but kids don't find that a problem. Similar shelf-stable packaging exists for rice and soy milk products. (Shopping tip: At the supermarket, these shelf-stable milk products are typically kept in the baking aisle.)

Portable DVD players or iPods: The downside of such devices is that television entertainment is available to your child anytime, anyplace. If used too often, children expect that there's always something for them to watch on TV and that every car ride comes with a movie. Hence, limits are needed. However, a two-hour movie can be an invaluable distraction for a child strapped into a car seat while stuck in traffic en route to a beach vacation. Another use: A portable, battery-charged media player can occupy your kids during a blackout or in a waiting or exam room when you have to drag them to your doctor appointments.

A diapering back-up plan: A time may come, if it hasn't already, when you are down to one diaper, either at home or while on the go. You need a plan B, short of racing to the store, or trying to divine—via "elimination communication" (a recent potty training trend)—when the baby might need to go. Among the options:

- Even if you're out of diapers, chances are you have some sanitary pads in the house or, if you're in a mall or restaurant, you can buy one from a ladies' room vending machine. Stick a highly absorbent pad into the diaper. If you're lucky, the pad will absorb the mess and enable you to just change the pads until you get more diapers.

- Keep adhesive tape on hand—at home and in your diaper bag—for when a closing tab is accidentally ripped off of a diaper. First-aid tape is generally the best, but you can try others.

- For when you're totally out of disposable diapers, know how to make a diaper out of a towel or dish cloth. Have diaper pins (or tape) in reserve. Since you probably won't have rubber pants handy to put over the diaper, consider fashioning a very temporary pair out of a plastic bag.

Car with tinted windows, ideally a minivan: Minivans equal space—for your own children, and for those you need to drive if you're in a carpool. Tinted windows equal privacy—for any quick-clothing changes, or to nurse a baby, let a child use a portable potty, or allow an about-to-start-puking-from-motion-sickness child to lay on the floor for a while. As noted earlier in the book, I have frequently crawled into the back of my minivan, thrown a blanket over myself, and taken a nap while waiting in the parking lot of my younger twin's preschool (which is in a rural area with little to do). My cell phone alarm clock wakes me at dismissal time.

My minivan nap might seem a bit pathetic, but it's not unheard of. Survey respondent Heather writes, "In the afternoon my sons are at school, and if I drive around, I can often get my daughter to fall asleep. I usually end up taking a nap with her in the car."

Sometimes car napping isn't intentional. When Lyn arrived early for the carpool pickup line at her sons' school, she figured that since her toddler was asleep behind her in a car seat, she'd recline her seat and close her eyes for a few minutes. As Lyn and her daughter snoozed, hidden from view, the other cars simply drove around the SUV. Next thing Lyn knew, carpool was over, and she was parked in an empty lot. (Her sons were fine, having been sent to the aftercare program when their mom didn't show.)

Another reason for the tinted windows: Passersby won't be able to look into your vehicle and see the stained upholstery, crayon-marked seat backs, and floor strewn with diapers, snack crumbs, juice boxes, toys, books, discarded clothing, school memos, water bottles, and other assorted debris.

Miscellaneous survival gear: Baby wipes are useful for so much more than just cleaning messy hands and bottoms, and are especially effective at removing stains on carpets and upholstery. A rotating collection of picture books is good for entertaining cranky kids. A travel pillow and blanket, kept in a car or stroller, can comfort the impromptu (or overdue) napper.

Is a Stay-at-Home Mom with a Full-Time Nanny a Stay-at-Home Mom? (Discuss)

If a man's home is his castle, as the old saying goes, shouldn't his wife be treated like a queen—rather than as a servant or a one-woman palace staff?

At certain economic levels, some Stay-at-Home moms do get to live like queens. They live in stately abodes, their children cared for by babysitters, au pairs, or nannies. The house is kept pristine by a cleaning person or crew. The woman's job is to supervise the work, and she can choose to engage with her children and her household at her convenience (say, when the kids aren't whining and when the kitchen isn't a mess). She's a mom who stays home as opposed to being employed in the workforce, but is she really a Stay-at-Home mom?

Who's to say? It's hard to judge without letting some envy seep in. And besides, such princess brides are awfully rare. Most women who are Stay-at-Home moms either have no help or have help but are still in the game—going to Mommy & Me classes, chaperoning field trips, assisting with homework. Often they have more than two children, and many times they are married to men who work long hours or travel.

When I put the word out about this book, a handful of women who volunteered to answer the survey later wrote to say they didn't qualify, according to *The Guide's* definition of a Stay-at-Home mom. "I have a full-time nanny," emailed one. "I have three children, ages five, three, and one. While I spend time with them, I'm supervising a major renovation project, and I do volunteer work. It's hard to be in all those places at once."

I appreciated this gal's honesty, along with that of the other women who said they weren't employed but had full- or nearly full-time childcare help. It's easy to think of a Stay-at-Home mother with a full-time nanny shopping and relaxing all day, but I find from women who have regular sitters that such leisurely living is generally not the case. Sheriene, a former business consultant, describes herself as a hands-on mom who starts her day at 6:00 AM. "I have a nanny, but I'm around most of the time," she says. The nanny works from nine to three, during which time Sheriene runs errands unencumbered, spends a morning at nursery school with one of her two preschoolers, goes to a mom's club meeting or other appointment, and catches a one-hour nap before her afternoon-into-night shift as a Stay-at-Home mom.

Julie F., a former bond trader, also answered the survey despite my no-nannies-please caveat. She actually has two nannies, a morning nanny (who works from 7:30 to 11:00 AM) and an afternoon nanny (11:00 AM to 7:00 PM). A large part of why Julie F.

has so much help is that she gave birth to three children within three years. At the time she contacted me, her oldest was just three-and-a-half years old. "Most mothers can't afford the choice I have," she acknowledges. "I have twelve hours a day of help divided between two wonderful gals. They do everything and anything that needs to be done. It's like having an Alice from *The Brady Bunch,* except she doesn't live with us. We're very lucky."

Luck helps. But so does years of hard work. With the growing trend toward older moms, many women achieve great career successes with years of lucrative income before having kids. When these women become first-time moms in their late thirties or early forties, as Sheriene and Julie F. did, they either take extended (if not permanent) leaves from their professions or reduce their workloads significantly. In essence, such gals self-finance their Stay-at-Home years as well as the childcare and cleaning people they hire to make their domestic lives more manageable and enjoyable.

I can understand why Sheriene and Julie F. and other women I know have chosen to hire regular help; every Stay-at-Home mom could benefit by not having to do it all alone. These gals are fortunate, and fortunately they're smart enough to understand and appreciate their unique good fortune. You can't begrudge a hard worker the benefits of her success. Nor can you begrudge a lottery winner her riches, unless she's so clueless and inconsiderate she judges you for not having the same.

For the majority of Stay-at-Home mothers, women who care for their children without hired help, it isn't easy to be generous of spirit and nonjudgmental upon meeting another Stay-at-Home mom who has her nanny clock-in at 7:00 AM so she doesn't have to drive carpool. It's easy to feel jealous, especially so early in the morning.

But mothering comes in various styles and always has. Some mothers are hands-on 24/7, some work outside the home by necessity or choice, and some are home but choose or are expected to delegate domestic duties to others. (Think of the Victorian ladies who presided over mansions served by cooks, gardeners, governesses, butlers, and baby nurses. At certain socioeconomic levels, mothers were and in some places still are expected to be more managers than mommies.)

Every woman makes choices from the options she's given and acts within the scope of her means. Even though our methods may differ—sometimes greatly—every woman who loves, cares, and provides for her children is a mother; some just get to change a few less diapers than others.

Money *Matters*

Most women are employed in the workforce before they have children. But when a woman devotes her energies to caring for children rather than a corporation, she can find herself with no means of making money for herself or her family. Even if a mom and her partner share equal access to the household finances, it's easy for her to feel panicked about not having an income of her own, and to feel guilty for spending money she didn't personally earn. Some women go the other way. Finally free of office hours, they shop til they drop as a way to fill the day and keep occupied while pushing a stroller or waiting for kids to get home from school.

Either way, how a woman handles working as a Stay-at-Home mother without a paycheck can make or break her self-worth, her future, and her family's finances.

Social commentators such as Linda R. Hirshman *(Get to Work)* and Leslie Bennetts *(The Feminine Mistake)* argue that it's a blatant financial hazard for a woman to stay at home full-time. As noted in Chapter One, of educated women who become Stay-at-Home moms, Hirshman writes "their so-called free choice makes them unfree dependents on their husbands."

I disagree. I believe—I know!—a woman can stay home with her children, leaving the workplace either for a period of time or permanently, and find economic equanimity. However, I do agree that women need to be cautious about, as Bennetts writes, "relying on the blithe assumption that there will always be an obliging husband around to support them."

Having lived through my mother's marriages and divorces (she's asked that I not give numerical details), I have never taken for granted Bennetts's concern. That I actually have a husband who is supporting me remains an amazement to me. It was a huge leap of faith for me to leave my career in order to care for my family and, in doing so, become financially dependent upon my partner. As much as I truly believe my husband and I will be together until one of us dies—so far having weathered more than two decades together and situations that have sent many to divorce court—before I left the workforce at age thirty-seven, I made sure I had a moderate retirement nest egg socked away. Another way I'm able to deal with my financial "dependency" is that I'm in charge of our household's daily finances, investments, and insurance portfolio.

On that point: Ladies, there is little excuse for any Stay-at-Home woman with children to be left a destitute widow. With proper financial planning, a mother and her children can be protected from financial disaster in the case of her partner's death. (For more, see page 131.) However, divorce and job loss are not as easily protected against, and Bennetts is on target when she says the possibility of a marriage collapsing or a breadwinner spouse losing his job are "harsh realities" that won't go away by "willful obliviousness." Fair enough.

For that reason, Stay-at-Home moms need to be financially savvy. I believe doing so is a job requirement, not a choice. This chapter provides examples of the various money management styles Stay-at-Home women and their partners have employed in an attempt to navigate the money issue. These arrangements run the gamut from women on allowances, to women receiving "paychecks" from their husbands (monies that are deposited into a gal's personal bank account), to the Stay-at-Home partner acting as the household's chief operating officer *and* chief financial officer.

As noted before, the last option is the approach we take in my house. When my employed friends ask how I can stand being financially dependent on my husband, I explain: "He makes the money, but I control where it goes." Other women spin from a similar theme: "He makes the money, but it's my job to stretch his salary as far as it can go."

These strategies are praised in the best-selling book *The Millionaire Next Door,* in which authors Thomas P. Stanley, PhD, and William D. Danko, PhD, note that wealth can be achieved in a one-income household if the person who *isn't* producing an income protects the family's finances by wisely managing the money earned by the other partner. When that doesn't happen, or if both partners spend without control, the investment banker with the million-dollar bonuses may wind up putting his house on the market and declaring bankruptcy while the high school teacher next door is doing just fine.

Most self-made millionaires, Stanley and Danko report, have wives who are "planners and meticulous budgeters" and are "a lot more conservative with money" than their spouses. Even in households where one or both partners earns a high income, they add, "a couple cannot accumulate wealth if one of its members is a hyperconsumer."

As discussed in the previous chapter, many of today's Stay-at-Home moms are in fact their family's CFOs. Even if she's not making the long-term investment decisions, the Stay-at-Home spouse is often the family treasurer and comptroller, responsible for daily cash management and bill paying. To continue the corporate analogy further, even if a woman has no hands-on involvement with her household's financial management, she should at the very least serve as an educated and aware member of its board of trustees, one who knows what accounts are where and understands her family's insurance portfolio.

For Stay-at-Home moms who aren't comfortable being the family's money managers, it's still essential that they have a thorough understanding of how the family's finances are set up. As we all know, life doesn't always go as planned. Breadwinners become disabled and ill, and sometimes they die. Couples divorce. For the welfare of herself and her children, a Stay-at-Home mom must never be in the dark about her family's finances.

THE "PRENUPTIAL AGREEMENT"

No, I'm not talking about an actual signed, sealed, lawyer-negotiated prenup. I'm talking about a conversation, and understanding, between two partners as to how they'll handle the financial aspects of being a family. Ideally, this discussion should occur before the wedding, and kids. If it doesn't, think of it as a postnuptial or postnatal agreement. Money management arrangements among couples vary greatly depending on each person's talents, time, financial history and, perhaps, age.

"I personally would have a very difficult time being 'dependent,'" says survey respondent Diane D., a "self-financing" Stay-at-Home mom who's refusing any financial support from her spouse and is living entirely off of her former earnings. "I think it would suck the spirit right out of me, perhaps because I'm nearing forty and I've had such a good career. I think the normal way of doing things for people at age twenty is very, *very* different for people who start parenting in their late thirties or early forties. In one's twenties through early thirties, a person might not have gone as far in his or her career, so they can blend their finances more easily with a partner."

While Diane D. is able to support herself as a Stay-at-Home mom, Anne, a PhD in avian biology, says her former salary wouldn't even cover the cost of childcare, which was a frustrating reality considering her years of education and specialized knowledge. "Many years ago, my husband and I developed a 'team' mentality," she says. "We were at the beginnings of conflict because his earning potential was so much greater than mine. I was peeved and felt undervalued by society because I was working as hard as he was but was making only ten percent as much money. We realized that money could be a big problem for us if we didn't nip this competition in the bud."

Their solution: "Money either of us earns belongs to us both. All money goes into the family pot, no strings attached. In our relationship, there is no correlation between earning power and marital power," says Anne. "Instead of feeling jealous that he earned more than I did, I became proud of his salary, and of mine too. We decided to look at the joint result as two equal partners in the marriage."

There was a time not long ago when a woman in the United States had, for all intents and purposes, no independent financial rights. In many parts of the world, that's still the case. While being a Stay-at-Home mom may require being financially dependent upon a partner's earnings, it needn't—and shouldn't—mean lacking financial power or a say in financial matters.

THE COMFORT ZONE

My one fear about marrying my husband was that he wasn't good with money. He was twenty when I met him, and when he had money, he spent it. From the get-go of our marriage six years later, we agreed that I would be in charge of our shared finances. He's grown much more responsible in his spending, and even though I don't have an income (that's right, after taxes, my advance for this book essentially covers one mortgage payment), I have much less anxiety than I thought I would about being financially "dependent" on my spouse.

Liz R., who is in charge of her family's daily cash management while her husband handles the long-term investing, has also been assuaged of fear surrounding her own lack of financial independence. "I have friends whose husbands pay the bills and question a lot of the spending they do. That would put me over the edge," she says. "It's hard enough to be comfortable with spending money when you aren't contributing to the income, let alone if someone is also giving you a hard time. It's important to plan together to make sure both partners understand the financial picture of the future."

In other households, the Stay-at-Home spouse is the overall money manager. Reports Lyn, a former trusts and estates attorney: "I handle all of the finances, and I think my husband prefers it that way. Paying the bills, filing insurance papers, organizing and paying taxes, and managing household finances and investments takes an immense amount of time and energy."

The following arrangements for how couples manage their financial responsibilities come from the women who responded to my survey.

1. He Makes It, She Manages It

This is actually the most common scenario among the survey respondents: He's responsible for earning the money; she's in charge of bill paying, checkbook balancing, account management, and record-keeping. Major purchases and long-term investments are generally done in concert with one another.

According to Lorraine McDermott, PhD, an Annapolis-based psychologist and marriage counselor, when it works, the "he makes it, she manages it" system is the healthiest among the financial arrangements used by couples with a Stay-at-Home partner. "It encourages mutual support and trust while providing each person with a measure of financial responsibility and control," she says.

The arrangement often stems from a Stay-at-Home partner's skills, as it has in Jen's household. "I'm a detail person, and my husband likes only enough detail to make a decision," she explains.

Another benefit is that as the household money manager, instead of feeling dependent and powerless about not earning an income, a Stay-at-Home mom not only knows where the money is, but she may be the one doling out the breadwinner's allowance. As Sarah B. points out: "My husband asks *me* for money."

2. Joint Accounting

Many couples don't divvy up the household money management. Each spends within an agreed upon budget and updates the accounts accordingly. However, to avoid confusion and possible late fees, bill paying is often assigned to one partner. Tracy says her husband does the actual bill paying, but "we both have access to Quicken, so we each make entries and know exactly where we're spending every month."

3. Yours, Mine, and Ours

Arrangements in which each person has his or her own pot of money and individual accounts, while as a couple they also hold shared monies, can take many forms—and involve many bank accounts. My husband and I used the "yours, mine, and ours" strategy while we were both working, pre-kids. We abandoned this setup when he quit his job to go to grad school and I became the breadwinner and sole financial manager.

"We divide and conquer," says Joni. "I keep an eye on the monthly cash. My husband watches the overall 'big picture' and keeps track of our long-term goals. We agree upon monthly deductions for saving, negotiate large purchases, and have our own accounts for day-to-day stuff."

Amy reports that in her house, "I handle all household bills and any expenses that involve the kids or me. My husband handles his own personal bills (like his haircuts, dry cleaning, etc.). We have a joint savings account, but separate checking accounts and no joint credit cards. A specific portion of his paycheck gets deposited directly into each of the following accounts: my checking, his checking, the joint savings, retirement plans."

Dixie describes a system that has worked for much of her twenty-five years as a Stay-at-Home mom. "I hate to ask for money. *Hate* it," she says. "So early on we allotted a sum that is automatically deposited into my checking account for groceries, household expenses, and whatever I think I can afford. I'm pretty independent with it. We're flexible, and it works."

4. He Pays Her Salary
After the birth of her son, Sarah G., then thirty-two years old, negotiated a part-time schedule for her managerial job at New York's Metropolitan Museum of Art. But with the reduced hours came a greatly reduced paycheck. "I had a big problem with it," she recalls. "So my husband and I came up with the idea that he would pay me a salary." He paid, she deposited the money into her checking account, and each contributed to the household expenses as they had done before kids.

But the system petered out after a few months. "It was too much like I was his employee, not his partner," she explains. "It also felt as if he was giving me an allowance, which it wasn't, because the 'salary' was not meant for household expenses. It was supposed to allay my fear of not being able to support myself. When I stopped working altogether five years ago, it didn't seem as big an issue to me. I suppose I grew up some and realized that my husband and I *are* partners, and we have to work that way."

5. She Supports Herself

"We are completely separate financially. We don't share accounts. I have my budget and he has his, and we discuss it when spending goes outside those limits," says Diane D., whom we met earlier in this chapter. "It helps that I have my own ownership over my capital, and vice versa. I'm not dependent on my husband one bit."

While Diane D. and her husband share household expenses, her account is funded by her own past and current earnings, the latter derived from early mornings at her home computer spent futures trading. "I raised my own capital to take this break, and I continue to manage my capital so during my break, what I don't need to use to sustain myself grows," she explains. Diane D.'s only financial worries have to do with her retirement: "I do get nervous about that. I hate to see my capital drain on daily expenses. But I budget and plan, so I'm not losing any sleep over it so far."

Diane D. knows her arrangement is highly unique and, like many things in all of our lives, it stems from a childhood experience. "I've had to earn my own money since I was about fourteen," she explains. "My dad had a severe heart attack. He had his own business, and it took him years to recover. I held two or three jobs most of the time I was in school. I learned to save and find ways to have my money make money so that, eventually, I wouldn't have to work so hard. It put me in a good place once my first baby was born."

6. He Controls the Purse Strings

Some couples go with the traditional approach: She handles the home, he handles the money. Among the reasons a woman's partner is solely in charge of making all the decisions, or why access to the accounts might be restricted:

- She has no interest in the task.
- He has more (nonkid) time to pay careful attention to the finances.
- She doesn't have the skills or aptitude for the job.
- He believes that, as the man and the breadwinner, he should be in charge.
- She has a bad track record—in finances, responsibility, or marital commitment.
- He feels less anxious about having one income when he knows where it goes.
- It's a mutually agreed upon division of labor.

Women living with a "he's in charge" partner have varying views about the arrangement.

"My husband basically handles all the money matters," explains Laura P., a former social worker. "It's something I swore would never happen. We were together for eleven years before having our first child and always kept separate accounts. But it feels too overwhelming to try to do the financial stuff now, especially because he's in finance and I'm not. That being said, every few months, we do sit down and talk about the financial situation. Still, if anything ever happened to him, it would take me a while to get up to speed. I should be more involved."

Says Emily about her home finances: "I'm the CEO and COO of our household. He's the CFO in charge of all the bills, investing, finances, and money matters. We collaborate on all big issues, but this helps keep the different tasks manageable and not overwhelming to just one of us." Maura, a mother of five, is understandably "too busy to deal with bills," she says. "I leave it all up to my husband."

If you and your partner haven't yet figured out a financial arrangement you're both comfortable with, try taking the *In Your Game of Life, Who Gets to Be the Banker?* quiz at the end of this chapter.

Smart Money Dos and Don'ts

DON'T be clueless about your family's finances by depending on your partner to take care of everything money-related.

DO take charge of your household's budget and finances, or at least share the responsibility for paying bills and saving money and balancing the checkbook—so you, or both of you, know what funds are where, and where the money goes.

DON'T put all the accounts or bills in your partner's name, such as having him be the sole owner of a credit card account (while you have only user privileges) or putting all of the utilities in his name.

DO keep some credit cards and other accounts in your name so you have a credit history independent of your spouse's.

DON'T rely entirely on his savings, or your joint savings. What if he one day decided to empty the account? (To be fair, such

> duplicity goes both ways: I know a philandering woman who did this to her husband.)
>
> **DO** keep your own retirement account and perhaps a savings account, both as a safety net and so you can have some money that's entirely yours.

SOCIAL SECURITY FOR STAY-AT-HOME MOMS

Another financial fact of life Stay-at-Home moms need to fully understand is Social Security—especially as it relates to women who leave the workforce in order to care for children.

For starters, let's avoid the argument about whether or not Social Security will even be around when you become eligible to collect benefits. Let's play this game based on the assumption that Social Security will continue to exist. In 2008, people born after 1960 can collect full benefits at age sixty-seven.

Now, here's the rub: A person's Social Security benefit—which is the value of the monthly check she will receive in old age—is based on having a total of thirty-five years of paid employment. For each year worked, a certain number of "credits" are provided, based on the amount of the earnings. You need to have forty credits to be eligible for your own benefits. To calculate the value of those benefits, the Social Security Administration averages the earnings from your highest thirty-five years of income. Using various rate sheets and tables, that sum is then translated into a benefit. Men generally have no problem meeting or exceeding a work life of thirty-five years. Women, however, are another story.

I'll use myself as an example. I collected my first official pay-check—income from which taxes were taken out or later paid—at age seventeen. I then earned Social Security–eligible income of some form for roughly the next twenty years, until leaving the paid workforce at age thirty-seven. While I have achieved my needed forty credits, for a full four years, which were spent as a mother and frequent volunteer, my earned income was zero. I need to put in at least another fifteen years of income-generating work in order for my zero (and near-zero) years not to drag down my overall average. But even if I go back to earning a regular or semi-regular income, it's unlikely that I'll ever hit the six-figure level I was at when I stepped off the corporate ladder. If I *never* earn another cent, my Social Security calculations will be based on two decades of varying income and more than a decade of *nothing*.

In an article available through the support organization Mothers & More (www.mothersandmore.org), Kristin Maschka, once the group's president, calculated that by leaving the workforce for seven years to stay home with her child she would be forfeit-ing $2,000 a month in future Social Security benefits. "Assuming I live to be eighty-seven," she writes, "that's nearly half a million dollars." (I applaud Maschka for being brave enough to face what she's forfeiting. I haven't. Although I know that I've gained many things by being a Stay-at-Home mom, I don't think it would be good for my psyche to have a hard number in my head of how much I've financially lost.)

Social Security Math for Stay-at-Home Moms

- The cost of a Stay-at-Home career varies for each woman. You can calculate both your future benefits and losses by visiting www.ssa.gov/planners/.

A note to readers who aren't yet Stay-at-Home moms: Use the Social Security website's calculators before you turn in your resignation. The information may help you and your partner with your decision-making and financial planning.

The unfairness of the benefits formula is that a woman gets zero—*zero*—benefit or recognition for the years she works round-the-clock as a Stay-at-Home mom. As women still earn less per dollar than men do, and women are more likely than men to step in and out of the workforce, a woman's Social Security check is commonly smaller than a man's.

In lieu of recognizing that Stay-at-Home motherhood is valid work, the government allows a married woman to collect off of her spouse's work history instead, if receiving 50 percent of his benefit is more than 100 percent of hers. (And this scenario is also true in the other direction, with the husband collecting on his wife's higher earnings.) For instance, if a gal and her spouse make it to retirement together and have been married at least a decade (pay attention to this important ten-year rule, it's a biggie), she can collect either her benefit or an amount that's half of his. An example: If John gets

$5,000 a month, Jane gets $2,500, so as a couple living together they bring in $7,500 monthly.

A divorced woman can also collect spousal benefits, so long as the marriage lasted ten years. In such a scenario, a divorced Jane who had ten-plus years vested in a marriage can still claim the 50 percent spousal benefit, but since she's no longer in the same household as John, unless she remarries, the Social Security income coming into her home is just $2,500 instead of the $7,500 she would have had access to had the marriage not dissolved.

Unfortunately, because of the decade rule, a woman who stayed home with her children for six years of her seven-year marriage receives *no* spousal benefits. A Stay-at-Home mom who has a child or children with a boyfriend or same-sex partner has *no* protection. If she has her own work history, she may have access to benefits of her own. But teenage or young mothers who continue to have minimal employment are at risk of becoming very poor old ladies.

Women leaving the workforce or staying out of it to care for children need to keep these facts in mind. And if a marriage ends before ten years, a Stay-at-Home mom should push that her divorce settlement take into account her ineligibility for spousal Social Security benefits.

Everyone, male and female, should review the "Earnings and Benefit Estimate Statement," your up-to-date Social Security future benefits report, which is provided each year by the Social Security Administration. Watch for yours to arrive in the mail a few months before your birthday. Make sure the report has your correct name (this is especially important if you changed your name upon marriage), address, and earnings history. An entire year of earnings was once missing from my statement. I had to provide tax-return information in order for the correction to be made. If your statement doesn't arrive on its own, go to the Social Security website, www .ssa.gov, to request one. For information about Social Security and women, go to www.ssa.gov/women.

Social Security: The Basics

According to the Social Security formulas for 2008, a worker earns one credit for every $1,050 in wages, not to exceed four credits per year. To collect your own benefits, you need a lifetime total of forty credits.

Social security survivor benefits: If one spouse dies, benefits are provided for the surviving spouse and minor or disabled children. Check your annual statement to see if you've earned enough credits to provide benefits for your family. But more importantly, as a Stay-at-Home mom, you need to review and be familiar with your husband's annual Social Security statement. You should know if you'll receive a benefit if he dies, and whether he and others in the family will be covered in case of disability.

Your social security disability benefits: If a spouse or child becomes disabled, a disability benefit is available, depending upon the type and duration of the disability. As a Stay-at-Home mom, it's likely that your only source of disability compensation will be whatever you might get from Social Security. (See page 136 for information about private disability coverage.) Unlike with private insurance, under Social Security disability, you needn't be leaving a paid job. You just need to be physically unable to work at a job—even if you didn't have children clinging to your body. However, the bar is high for collecting. First, the benefit doesn't pay out until you've been fully unable to "perform any substantially gainful work" for five months. Secondly, it must be predicted that your disability will last for at least twelve months or else cause your death.

The spousal benefit: Because the lifetime earnings of a woman with children tends to be so much less than a man's, the chances are good that a Stay-at-Home mom will secure a more generous retirement benefit by piggybacking on her husband's earnings and choosing to receive a check half the size of his. While the spousal benefit is the main accommodation the program makes for Stay-at-Home motherhood, the bitter pill of it is that with this calculation, a woman's years of earning her own income is entirely ignored. On the plus side, for women and couples who come to this awareness ahead of time, it can mean less fretting about whether or not, for Social Security purposes, a woman needs to get back into the traditional workforce postkids.

Make the most of your benefits: A Stay-at-Home mom can improve her chances for receiving somewhat meaningful Social Security benefits by . . .

- working until she has achieved her forty lifetime credits
- staying married for at least ten years
- getting back into the workforce full-time (or via lucrative part-time work) at some point after staying home to care for children

However, despite your concerns and best-laid plans regarding Social Security, the reality is that even if Social Security is around when each of us becomes eligible to collect it, the amount provided is rarely enough to retire on comfortably.

SAVING FOR YOUR RETIREMENT

401(k)s: If you had a 401(k) account when you were in the workforce, keep those monies working for you in an individual retirement account. (If such funds aren't already in one plan, consolidate the varied accounts. When wisely managed, pooling the money generates more income overall.) By diversifying the assets into stocks, bonds, and money market funds that have varying levels of risk, you can achieve a balanced portfolio that can make and protect gains. If you are uncomfortable doing this yourself, put your funds into the hands of a professional money manager or investment advisor (such as with a company like Morgan Stanley or Citigroup Smith Barney, or a smaller investment firm you know). Interview investment advisors, get referrals from people you trust, and do your research about fees. Banks also offer IRAs, so you can consider using a bank or banker you have a relationship with.

To avoid paying taxes, any 401(k) funds you take from a job *must* be rolled over into an individual retirement account in your name. (IRAs cannot be joint accounts.)

If at all possible, avoid dipping into your 401(k) proceeds after (or even before) you leave the workforce. Doing so will require that you pay taxes and a penalty or pay back to yourself (with interest) the amount that you withdrew. Also, *do not* let a partner talk you into dissolving your account to use the money for, say, bills or a down payment, "because the two of you" will retire on his 401(k) and savings. *Your 401(k) income is your money. It's money you earned, and it may be the only money you'll ever have again that is entirely yours.* When you and your spouse retire together, you'll live off the funds from both of your accounts. If for whatever reason you don't make it to retirement together, your retirement money is still yours and yours alone. *I repeat*: If you and your partner need a chunk of money, pull it from his 401(k). He's still working; you're a Stay-at-Home mom or will be. He has more of a chance to recoup the loss in his retirement nest egg than you ever will in yours.

Individual Retirement Account (IRA): If you have a 401(k) rollover, that money needs to be put into an IRA. If you earn some income during your Stay-at-Home years, you can add money to that account, or open and contribute funds to another IRA in your name. But since IRAs are a way of deferring taxes on earnings and interest, the funds need to come from earned income (as reported on your tax return). The contribution may be deductible on your tax return, depending upon your earnings and whether your spouse has a work-sponsored retirement plan.

Saving for your kids: While this isn't exactly saving for your retirement, socking money away now for your kids' education expenses and letting it grow will keep you and your spouse from later cutting into whatever retirement money each of you has saved. Look into opening a 529 Plan or an Education IRA (sometimes called a Coverdell IRA), both of which allow income to grow tax-deferred. In some states, contributions to 529 Plans are tax deductible (generally up to $2,500 or so per account holder per child), which can help reduce your family's taxable income in a given year.

Many plans extend tax saving benefits to others (grandparents, a rich bachelor uncle) who choose to open and invest in a college savings account for your child.

INSURANCE ASSURANCE

When you become a parent, it's important to establish an estate plan (a will) and a guardianship plan for your children. The reality is, many parents haven't written their wills, planned for their estates, or spelled out their wishes for their children. But even if you don't have a will in place, at the very least you need to have life insurance coverage. As a Stay-at-Home mom dependent on the income of your working spouse or partner, it is *essential* that the income-earning member of your family carry life and disability insurance, and a good amount of it. If you don't want to deal with so much death planning at once, put the will on the back burner for a bit but *absolutely* get the proper insurance coverage in place.

LIFE INSURANCE: Life insurance for a couple in which there is a dependent spouse and/or children should serve three purposes:

- **Debt reduction,** which includes paying off a mortgage, loans, and credit card balances.

- **Income replacement,** so the Stay-at-Home parent can continue to care for the children without being forced back into the workforce. With this as the goal, the insured needs to determine how much income would be needed and for how long so, for instance, the surviving spouse can care for and get the kids into college and then support herself until her death. (Worth noting: Life insurance proceeds aren't subject to income taxes, in large part as an incentive by government for people to take responsibility for protecting and providing for themselves and their dependents.)

- **Child specific costs,** such as school or college tuition and special medical issues, all need to be factored in.

With the proper planning and the right amount of insurance, being a widow (or, for that matter, a widower) needn't mean destitution. In fact, it can mean just the opposite. As a woman in a mother's group I belong to commented when the subject of financial dependency was addressed in our newsletter: "Thanks to an awesome financial planner, my husband is worth much more dead than alive, so if, God forbid, he were to pass away, our family would be okay financially."

It may sound morbid, and you may feel weird about pushing the issue, but you need to ensure that your husband is properly insured. (If you're a Stay-at-Home mom in an unmarried relationship, you need to make sure that your partner is insured, and that you and your shared children are named as beneficiaries.)

"Some husbands actually think their wives can just go back to work or remarry if anything happens," says Catherine A. Mullen, an attorney who is a licensed financial representative and insurance agent with Northwestern Mutual in Manhattan. "That's not a responsible plan. The only thing in life that we're all guaranteed is we're going to die. We just don't know when."

When thinking about your insurance needs and portfolio, Mullen recommends you keep the following in mind:

Term insurance: This is the most affordable insurance, and can be particularly low-cost for nonsmokers. Whole life, variable life, and universal life policies, which are more expensive, offer additional benefits, such as providing dividends and cash back if you cancel the policy before the insured dies. But if those added options prove too pricey or unneeded, it's better to get straight term insurance, which only pays out upon death, than to have nothing at all.

Employer sponsored policies aren't enough: Life insurance received or purchased through a job might not be transferable if the holder loses or leaves the job. Also, if your spouse is healthy and relatively young, he might get a better rate on his own than through his employer (who has negotiated fees based on having to cover folks of diverse ages and health status). It's best to buy as much insurance as you can when you're young, and hold on to it. Most employers who do offer life insurance only provide coverage equivalent to a one-year salary. Unless you're a Stay-at-Home mom with a huge savings account or rich parents, one year's salary is not enough life insurance to have on your breadwinning partner.

Follow through on the medical: Many policies require that the insured submit to blood and urine analysis and perhaps a physical including an EKG. Several applicants Mullen was working with were in the World Trade Center on 9/11. Because their medical screenings had not been completed, due to their own procrastination, some died under- or uninsured; others who survived, but were left with disabilities, found it very difficult to procure coverage.

It's important to insure yourself too: Don't let anyone tell you that because you don't "work" you don't need to be insured. If you died, could your partner afford to hire a nanny and housekeeper so he could still work? Perhaps he and the kids would be so distraught by your passing that he'd need to quit his job to help himself and the children deal with their loss. A life insurance policy on you would help finance those costs.

"A $250,000 term life insurance policy on a healthy thirty-year-old female nonsmoker can cost less than $200 a year," says Mullen. "But the same people who are buying a third or fourth flat-screen TV for their home are the ones who claim they can't afford any additional insurance."

Check the suicide clause: Many insurance policies won't pay out if the insured dies by suicide. Some will pay so long as the policy has been in force for a certain period of time. Know what your insurance carrier's provisions are for suicide. I'm personally aware of families in which the mother killed herself, the breadwinner father killed himself, and another attempted suicide. Depression and mental illness are not uncommon. And sometimes people get into panicked situations in which they consider suicide to be the only option. It's important that a Stay-at-Home mom and her children be protected against a possible, though unlikely, spousal suicide.

Know the exclusions: If your husband perishes while jumping out of an airplane (for fun or as a paratrooper in the military), many policies won't pay. If your spouse partakes in dangerous hobbies or work, shop for a policy that will cover those risks.

Account for inflation: A man leaving his wife and kids $1 million in life insurance might sound like a lot, but you have to remember that prices for everything will be more in the future than they are today. Inflation generally increases at a rate of 3 percent a year. The cost for higher education has been increasing about 5 percent annually. When thinking about the amount of insurance you'll need, consider both your future cost of living and whether putting the insurance proceeds into a professionally managed investment account will be able to provide added income from dividends and interest.

Tell the truth: If you or your spouse is a smoker, you'd better say so. Policies can be denied during the application or voided upon death if it's discovered that a person didn't fess up about a medical condition or risky behavior.

Buy insurance from a reputable agent or agency: Shopping on the Internet is convenient and quick, but for life insurance it's not always the wisest way to go. A responsible, licensed insurance agent will look at your entire financial picture and goals in determining your needs. She will then work with you to acquire the amount of coverage you can afford, and find an insurer that fits your needs, such as if you have a preexisting condition. Many insurance agents are independent contractors, which means they are able to choose from any company, so long as they always consider the products being offered by their sponsoring insurer. In the event you need to collect on the policy due to a death, you want an agent you can call and a company that will pay promptly. (Among the indicators that it will: Having high financial ratings and a low complaint history.) Says insurance agent Mullen: "The better the company, the quicker the benefits are paid out upon a death."

Have access to other money: Some insurance companies can pay out within forty-eight hours of receiving a copy of a death certificate. But there are many cases when a death certificate isn't issued promptly, or is significantly delayed due to the death being accidental, mysterious, or a body not being found (such as what happened after the attacks on 9/11). You need to have access to money and the ability to pay your bills while you wait for an insurance settlement.

You can't insure someone on the sly: Hollywood storylines often have one spouse taking out a secret insurance policy on another, and then having that person killed in order to collect the million-dollar policy. In the real world, it's difficult to get anything more than $10,000 or so of coverage without the insured's consent and participation.

Naming beneficiaries: There are many ways insurance money can be paid out. It can all go to one person, such as the surviving spouse, or it can be divided between the spouse and the kids. The funds can be directed into a trust fund, or to a guardian. If you have a disabled or special needs child, you might want to consider establishing a trust specifically for him or her.

DISABILITY INSURANCE: Another insurance *must* is that a breadwinner carry disability insurance. Adults are more likely to become disabled young than die young. I know a man who was in his early thirties when he was diagnosed with cancer. At the time he was a partner in a small business and the sole support of his Stay-at-Home wife and two children. He had health insurance but no disability coverage. The man managed to work part-time despite undergoing surgery and chemotherapy. His cancer was cured, but it's likely he'll never be approved for private disability insurance or, if he is, he may very well be paying a higher premium and it might have a cancer exclusion. Many families aren't as lucky to be able to bounce back financially from such a disability.

As is true of life insurance, with disability insurance it's best not to rely solely on coverage your spouse might have from work.

Employer-sponsored policies typically provide only a portion of a person's salary (often a maximum of 60 percent as opposed to the 80 percent recommended by financial planners) and the insurance usually can't be retained when an employee leaves the company. And don't just count on getting coverage from the next job. What if the next job is working freelance? If your husband doesn't have adequate, retainable, inflation-adjusted disability insurance, contact an insurance agent who specializes in disability and pursue buying individual coverage. According to Mullen, "The most important piece of a disability plan is knowing it will pay when there is a disability. Most people focus on cost alone, but you get what you pay for."

My husband and I pay for two individual disability policies on him, in addition to a group policy through his work. While there are no tax breaks for disability premiums, if a person becomes disabled, the income received is tax-free. Interestingly, unlike with life insurance, disability insurance tends to be less expensive for men than for women. A primary reason: Women live longer and linger, men just die.

Unfortunately, a Stay-at-Home mom can't buy a disability policy if she is not earning an income. While there are instances, depending on the company and the policy, when a Stay-at-Home mom can collect benefits if she suffers a disability, most often she's out of luck. Private disability insurance exists to replace income lost due to disability. It does not provide previously nonexistent income. (I wonder: If a woman is paid on the books by her spouse for being "a professional nanny," might she be able to qualify? *Hmm?*)

Disability insurance is complicated. I took out a policy when I was twenty-five years old, and it actually paid me when I was on bed rest with my twins a dozen years later—because, at the time, I had been working part-time. While the policy likely wouldn't cover me as a Stay-at-Home mom with no income, I still pay the premiums, so I'll have the coverage if or when I return to paid employment. If I had to reinsure myself in my forties, I'd be paying a lot more in premiums than I do at the rate I locked in nearly two decades ago.

THE MONIED MOM

While it's not uncommon that the breadwinner in a Stay-at-Home household makes a lot of money (hence the ability to live on one income), in some couples it's neither the husband nor wife who supports the family with a Stay-at-Home parent. Instead, it's Father or Mother or Grandfather.

A few respondents to my survey referred to how "family money" helps ease their anxieties about forsaking work for home. In my own circle of friends, I know couples whose financial burdens are greatly relieved by old money, as well as one woman whose father-in-law provided her with a salary for staying home. Although these couples do fret over their routine bills (the mortgage, car payments, groceries, utilities), they often don't pay for their vacations (which are taken at family homes), and they rarely worry about the costs of their children's educations, which are or will be paid for by a grandparent or trust fund. In some cases, these couples needn't even save for their own retirement, since an inheritance awaits.

As a Stay-at-Home mom, you're going to encounter Stay-at-Home women from a variety of socioeconomic levels. If you and your partner are struggling to make ends meet on a single salary, it can be hard to be around Stay-at-Home mothers who spend frivolously or think nothing of hiring a sitter so they can get a manicure, shop, lunch, or work out with a trainer. Turning the tables, if you don't have to pinch every penny, it can be tiresome to have a pal who can't do much with you because she can't afford a sitter, a shopping spree, or a night on the town. Ideally, every Stay-at-Home mom needs to surround herself with friends who can see beyond their own unique circumstances and relate to who she is and how she lives.

"Intereconomic" friendships are absolutely possible. One of my best friends has two homes, several luxury cars, and children whose current private school and future college tuitions are trust fund–financed. When she's stressed, she treats herself to a few days at the exclusive Canyon Ranch spa. But this friend doesn't look down on me for driving a beat-up minivan, and when we go out, we do so according to my budget, not hers. She has never made me feel I have to live up to her level of luxury and spending. On the other hand, I've been acquainted with Stay-at-Home women who couldn't fully appreciate why my financial situation prevented me from hiring help when my husband lived weekdays out of town and I was home alone with the kids.

If you know a highly financed Stay-at-Home mom, here's hoping she's humble and generous of spirit. If she is, and you're her pal, you and your kids might be invited to the family ski lodge or beach house. If you're the one living the good life, know that it can be really nice to have a close friend who isn't part of the country club/private school clique, and who isn't trying to keep up with the Joneses—or you.

DIVORCE AND THE STAY-AT-HOME MOM

Andrea married at age twenty-five and stopped working, as an administrative assistant, when she had her first child the following year. Her second child arrived seventeen months after that. Almost eight years into her marriage, Andrea discovered that her husband was having an affair. Now thirty-five, she's back in the workforce as a divorced mother of two.

Andrea's Story

No one likes to think about it. But statistics tell us that half of all married couples will divorce. This is what Andrea says she wishes she knew when she got married and became a Stay-at-Home mom:

Coming from a long line of solid marriages, divorce was something I never expected to touch my life. But it arrived smack at my doorstep when my husband found himself unable to resist an old flame who got a job working at his company. He and I spent months in couple's therapy and the better part of a year trying to get past this bump in the road of our marriage. In the end, he couldn't get past her. So I got a backbone and started divorce proceedings.

When I was warned that getting a divorce could take up to two years, I laughed at the absurdity of it taking so long. Well, two years later, the final papers were finally signed. I lived through a hell I wish on no woman (well, maybe just one woman), but I've come out stronger, wiser, and even better off emotionally than I've ever been.

> No one plans for divorce, wants it, or comes out unscarred from
> it. Sadly, the statistics are such that being as naive as I was about
> it happening to me was foolishly unrealistic. You have insurance
> for your house and car. You also need some for yourself.

Because of her experience, Andrea has the following advice for
all women:

Handle the household finances: You're essentially the COO of
your household—become the CFO as well. Being unaware, unedu-
cated, and uninvolved with how your family's money is handled,
where it goes, and how much even exists is simply ignorant. In a divorce situation, it can cost you hours, and thousands of dollars, to
sort through bills, estate planning papers, insurance, investments,
you name it. To protect yourself and your children (as it's often the
mom's job to do this in a divorce), you need to take care of your
family's finances yourself, or else have a strong handle on what's
happening with your household's money.

Keep good records and files: Be vigilant about good record-
keeping—of household bills, legal documents, insurance policies,
mortgage papers, tax returns. In general, it's a good idea to have
proper files, but if your marriage goes off course, such records will
make the legal process much smoother.

Have some money of your own: If at all possible, keep a fund
tucked away *for yourself* that is *accessible only by you.* Add to
the account, in any amount, regularly. Divorce attorneys generally
require a sizable retainer up front. If you wind up never needing an

attorney, all the better. You can someday splurge on yourself for saving so well.

Own a car in your name: If your name isn't on the title to your car, and the break-up with your spouse gets acrimonious, you could lose access to the vehicle during or after the divorce. If your household owns more than one car, try to have at least one (preferably paid-off) vehicle titled in your name.

Keep your résumé current: Every little thing you do as a Stay-at-Home mom (such as when you organized the community yard sale) builds your skills set. Even if you're only volunteering, you can list those efforts and achievements on your résumé as examples of your marketable experience.

Know that alimony isn't automatic: Divorce settlements aren't always as supportive as you'd expect toward a spouse who either left her career to care for children, reduced her working hours, or never had as lucrative a job as her mate's. A typical alimony award extends for roughly half the duration of a marriage.

Always remember—you're a partner, not a dependent: Just because you're not earning an income doesn't mean you're not an equal contributor to the family. You work for your family, and your home is your office. You need to have an equal say and awareness in all financial decisions.

What's His Is Yours (and Vice Versa): Marital Assets

If possession is nine-tenths of the law, a Stay-at-Home mom must know exactly what she owns. Although there are exceptions, most property or assets acquired during a marriage are referred to as **marital** or **community property.** Even nontangible assets can be considered joint property. For instance, when my husband quit his job to attend graduate school, during which time I served as the sole earner supporting our expenses and rents in two cities, my lawyer sister-in-law reminded us both, "That master's degree is half hers!" (Thank you, Barbara.) Items considered **separate** or **nonmarital property** are assets that a spouse acquired before a marriage, or during a marriage by means of inheritance or receiving a gift.

Although a Stay-at-Home mom isn't necessarily earning income, her spouse's income (including bonuses and retirement plan) is legally hers. What portion is hers can vary, except in **community property** states, where assets are divided equally no matter who contributed the lion's share, or why. Currently, Arizona, California, Idaho, Louisiana, Nevada, New Mexico, Texas, Washington, and Wisconsin are the only community property states in the country.

Credit and credit cards: Like assets, a couple's debts are also shared, especially in community property states. The primary exceptions to having one partner held liable for another's over-spending would be if, for example, the credit card was not a joint account *and* the purchases were not for the benefit of the family. So, if a man charges up his personal credit card by calling phone-sex hotlines, and the couple breaks up, that's his debt. However, if a wife used her personal credit card to pay for groceries and

▶

doctor co-pays, that's a family expense, hence the responsibility for paying the bill post–break-up is at the very least shared.

A related tidbit: Unless a couple resides in a community property state, one partner *can* open an individual credit account without the other's knowledge or permission. In fact, it's actually wise for a Stay-at-Home mom to maintain or open at least one of her own financial accounts in order to secure her personal credit profile and credit worthiness. It's worth remembering that not so long ago, prior to the women's movement of the 1960s and '70s, wives could not receive credit separate from their husbands. As a result, women were essentially treated as having the financial history of a child. If they divorced, they were routinely hampered in securing financing (such as a mortgage) or establishing charge card and credit accounts.

Taxes: The payment of taxes, and the accuracy of a filer's tax return, are also shared liabilities. The only way a spouse can be protected from the inaccuracy or intentional deceit involved in a tax return is to complete a return as "married, filing separately." Unfortunately, in situations involving disproportionate income, such as in a family with a Stay-at-Home spouse, "married, filing separately" typically results in a larger tax liability than the more economical joint return.

REAL ESTATE AND FINANCIAL ACCOUNTS

For couples that own property or have investments, attention should be paid to how the ownership of such assets is recorded. What's right for each couple varies, but no woman should ever face the nightmare of learning that the home she lives in isn't really hers. (As might happen if the deed to the family home was registered in the husband's name only.)

Following are the typical ways property can be co-owned by a couple. For determining your specific needs, and what's allowed in the state where you live, speak with an accountant, attorney, or estate planning professional.

Joint tenancy: Sometimes called *joint tenancy with right of survivorship*, this type of ownership holds that if one partner dies, the survivor becomes the sole owner of the property. However, if the deceased partner has unsatisfied debts, a creditor can force the survivor to sell the property in order to receive payment of the debt.

Tenancy by the entirety: This type of title can only be used by married couples. It varies from joint tenancy in that a creditor of the deceased partner *cannot* force a survivor to sell the property to repay the debt.

Tenancy in common: Available to unmarried people as well as married couples, each partner in this ownership agreement retains control of a share of the property, equal or not. A tenant in common has no right of survivorship. Instead, if a partner dies, his/her share passes to the heir(s) designated by that person's will. (Such an heir or beneficiary is usually the spouse.) Couples with significant financial assets often choose to title property in this manner due to the benefits it can provide in reducing estate tax liabilities.

Voices: How Do You Feel About Not Having an Income of Your Own?

"A little scared. Sometimes a lot scared. I have just a small 401(k) from working, and it's scary that I'm in my thirties and don't have much saved. The divorce rate makes it scary too. I'd like to work again at some point to have more savings for my husband and myself."

—Kara

"It totally bugs me. I was a fiercely independent person for such a long time. It's a bitter pill to swallow. I just try and take the long view. Hopefully I'll go back to work in a few years and he can take some time off!"

—Gerri

"Horrible. I still have income from some work, but it's very minor. I could not support our family. I feel this puts a lot of stress on my husband. I also worry about what if something happened and I could not rely on him. How would I survive?"

—Cindy

"I hate it. My husband is not selfish with our money, he doesn't play any monetary power trips, but I liked making my own contribution, and I liked having more money and feeling more secure."

—Erin Z.

"I don't feel financially dependent. I brought a considerable amount of assets into this marriage—we live in a house I bought— and it's because I did that we have the ability to dispose of my

▶

husband's income in ways that we do. Also, I feel he's getting a fantastic financial deal: Fabulous children, a wife with interests, decent meals ready when he manages to get home. Everyone should be so lucky."

—Sandra

"This was one of the hardest things for me to adjust to. I especially felt like I was a 'nothing' when it was time to buy gifts. On my husband's birthday I would think, 'Why am I even wrapping this present? I'm using his money to buy him a gift.'"

—Ginny

"I don't have strong feelings about being financially dependent on my husband. He's dependent on me for pretty much everything else."

—Nicki

"I think you have to make the decision that is best for you and your family now, in terms of whether you work full-time, part-time, or not at all. While I do plan for the future as much as I can, I could get hit by a bus tomorrow, and all of my best-laid plans would be for nothing. I intend to go back to work when my kids are in school. I fully realize I won't be stepping into a position or salary that I would have if I hadn't stopped working, but I'm fine with that. I think I'll eventually make up that difference."

—Jen

"I don't really see myself as being financially dependent on my husband. He has the freedom to work and travel for his job because I stay at home. I manage the finances. In a manner of speaking, he's financially dependent on me!"

—Molly

▶

"I don't miss my income because I feel that being at home is much more rewarding and valuable to our family. The kids and I are financially dependent on my husband, no doubt. When I decided to stay home, there was no problem with both of us falling into our roles as breadwinner (him) and head of household (me). We wouldn't have it any other way and almost daily say how happy we are that we can afford for me to stay home."

—Colleen

"I thought it would bother me and I would feel awkward, but my husband always reminds me that the money he brings in is our money and not his."

—Julie C.

"I don't feel guilty at all about not providing a paycheck to our family. What I'm providing is infinitely more important than whatever my paycheck was."

—Amy

"Are you kidding? I earn at least half of his income by raising our children!"

—Joni

IN YOUR GAME OF LIFE, WHO GETS TO BE THE BANKER?

Some people are just better with money than others. If it's not readily apparent who the Financial Wizard is in your household, grab your partner and a pencil and take this quiz.

Select the answer that best applies.

1. Which one of you is detail oriented?
   a. Me
   b. My partner
   c. Both of us
   d. Neither of us

2. Prior to getting together, which one of you paid off your credit cards each month?
   a. Me
   b. My partner
   c. Both of us
   d. Neither of us

3. If given $10,000 with no strings attached, you would:
   a. Buy a luxury item you've wanted but otherwise couldn't afford (such as a piece of jewelry or home entertainment system)
   b. Pay bills
   c. Put it into savings
   d. Use it on a home improvement, family vacation, or romantic getaway

4. How do you pay for purchases?
   a. Cash or debit card, sometimes overdrawing the account
   b. Cash or debit card, spending within a budget and/or available cash
   c. Credit card (and carry a balance)
   d. Credit card (and pay the bill in full when it's due)

5. When out shopping, how likely are you to make an impulse purchase for items sold at the cash register? (e.g. a magazine, toiletry, food item, beverage, gadget, etc.)
   a. Very likely
   b. Somewhat likely
   c. Unlikely
   d. Hardly ever or never

6. How much does each of the following typically cost your household? (Don't do any research, just guess. Points go to whoever answers closest to reality.)
   a. Your monthly mortgage or rent: _____
   b. Your monthly utility costs (gas, water, and/or electricity): _____
   c. Your nonmortgage loan payments (car loans, student loans): _____
   d. Your weekly grocery bills: _____
   e. The going hourly rate for a babysitter in your area: _____

7. Name the following companies you have accounts or policies with. (One point for each category with a correct answer.)
   a. Auto Insurance: _____
   b. Health Insurance: _____
   c. Life Insurance: _____
   d. Disability Insurance: _____
   e. Homeowner's/Renter's Insurance: _____
   f. Checking Account: _____
   g. Savings Account: _____
   h. Investment Account(s): _____
   i. Credit Card Account(s): _____
   j. Number of open credit card accounts you have together (or individually, if you keep separate accounts): _____

8. Assume that you and/or your partner has an IRA or 401(k) retirement account and you make a withdrawal from it. Which of the following scenarios is true?

   a. The money can be used without penalty if put toward the purchase of a primary residence.
   b. If you are no longer employed, the money is yours to withdraw and do with as you choose.
   c. If you aren't of retirement age, you'll be taxed on the withdrawal, will be accessed an early fee, and/or may need to repay the funds with interest.
   d. Such funds are saving accounts that you can dip into, regardless of your age or employment status.

9. Which statement best reflects your feelings about shopping?

   a. I love, love, love, love shopping!
   b. I like shopping.
   c. I can take it or leave it.
   d. I shop only when I have to.

10. Which statement most accurately describes your shopping strategy?

    a. I grab and go.
    b. I look for bargains and use coupons when I have them.
    c. I buy what I want or need, regardless of cost.
    d. I shop with a list (either written or in my head) and pretty much stick to it.

11. What do you do with your ATM slips and other financial receipts (credit card slips, doctor's visit receipts)?

    a. Toss them in the trash
    b. Shove them into my purse/briefcase/pocket
    c. Record the transactions or put them in a safe place for recording later
    d. Give them to my partner to do something with

12. What do you do when the mail arrives?

   a. Sort and open it right away, putting the bills in a special spot
   b. Put it all in a pile and open it when I get a chance
   c. I don't know, my partner deals with the mail
   d. Hmm, good question

13. It's tax time. What will you do?

   a. Pull out a folder of tax receipts and documents
   b. Start looking for your tax receipts and documents
   c. File for an extension
   d. Hope that your partner, accountant, or someone else will figure out your tax situation

Scoring:

A perfect score = 100 points

1. a = 10   b = 0   c = 10   d = 0
2. a = 10   b = 0   c = 10   d = 0
3. a = 0   b = 10   c = 10   d = 5
4. a = 0   b = 10   c = 0   d = 10
5. a = 0   b = 3   c = 5   d = 10
6. 1 point per question for whichever partner's answer is closest to the real cost
7. 1 point per correct answer
8. a = 0   b = 0   c = 10   d = 0
9. a = 0   b = 2   c = 3   d = 5
10. a = 0   b = 5   c = 0   d = 5
11. a = 0   b = 2   c = 5   d = 0
12. a = 5   b = 3   c = 0   d = 0
13. a = 5   b = 3   c = 2   d = 0

How did you do? Whoever scored higher may be the more suitable banker between the two of you. If you both have high scores, think about ways you can share the money management duties. If you both had low scores, as a couple, you might want to consider financial counseling, or else seek out some financial strategies that can work in your home.

Ms. or Mrs. Smith?

When I was in my twenties, I worked for a talented editor who was and still is a super successful publishing executive. One day, Alan (not his real name) and I were in an office kitchen at the same time. I was grabbing a soda and saw him staring at the coffeemaker. "Do you know how this thing works?" he asked. I didn't—I wasn't a coffee drinker—but after looking at the machine for a moment, I figured out its parts, put in water and coffee grounds and then pushed a button. Voilà, the coffee started brewing. "Wow, thanks," said Alan, relieved. "You're so domestic. I don't know if that's a good thing or a bad thing."

Huh? It's a good thing, thank you, if, as in this example, being domestic involves both practical intelligence and practical life skills (like being able to prepare yourself a beverage). Yet, perhaps because domesticity is most often associated with women, those talents are easily demeaned, even though they're essential to human survival. As my father, borrowing from Woody Allen, often joked about his own parents: "My mother dealt with the mundane matters, like where we should live, go to school, what doctors to go to, feeding the family, caring for the children and house. My father took care of the important stuff, like whether our family should recognize Red China." To us smart, capable, twenty-first-century women, the question is this: Does being a homemaker, housewife, Stay-at-Home mom, full-time mom—whatever you call yourself— automatically make you a "traditional" wife and mother?

For a woman used to a fairly egalitarian relationship with her partner, becoming a Stay-at-Home mother can be a difficult adjustment. Not only does her daily life change enormously, there's no natural equality in having one partner go to work and the other stay home.

Lorraine McDermott, PhD, an Annapolis-based psychologist who specializes in marriage and family counseling, notes that the traditional family model—dad as breadwinner, mom as homemaker— can actually be hazardous to marriages. "It forces couples to live parallel lives," she says. "A man spends his day at a job, where he interacts with other people. A woman spends her day at home, either alone or in the company of only children. He is paid for his efforts; she isn't. She knows the workings of their family and home and community; he often doesn't. At night, the roles continue or, in some cases, are reversed, because she needs a break from the kids and he actually wants to spend time with them. The demands can cause each person in the marriage to have separate needs and interests, which over time can lead the partners to have less in common with one another and spend less time together as a couple."

I can totally see how such a scenario is possible. But is it any better for a marriage to have both parents working full throttle, with one or both also attempting to manage the care of the kids and home? Essentially, marriage is hard. Adding children to the mix makes it even harder. For many reasons, it's a miracle *any* marriage survives children.

A marriage can be structured in myriad ways, and each arrangement has its perks and pitfalls. That said, there are challenges unique to a marriage in which the woman's career and income is forfeited so she can stay home to care for children. While the pressure on a man to provide for his family can cause immense stress, a woman who is dependent on her spouse or partner for her own financial welfare, and that of her children, may experience a different, but similarly worrisome, level of stress and concern. Because she intentionally put herself into such a dependent situation, a woman might also begin to question her own judgment, abilities, and worth.

While women often experience the anxiety and uncertainty that comes with making tough personal decisions regarding work and family, men generally don't have to make the hard choice: They just assume they can have both. Their work versus family burden is eased a bit more since women today routinely work for pay outside the home, which enables many men to have a career *and* family without also bearing the 1950s-era responsibility of being the sole breadwinner. An argument can be made, and often is, that because women today are so capable, irresponsible guys are never required to fully grow up, including when they become fathers.

In light of today's norms, it can seem like a blast from the past when a household has a breadwinner dad and a Stay-at-Home mom who shoulders all or essentially all of the family's domestic duties, such as all childcare and housekeeping. Some Stay-at-Home women

do so because their husbands have demanding jobs and work extremely long hours. But several do so because the homefront is considered her responsibility. I have a friend whose husband feels that
since he works full time and endures a horrendous commute, he
shouldn't have to ever take sole charge of the kids on the weekend.
So other than for occasional sitters, my friend is on full-time domestic duty seven days a week. "If you don't like it," her husband tells
her, "go back to work."

Such a statement, and attitude, harkens back to the days when
fathers didn't change diapers and a wife was unapologetically referred to as "the little woman" or, worse, the "ol' ball and chain."
There are still plenty of guys out there who think their wives don't
work, because "all they do" is care for the kids and the house.
There are men who think their Stay-at-Home wives are so lucky "to
not have to work." I had a heated conversation with one friend's
husband who announced at a party that "women these days have it
so easy" because, unlike in his parents generation, fathers today are
so hands-on with their kids. While not disputing his mom's hard
work caring for her children and a home, I pointed out that during
his parents' generation, most all moms stayed home and dads went
to work, whereas today, most women with children also have paid
jobs. I threw his comment back at him, saying "Men today have it
so easy. They don't have to be the sole support of their families."
(Amazingly, the self-employed father of three with whom I was arguing had an employed wife whose career provided the family's
health insurance.) I added that even if a woman today is "lucky to
not have to work," chances are good that the money she earned

while employed helped buy the family's home, or has helped finance one parent being able to stay home with the kids.

Survey respondent Erin Z., a former Wall Street trader, noticed that some disregard and traditionalism emerged in her husband once she became a Stay-at-Home mom. "Even though I was making more money than he was when I left my job, the past six years have completely erased my credibility as an equal," she says. "There is no more sharing of household chores, because this is now my 'job.' He uses the 'I work' speech as much as he can, when I know his days are so much more sane than mine. Some nights I just cave in and avoid the fight, but when I do have a brilliant moment of clarity and all my arguments make complete sense, I'll get a week or two of kitchen cleanup, an occasional dinner cooked, and he will supervise the kids in putting their laundry away."

Speaking up and standing your ground in any setting is tough. Having to do so with your partner, upon whom you rely for so much and with whom you don't want to argue (especially when the kids are around), can make you shrink from the fight. But it shouldn't be a fight. In a moment of peace, make the point that what you do *is* work and, like him, you need time off from work, or at the very least a change of routine. (The truth is, parents are always working, so few people with children ever really get any time off.) Just as you don't expect him to be at the office or at his job 24/7, he can't expect such endless labors of you. Assuming that both of you chose to be parents, he needs to recognize that while you're "lucky" to not have to worry about earning an income, he's *damn* "lucky" to have you at home caring for his kids.

THE TRADITIONAL AMERICAN FAMIILY

I worked at *LIFE* magazine in the 1990s, nearly half a century after the magazine's 1950s Golden Age, an era many Americans believe to have been the heyday of the traditional American family—a time when dad went to work wearing a suit, while mom wore a crisp apron and stayed behind to care for Junior, his pig-tailed sister, and the foursome's lovely home. *LIFE* magazine, my modern-day bosses often joked, was "a mythical bridge to a time that never was." The comment stems in part from the fact that if you looked beyond the white picket fences, all was not hunky-dory on the homefront, especially not with mom.

In 1963, the now iconic book *The Feminine Mystique* first appeared on shelves. Within its pages, Betty Friedan, a married mother of three and part-time writer, examined the lives of women in the fifteen preceding years of post–World War II America. During that time of celebrated American prosperity, women had been pushed out of the workforce by returning war vets, and more female students dropped out of college in order to walk down the aisle than actually graduated. In her research, Friedan found that middle-class American women, many of whom had aspired only to marry and have children (a goal typically achieved by age twenty), were suffering from "the problem that has no name." While these women had difficulty pinpointing their discontent (after all, they were living the dream), the underlying cause was repeatedly revealed to be the mind-numbing drudgery and isolation of life as a housewife. The book hit a nerve, so much so that *The Feminine Mystique* and Friedan (who in 1966 founded NOW, the National Organization for Women) are credited with launching the women's rights movement.

In trying to identify the problem and its causes, Friedan interviewed homemakers (then called housewives), many of whom had been her Smith College classmates. In the book's opening chapter, she introduces a doctor who grew curious as to why so many of his female patients were complaining of overwhelming tiredness. She writes:

> He found, surprisingly, that his patients suffering from 'housewife's fatigue' slept more than an adult needed to sleep—as much as ten hours a day—and that the actual energy they expended on housework did not tax their capacity. The real problem must be something else, he decided—perhaps boredom. Some doctors told their women patients they must get out of the house for a day, treat themselves to a movie in town. Others prescribed tranquilizers. Many suburban housewives were taking tranquilizers like cough drops. 'You wake up in the morning, and you feel as if there's no point in going on another day like this. So you take a tranquilizer because it makes you not care so much that it's pointless.'

While the potential sadness experienced by today's Stay-at-Home moms generally isn't the result of domestic imprisonment at an early age, nor gender roles as constrained as those during the '50s, many women do experience anxiety and uncertainty surrounding their family choices.

I know that there have been times, many times, when I just couldn't muster the will to clean the high chairs and put toys away, yet again, and instead flopped onto the couch, my mental exhaustion manifesting itself as a physical shutdown. I've also had countless instances during which the intellectual boredom, endlessness, and isolation of my Stay-at-Home mom obligations made me feel like a caged tiger. Choices are wonderful to have, and as women, we now do have choices (about whether or not to have children, to combine family with paid work, etc.). While it's not entirely fair that men don't have as many societally acceptable options, they generally don't have to make the hard choice between work and family. (Men are expected to be able to have both, typically with a wife managing the latter.) The balancing act is a burden still unique to being a woman.

1950s REDUX?

Just as men these days don't necessarily grow up thinking they will someday be their family's sole breadwinner, women don't necessarily grow up thinking they will someday become financially dependent on a spouse. (If a young woman is counting on a man to support her someday, she shouldn't be.)

During the many years I dated my husband, I never imagined him becoming the sole wage-earner for our future family. I always intended to work. But after our son arrived, my husband understood before I did that the best arrangement for our family would be for one of us to stay home. By the time I left my job, he had wrapped his head around being the breadwinner and my staying home, while I was still getting used to the idea.

In truth, he's super with the kids and without a doubt would have made a great Stay-at-Home parent. Had the financial potential of our occupations been different, if society were more accepting of men as full-time caregivers, and if the workforce were more welcoming to returning Stay-at-Home dads, we might have chosen that option. We didn't; it took us several years to fully understand the impact that my transition from work to home (and then going from one child to three) had on me and on us as a couple.

Because while my husband does have the pressure of bringing home the only paycheck, for better or for worse, his day-to-day really hasn't changed in twenty years: He goes to work, he interacts with adults, he's paid for his efforts, he moves about freely. By contrast, my life turned upside down. The *me* at the end of my actually endless workday is different from the *me* I used to be. When I worked in Manhattan and was away from my son all day, I cherished the dinner, bath, and bedtime routines my husband and I would share with our small child. While Brian still looks forward to family time at the end of his day, by nightfall, I need time away from parent–child togetherness. I suspect he would feel as I do if the tables were turned.

Would I want the tables turned? Not necessarily. When my husband quit his job to go to grad school, I supported us. We had no children at the time. And although I was financing rent in two cities, we had no mortgage to feed. The pressure made me never want to repeat that one-year experience. Being financially responsible for a family is a huge responsibility. Yet, while it's essential that a man (as it's typically a man) devote his energies to his job, having a Stay-at-Home wife shouldn't mean his familial duties end with a paycheck. Accordingly, working late is one thing, partying with coworkers nightly after work is another. A Stay-at-Home mom isn't a round-the-clock maid and nanny.

Although an insensitive guy might treat his Stay-at-Home spouse as a live-in sitter, a stressed-out husband may look at his

Stay-at-Home wife and think about all the money she's not making. It's understandable how a man who has a bad day at work, or is facing a possible layoff, would look at his highly educated, highly capable wife and see nothing but lost income.

Such a scene recently played out when the husband of one of my best friends, stressed from a bad day at work and feeling the pressure of providing for a family of five, asked his wife how long she intended to be a Stay-at-Home mom.

"Is this really all you want to do?" he inquired of his master's degree–holding wife, a woman who twice embarked on relief work assignments in Third World countries. "What happened to all your ambition?"

"We have three small children," she responded. "I'm doing what I need to do at this time in their life, my life and, whether you can see it or not, our life together."

End of discussion.

THE LITTLE WOMAN?

Survey respondents had a tough time answering my question about whether they consider themselves traditional wives and mothers. Only one woman made a comment that was in any way close to *traditional* traditionalism, which I'd describe as statements along the lines of, "A woman's place is in the home" or "My husband is the head of our family, and I obey what he says."

That mom, a thirty-seven-year-old business school grad and project manager, now home with a newborn after an office layoff, wrote: "Being a Christian and believing that you cannot have two leaders in the army, I am learning to be more traditional."

Colleen, a mother of four (with her fifth on the way), responded that, although she does consider herself to be a traditional wife "to an extent," she does so in a relationship of mutual support and responsibility, not of one member's authority. "My priorities are the children, then myself and my husband, and then the house, in that order," she says. "I think it's important for there to be a hot meal most nights of the week, with the house smelling good when he walks in the door, although I don't cook on weekends. I try to keep things neat and organized for less stress, but if there's something that hasn't been done, or I need help with, my husband is there with no complaint. I expect him to have a good job with benefits and a good salary. I keep the home fires burning."

But other respondents expressed confusion and bewilderment when having to consider the traditionalism of their lives. "I'm not sure what traditional is anymore, but I know I like to have home-cooked meals on the table for my family and I do keep house," says Robin, a former U.S. Air Force airman. "Gosh, does that make me a housewife? *Agh!*" Adds Laura: "What does that mean? I guess I am pretty traditional. I stay home; keep house; feed, clothe, and bathe the kids; do the shopping. I have to say, it goes against everything I thought I would be. I was always an independent woman. I lived on my own. I was in the U.S. Army for four years, for goodness sake, and here I am, a housewife. It's weird."

Several women explained that they are, and *aren't*, traditional. "My husband is an executive at a big company. I stay home and take care of our two kids. In that sense, we live a traditional life," says Gerri. "The difference for me is how our relationship originated. When we met, my husband was in school and I was the bigger earner for most of our pre-baby relationship. We paid for our first house equally. I paid his student loans and for his car. I think our having that equal start helps me now."

Stacey explains her dual identity, saying, "I'm a variant of what I consider the traditional wife and mother, which was my mom. I stay home; handle all the cooking, shopping, doctor appointments, etc.—but I take care of the finances, which my mother never had a clue about."

Molly adds, "I feel like I'm filling a traditional role, but with some differences. My husband offered to be the Stay-at-Home parent. We've entered into our roles by choice rather than expectation or assumption." Cindy, an attorney, states, "I'm traditional, but I don't feel powerless. I'm a player in this relationship."

A few women, however, firmly explained that, appearances aside, they are not traditional. "I think of 'traditional' as not questioning your husband, letting him make all the decisions, manage all the money, and basically run the show," says Liz. R. "I think of myself as running the show at home. He looks to me to let him know what we are doing on the home front."

Joni, who is thirty-one, answered the question by looking back to the generation of women before her own. "Traditional wives and mothers are now grown Baby Boomers who are divorced, depressed, and generally unhappy with the way they sacrificed their youth," she says. "I refuse to never go out, always have dinner on the table, or anything else so sacrificial that my marriage and happiness will suffer."

Voices: What Do You Say When You're Asked, "What Do You Do?"

It's a simple question. But as anyone who has been between jobs (or in a job they don't like or aren't proud of) knows, the question can become hard to answer. The same thing happens when Stay-at-Home women are asked what they "do." Many hem and haw over how to give an answer that's honest to their present, while also acknowledging their past and possible future.

Of the many surveys I received, only a handful of women were like Elizabeth, a Maryland mother of two toddlers who says she simply states: "I'm a mom."

What remains unsaid with Elizabeth's brief response is that she's a Harvard University graduate and member of its championship ice hockey team. She also has a master's degree in forensic science and, prior to becoming a mom, was an intelligence analyst for the U.S. Navy's criminal investigations unit. Following are some other moms' answers:

"It's a hard question sometimes. Most people don't think staying home is a career or a job."

—Denise

"I just say I don't work and I have two kids. I try to downplay it because I don't want to come off like I'm bragging about being a Stay-at-Home mom. I guess I don't want the working moms to feel bad."

—Kara

"I've been working really hard to say I'm an attorney, without qualifying it by saying I'm taking time off to raise my kids. I've realized that once most people figure out you stay home, they don't think you have anything important to say."

—Jen

"If I say, 'I stay home with my kids' in a proud manner, I'm afraid I'll come off acting superior. If I tell them I stay home, but I also do some theater work and freelance writing, I feel I sound desperate to validate myself. I think you can't act too happy about staying home, and you can't act too miserable about it either."

—Laura

"I used to say, 'I'm just a Stay-at-Home mom.' But then I noticed people saying to me, 'Just a Stay-at-Home mom? It's a lot of work taking care of kids.' It is a lot of work, and what I do should be given its proper place as work. I've started feeling more comfortable saying 'I'm a Stay-at-Home mom' and taking out the 'just.'"

—Whitney

"I tell them I got laid off during maternity leave. That's a conversation in itself. I say it was a blessing in disguise and now I don't know when I'll go back."

—Lisa

"I always give it to them straight and say I'm a homemaker. I tend not to say I'm a lawyer or a cellist unless it comes up. I watch their reactions. It's no loss to me to not spend time with a person who's so stupid as to actually think that because someone cares for the most important asset society has, she has nothing to offer the conversation."

—Sandra

"I say I'm at home with the kids right now, but I hope to go back to being a physical therapist at some point. I do feel a bit defensive when I'm asked this question, and I hate when people end it right there, like they have nothing left to say to me and I have nothing of interest to say. I feel like yelling, 'Okay, so I'm not working right now. But I run marathons. I read The New Yorker. *I love talking about politics! I can talk about something other than my kids!' In fact, I really want to talk about things that don't have to do with parenting and being a mom."*

—Deb

"I say I'm currently not working because I'm home taking care of small children."

—Diane A.

"I say that I am an executive recruiter taking a long-term break to manage our household and three boys."

—Annabel

"I'm very proud to say I'm a Stay-at-Home mom. There aren't many women in our neighborhood who can afford to stay home. I feel it's a great luxury and I appreciate it every day."

—Debbie

"My gut reaction is to say, 'I just stay at home,' but I learned a better response from being a member of Professional Moms at Home. I now say, 'I'm taking a break from my career to raise my son.' This opens up the conversation to discuss kids, or my career that's on hold. I think it puts others at ease too."

—Molly

"I tell them I'm a Domestic Goddess."

—Samantha

If a traditional wife and mother is a woman who submits to her husband's will, then I'll speak for the team and presume that most Stay-at-Home women are *not* traditional wives and mothers. But if a traditional wife and mother is a woman who cares for children and the house, and doesn't have a paid job, then yes, we're all traditional wives and mothers—with two important caveats. Unlike the archetypal, though fictional, 1950s TV housewives June Cleaver and Harriet Nelson, many of us had significant careers before motherhood. Also, in many of our homes, Ward Cleaver and Ozzie Nelson change diapers and go grocery shopping.

"When he's home, my husband dives right into the childcare. He cooks and cleans, does dishes and vacuums, folds laundry and changes diapers," notes survey respondent Anne. "He does everything that I do. This is far from the traditional arrangement in which the husband does little or nothing around the house. My father was a traditional husband. He brags about how few diapers he changed—four, one per child. He can't scramble an egg, and he has no idea how to run the dishwasher. He is totally helpless and is proud of it."

The jobs my own husband and I now do have us falling into stereotypical roles—Mom stays home, Dad goes to work—but as with Anne and her spouse, the boundaries of who does what are fluid. I may do the laundry, but my husband almost always does the sorting and folding. On weekends, I do the banking, much of the home repair, and play second fiddle in kid care; he takes charge of the children and most of the cooking. Survey respondent Pat says about her husband, "I mow the lawn, he does the ironing." For other couples, however, the division of labor does fall along more traditional gender lines.

"Because I stay at home, it's presumed that taking care of certain tasks all the time are part of 'my job description,'" says Ginny, a mother of four (now mostly grown) children. "I get no help from my husband with laundry, grocery shopping, cooking meals, doing dishes, or the basic cleaning and upkeep of the home."

While there are still many American men who just won't do "women's work," their numbers are dwindling, even among those men who have Stay-at-Home wives. In comparison to her mother and father's "traditional" marriage, Anne writes: "I have the best of both worlds. We can afford the luxury of having me stay home with my children, *and* my husband shares the household tasks and childcare."

In her survey, Anne also gives credit for the life she lives today to the achievements of feminism, which is a term many women younger than fifty either shy away from or outright reject. "By choosing to stay home with my children, I often feel as though I'm tossed into a bucket with the antifeminists who believe women should be chained to the stove and pumping out babies," says Anne. "Choosing to stay home is not considered a modern choice, a feminist choice. But I'm a modern feminist, a highly educated and very lucky woman who has considered her many options and has freely chosen to stay home."

Having children and staying home to care for them is not the same as entering a time machine going back fifty years. The Stay-at-Home moms represented in *The Guide* are wives and mothers, but not "traditional" ones. Similarly, many are feminists, whether they use the term or not. Sometimes it's good to shake up tradition.

P.S. For methods about how to equalize your roles—and to still be the person you were, are, and want to be—see the chapters about money (starting on page 111), coping (page 285), and having a life and activities independent of caring for kids (Chapters Eleven and Fourteen).

True Love + Kids = Real Life

Before having children, Whitney and her husband spent a lot of time doing fun things together. "We went hiking or biking every weekend, as well as backpacking up in the Sierras and some camping too," she says. "Then, when we had our daughter, we couldn't do those things, or if we did, we'd have to do them separately. So in a sense, we pretty much lost our 'former lives' together. That was a huge change." Now parents of two children under age three, Whitney and her spouse do connect over their shared love and interest in their kids. Yet, like many couples, they sometimes mourn the duo they once were, and the freedom they once had to enjoy being together. (And I'm not necessarily talking about sex, which will be addressed at length in the next chapter.)

It's an amazing experience to create a child with the person you love. It's an amazing experience to share a child—through birth or adoption—with the person you love. But with the rise in single parenthood, and with the divorce rate being what it is, it's also considered amazing when a couple stays together for the rest of their lives, or even stays together through the years they're both needed to love and care for their growing offspring. Children can be a cement that joins two people together in a strong and long-lasting bond, but they don't work that way for all relationships. In one respect, having a Stay-at-Home partner means there's one less person in the household having to juggle the demands and distractions of the workforce. However, it also means that, compared to their pre-kid lives, one partner (typically the female) has less independence, and the two have less time to simply be a couple overall.

"From a family perspective, I feel like our time together with 'Dad' is more fun," says Mary, a mother of two preschoolers. "Since I don't work, I can do the errands and most cleaning and paperwork during the week." The challenge, Mary notes, is that, "our schedules don't line up. I stay up late to get stuff done. My husband goes to bed by 9:00 PM since he has to get up early. I know we should spend more time together without the children, but a night out, after paying for a babysitter and wherever we go, costs at least $150. We try to spend time together after the children go to bed, but it seems all we have is between 7:30 and 9:00 PM. That hour-and-a-half can fill up quickly with dishes, computer work, and other things that need to get done."

Jennifer, a new mom in Wyoming, has the same concerns: "Sadly, I feel a distance from my husband. I know much of that is because of the sleep issue. I'm exhausted all the time, and we don't go to bed at the same time anymore because I have to be in bed within an hour of the baby going to sleep or I'm worthless the next day. We rarely see each other anymore."

In her book *A History of the Wife*, women's studies professor Marilyn Yalom cites surveys showing that "however much children added to marriage, they also put strains on it." Unfortunately for all of us Stay-at-Home moms with babies and preschoolers who think things are tough now, studies show that the most significant strains on marital satisfaction occur when a couple's children are adolescents.

In other words: Life is challenging in these preschool times. If you're lucky, you'll coast a bit during the elementary school years. Then you'll be smacked with the angst of middle and high school. (This time around, experiencing it from the parent's perspective.) Alas, there is light at the end of the tunnel. "Even though the course of marital satisfaction ran downhill for the first two decades," writes Yalom, "it eventually turned upward again. Once the children had been launched, marital problems diminished." The reward for the couple left standing: a second honeymoon.

While it's reassuring to know that nirvana awaits those of us whose marriages survive parenthood, that glorious time is some two decades away! In the here and now, we're just trying to get through the day while keeping our children and marriage alive.

Megan, who has two preschoolers, says she and her husband keep their relationship strong by acknowledging one another's contributions. "I think we respect each other more now because we see what the other is doing for the children," she says. "We recognize when the other person is making a sacrifice to do something meaningful for the partnership."

Dixie, whose grown children live most of the year on their own or at college, points out that a couple's relationship pre-kids can be a lifeline when the going gets tough. "My husband and I were married for four years before our first child was born," she says.

"During that time, I learned that he was a fair-minded, sensitive, honest, and supportive partner who was deeply committed to our marriage and family. Knowing that about your partner helps when, after the children arrive, you're sleep-deprived, you have stringy hair, you smell like fish sticks, and you have to sweep Cheerios out of your bed. Real-life issues change relationships, but it's all just part of life moving along. There will always be peaks and valleys."

Debbie and her husband have three children, ages eight, seven, and five. She says a marriage's magic does return after the toddler years. "When I had a three-and-a-half-year-old, a two-year-old, and a newborn, I was so busy changing diapers, nursing, and cleaning spit-up that I was hardly aware my husband was even around," she explains. "We simply didn't have time to sit and chat for hours. Now that the children are out of that stage, we get along great. I hope people remember this if they're contemplating divorce when they have toddlers in the house. Things improve. Try to stick it out together!"

Personally, as a child of divorce, I second Debbie's advice. I'm of an age (early forty-something) at which a number of couples I know with children are now divorced, divorcing, or working hard not to. In each of the half-dozen situations I'm privy to, the cause seems to be due to one partner's frustration with the expectations and responsibilities of marriage and children. In each case, the "strayer" claimed to be ignored by his or her partner or too restricted by their lifestyle together and thus sought attention and freedom outside the relationship by partying, carousing, spending to excess, cruising for sex via the Internet, or outright dating. In this microcosm, two of the initiators were Stay-at-Home moms (notice the past tense) and four are men. The commonality in each relationship is that once two or more small children entered the mix, the guy or gal who was used to being their partner's, or their own, primary focus, had their needs usurped by the needs of the children. In all but the couple still on the mend, the partner who desired the freedoms of younger days eventually got his or her way—three by bolting from the marriage, two by being kicked out.

Long-term relationships are hard, and even cautious dating beforehand can't predict what will happen to a couple once children arrive, or a partner hits a certain age, or experiences a significant achievement, event, or disappointment. In my own marriage, to a man I spent thirteen years with before deciding to start a family, having three small children has changed us both individually and as a couple. Relaxed time alone together is now extremely rare. The three kids, combined with our personal changes, have put stresses on our relationship that we have to work to manage—and that's not even taking into account the outside pressures most everyone experiences from work, extended family, friends, and life.

It's important for both partners in a committed relationship to recognize that kids do change everything (for better and worse), and once children arrive, you just can't be the exact same person or twosome you once were. The hope for all couples is that each partner can deal with the new person they are, and are with, enjoy the children they share, prop each other up during the challenges of parenthood, and come out on the other end intact and ready for new experiences—together.

Voices: Does Your Partner Understand What Your Life Is Like?

"No, no, and no!"

—Jennifer D.

"I'm not sure anyone can really understand it who hasn't lived it. Even when my husband has been with the kids for a weekend alone, it's different. The kids aren't as needy with him as they are with me, and on weekends, he has less to manage. Besides, being in charge of the kids for one day is different than doing it for seven years."

—Deb

"No. Just as I will never fully understand his load as the sole provider."

—Joni

"No, he often tells me he works hard and needs time off, but he doesn't understand that I work hard and need time off too. He plans at least four 'male bonding' trips a year. I haven't been away from my kids since they were born. When we discuss that, he says, 'So tell me when you want to go away. I'll take time off to stay home with the boys.' While that seems like a nice offer, it isn't the point. I don't need a week away. Sometimes just a trip to the grocery store alone will do the trick."

—Elizabeth

"Yes. He has done it quite a few times and realizes that it's not all bonbons and Oprah."

—Sarah B.

> "No. He thinks I'm at home hanging out, having fun and no stress and nothing to do."
>
> —Heather
>
> "Yes. Whenever he spends the day alone with both kids, he says to me, 'God bless you and what you're doing for our family.' We're not particularly religious, but that's how strongly he feels about it. I think my being home with the kids has elevated his respect for me even higher."
>
> —Amy

THEM'S FIGHTIN' WORDS

Because it's so easy to take each other for granted, or become angry and resentful, couples need to set boundaries and define their expectations of each other. Otherwise, the disconnect can create a typical he said/she said dynamic. Recognize any of these?

She: "He comes home at the end of the day and won't take over caring for the kids. He says he needs some 'transition time.' His drive home was his transition time. I've been with the kids all day. When he's home, he either has to take them so I can have a break, or we need to do the kid stuff together."

He: "I work the entire day to put a roof over my family's heads and food on their plates. I shouldn't have to work a second job when I get home."

She: "He doesn't want to listen to me talk about how I couldn't take a shower or get out of the house because the baby was napping and the kids were fighting me. I can't blame him. I'm bored listening to myself. But I have no one else to talk to, and caring for kids is the only thing I do."

He: "The baby being cranky and kids acting up comes with the territory. What does she expect? That's her job. I have bad days at work too. When I get home I need to relax and reenergize so I can go to work the next day."

She: I'm so tired.

He: Why is she so tired? She stayed home all day.

Laura recalls a similar dialogue: "During the first two months of my first child's life, my husband would come home and say, 'What did you do today?' and I would want to kill him—because I didn't stop *doing*, but I didn't *do* anything. What was I going to say? 'Let's see, I changed twelve diapers, nursed for about five hours, ate some food, had three fifteen-minute naps, cajoled our crying daughter, did laundry, emptied the Diaper Genie.' I could have continued, but he would have stopped listening after the third exciting item."

Chances are, domestic scenes like Laura's, and those relayed throughout this book by other women, play out in many Stay-at-Home mom households.

KEEP IT CLEAN

Karen rarely loses her temper. She handles three kids, the construction chaos of a fixer-upper house, and hours on end alone with no help without snapping at her children or her spouse. But one day her husband came home from work and—upon surveying the kitchen sink with overflowing dishes, the trash can with overflow-ing garbage, the toys and craft supplies strewn throughout the house, the children running around in various states of undress— blurted out, "Look at this place! It's a mess! Aren't you ashamed to have the house look like this? Don't you take any pride in keeping the house clean?"

That's when Karen, by her own description, *lost it.*

"Pride in my house? No!" shouted this women's studies major who spent her pre-motherhood career working and advocating for women's and children's health. "My self-esteem and self-worth are not based on how my house looks. I take care of three children all day. That's my priority." Karen then made it very clear that never, ever again was her spouse to judge her based on how the house looks when he gets home.

Debbie (giver of the "life gets better after the toddler years" ad-vice) had an eerily similar experience. "One day my husband came home and said, 'I would really like it if you could just have the house look nice and neat when I come home,'" she recalls. "That didn't go over well. I had three children under four years of age to attend to all day, and being tidy wasn't too high on my list at the time."

Instead of simply writing these guys off as jerks, consider a theory for this type of reaction that author Gary Chapman, a pas-toral counselor, notes in *The Five Love Languages: How to Express Your Heartfelt Commitment to Your Mate.* Men who grew up in homes in which the mother did all things domestic often look at a woman's cooking or housekeeping as a symbol of love. Mom loved and cared for him (and his dad), and she made every meal and kept the house clean. Therefore, a husband might be thinking, if his own wife (you?) *truly* loved and cared for him, she (you?) would do the same.

BIG WORK, SMALL RESULTS

It's wonderful to have a spouse or partner who recognizes that caring for children and a home all day is an achievement, and something to be proud of. It's important for Stay-at-Home moms to remind themselves that what they do each day is an accomplishment. It's when we compare the work we do on a daily basis to the other accomplishments in our lives, and in the lives of others, that we have difficulty taking pride in what we do.

When we worked outside the home, we got paid. Hopefully we also enjoyed our jobs and received praise and promotions. If we were good students or athletes, we were celebrated for our hard work and successes. If we dressed for a night out and looked good, we got noticed. Stay-at-Home motherhood doesn't come with that outside affirmation. While employed parents get to be both parents and, for example, doctors, lawyers, or corporate executives, Stay-at-Home moms get to be moms, every minute of the day. Doing the same thing over and over and over again can make a gal unmotivated—and cranky.

"My husband has said, 'You should *enjoy* taking care of the kids and the house,'" reports Ginny, a Stay-at-Home mother for sixteen years. "'You should prove your love for us by being happy about taking care of us. If you're complaining, it must mean you aren't happy and don't love us as much as I thought you did.'" Ginny's response: "I wanted to . . . well, let's just say I let him know exactly what I thought of his comment."

Voices: How Does Your Partner Not Help You?

"While my husband plays with the kids and takes them to sports practices and games, he doesn't actively jump in to help with tasks around the house. I'm not even sure how we arrived at our division of labor. It just sort of evolved. I would advise couples to make conscious choices about their division of labor."

—Lyn

"He says 'Can you just [insert an errand or chore]?' This is when he asks me to run what he thinks is a simple errand, not realizing that with two kids in tow, it's really difficult and takes half the day. He sometimes forgets how long it takes me to accomplish some things."

—Megan

"He gets upset when he doesn't have black socks in his drawer. I get upset because I fold, wash, and put away the kids' clothes. He could at least take care of his own socks. It makes me feel like I'm the maid."

—Denise

"He's unrealistic about how long it takes to get things done. I'll rattle off the ten things that we need to do before going on a trip the next day, and he'll say, 'I'll just do it all.' I find it a little arrogant."

—Liz R.

"He assumes I have my period when I'm cranky. I want to know what his excuse is."

—Nancy

Another challenge to believing that caring for kids is an accomplishment is that caring for children never ends. Remember the forty-hour workweek? Welcome to the 168-hour work week. And there are few tasks that can be checked off on a to-do list—as soon as you've finished them, they need to be done again.

It's a downer to think about the endless nature and monotony of your work, and it's so important for your partner to understand that frustration. "He knows I don't entirely love the role and therefore I get resentful and moody every now and then," says Liz R., who has been a Stay-at-Home mom for nine years. "It's true that when you love what you do it makes everyone around you happy. I love *parts* of what I do, but not all of it. And that resentment about what I'm missing does come up occasionally. I know I'm lucky my husband is so appreciative of my role as the Stay-at-Home parent. If he didn't get that it's a tough job, I can't imagine how we would survive."

THANKS FOR THE "ADVICE"

Often, when I describe the frustrations of my day to my husband, explaining how I'm so tired of having to, for example, search the house for lost sippy cups before the milk in them curdles, he might then respond: "Well, why don't you just stop giving them sippy cups?" Whether he means to or not, the "Why don't you just . . ." construction sounds a lot like, "Why don't you just stop being such a moron and . . . ?"

The even more infuriating part of such a response is that it implies the problem is so utterly simple to solve. "Just stop giving the kids sippy cups," or "Just make them sit at the table." Yes, that would solve the problem, but as every Stay-at-Home mom knows, we often don't have total control over our little charges. We knock heads with our wee ones a lot.

In some professions, doing a job every day makes you an expert. In full-time, hands-on, 24/7 Stay-at-Home parenting, the job and the battles it brings often sap the most experienced mom of strength, and make it more likely she'll do just about anything to ensure some moments of peace. In the case of the traveling sippy cups, it's often easier to retrieve the cups than to have to deal with a screaming, whining child who doesn't want to drink only at the table (or will spill the open cup you place on the table). Giving in isn't the right thing to do. It's just what happens.

HE SAID WHAT?

The first group of phrases are sure to unleash the fury or silent fuming of any Stay-at-Home mom, especially when delivered in a patronizing or inpatient tone. Those that follow represent more diplomatic efforts and the praise we all long for and deserve to hear.

Better left unsaid:
- Just say no.
- Why can't you . . . ?
- Why don't you just . . . ?
- Calm down.
- What's the big deal?
- You shouldn't let them . . .
- Can't you clean up?
- What did you expect?
- Why didn't you make anything for dinner?
- I won't be home by . . .

- I'm going out after work.
- I just got home, let me relax.
- My mom managed fine.

What we all long to hear:

- Wow, you look beat.
- You need a break from the kids.
- I can handle it.
- Let me do that for you.
- How can I help?
- Can I pick up anything on the way home from work?
- I'll stay home tomorrow so you can have the day off.
- Great dinner.
- Thank you.
- You're right.
- I'm amazed you can handle all of this.
- You're great!

Ideally, the second batch of comments should be expressed without prompting or a specific request. "After more than four years, I wish the presumption would be, 'Wow, you probably need a break,'" says survey respondent Laura, "but that still doesn't happen."

Perhaps her spouse needs to take some tips from Anne's. "On the occasions I've had a truly horrible day, a day that leaves me shaking from stress and aggravation and on the verge of tears, he doesn't even have to ask what's happening," says Anne about her husband. "He just comes home from work, picks up our daughter, mixes me a cocktail, and sends me to read a book or relax in a quiet room. I've had only three totally miserable days in the past twenty months that have called for this level of TLC, but my husband came through for me every single time." *Aww.*

Voices: How Does Your Partner Help You?

"My husband does all of the laundry and vacuuming."

—Tracy

"When I'm at my wits end, he can always come up with something brilliant to get everyone calmed down and happy."

—Sarah B.

"He's very present in the mornings and the evenings, and also on weekends. But he wasn't always like that. It took some training after our first child was born for him to realize he couldn't just do what he wanted when he wanted. He had to function on other people's schedules and do what they needed, and wanted."

—Nicki

"He keeps me sane and helps me put my emotions in check when they run amok. He gives me lots of praise and gratitude for the choice I've made to stay home. He knows I've sacrificed my career, and he's very respectful of that."

—Megan

Sex and the Stressed-Out
Stay-at-Home Mom

When I was twenty-three-years old and working in the articles
department of *Redbook* magazine, I was given an article
to fact-check called "Too Tired for Sex." At the time, I scoffed at
the story's title and premise. I was finally living with my boyfriend
of four years (now my husband), and we were so happy to have
a place of our own—and the freedom to have sex whenever we
wanted—that I couldn't imagine ever being *too tired* for sex.

Two decades later, I can relate to that article more than I can
to my former twenty-three-year-old self.

First of all, after being cooped up with kids who, at various
times during the day, have been clinging, crawling, and drooling on
me, the last thing I want is to be touched by someone else. Secondly,
by the time a Stay-at-Home mom, like me or you, has spent the day
caring for kids and keeping a house together gets into bed, she's
pooped. Not just physically tired, but mentally and emotionally
tired as well. Not a great recipe for getting turned on.

But wait, that's not all! Even if there *is* a spark of sexual desire,
the timing can be all wrong. "I get frustrated when my husband

comes to bed late after I'm asleep and wants to be intimate," explains Erin S., who's home with two preschoolers. Or it's the opposite situation, a problem I experienced for a while: My spouse would get into bed by ten to read, but he'd instead fall asleep. When I dragged myself upstairs at midnight or later, having finally regrouped from my day with the kids and gotten a head start on the next morning, my getting under the covers would wake him up. Refreshed from his nap, he was raring to go. Having already put in an eighteen-hour day, all I wanted was to go to sleep and stop serving my family's needs, especially their physical needs. Until we finally had a discussion about our disconnect, my husband would fall back asleep angry that I had rejected him, and I'd go to sleep angry that he was angry at me—for being tired! Some nights, to avoid the potential bad feelings, I'd crawl into bed with one of the kids or crash downstairs on a couch.

When she's a mother, a woman can sometimes be left feeling as emotionally and physically drained as a vampire victim. Everyone takes from her what they want to satisfy their own needs. After a while, with so many people taking, there's nothing left to give. "He gets pissed off," reports a Connecticut mother of three about the times she's so tired she turns down her spouse's advances. "I then get angry at him for being angry at me, but I don't lose any sleep over it."

Some women do lose sleep over not giving a partner the sex he wants when he wants it. I was once on a girl's weekend getaway with a woman who was feeling guilty for not having sex with her husband before she left for her trip. After a crazed day preparing to actually be able to leave the house and their children in his care, she collapsed into bed late at night unshowered and exhausted, with no energy left to play. It took convincing from her friends to accept that she had had very good reasons for not wanting to have sex at that moment.

Voices: Why Sleep Is Often Better Than Sex

"I'm so pawed over and touched during the day by my kids that I really don't want to be touched at night. Sometimes I actually try to get as far away as possible from my husband in our king-size bed. It makes me sad because we used to snuggle. Now, sometimes, I secretly wish I had my own bed. I fantasize about going away to a really fancy hotel by myself to get a great night's sleep. I also don't feel as great about my body or just myself in general, which makes me feel less sexy and less womanly. It reminds me of that Saturday Night Live skit about "mom jeans," where the actress playing the mom says, "These jeans tell the world I'm not a woman anymore, I'm a mom."

—Deb

"Having children clearly impacted our relationship both positively and negatively. At times it zaps my energy, and I feel like I've been crawled over all day long by children, so the last thing I want is my husband crawling over me too."

—Linda

"Sometimes it's a chore to find the time to give to him. He takes it personally. It makes me mad that he doesn't understand how tiring it is being home all day with small children."

—Diane A.

▶

> *"The amount of physical attention that babies require can tire you in a different way. I find I've even become a horrible pet owner since my son was born. I just have no love left to give at the end of the day."*
>
> —Jennifer
>
> *"It definitely annoys me if he belittles my reasons for not being in the mood. But I'm very stubborn and spiteful, so one stupid comment can get him many lonely nights. Knowing that, he tries to curb his comments."*
>
> —Erin Z.

According to the many relationship "experts" who parade across the morning talk shows—especially during the domesticized post–nine o'clock segments aimed at the Stay-at-Home moms— women shouldn't refuse their husbands sex. I've heard that advice before. At the end of my *Redbook* career, I was assigned to fact-check an article in which the author, a relationship expert of some sort, discussed how women could keep their husbands from having affairs. One bit of wisdom was that after a woman has a baby, she has to make a special effort to give her spouse the attention he needs. Even back then, pre-motherhood, the advice offended me, and I ranted to my boss: "A woman carries a pregnancy, gives birth, wrestles with hormonal changes, pain, and body changes and gets no sleep due to being a new mom, but *she* has to ensure that her husband is getting the attention *he* needs, so he won't leave her for another woman?" My immediate boss was similarly bothered by the piece, but such drivel was (and often still is) part and parcel of women's service magazines, which within a single issue are able to both inspire women to greatness and knock them down a few pegs.

It's not that women with children don't want to have sex. Intimacy and affection are essential, and sexual activity produces feel-good endorphins. Plus, sex can be intricately tied to a woman's self-esteem, especially since many of us don't feel so alluring in our postpregnancy bodies. As a first-time mom with a three-month-old explained, "My husband hasn't made any advances, I think because he knows how tired I am. But I really wish he *would,* because I'm feeling like a frumpy wife since I'm still carrying pregnancy weight."

Having sex and feeling attractive and desired is a must for Stay-at-Home moms. The hitch is that time and place and context now matter. In addition to oftentimes not having the physical and emotional energy for even the simplest bedroom gymnastics, it can be hard for a woman to intellectually switch gears from mommy to vixen. Says survey respondent Rachel, echoing many: "I feel bad and guilty when I can't get my brain in the right place." (It should be noted that a similar exhaustion hits moms who work outside the home and land in bed after a day of juggling kids, commuting, work, kids again, home, and maybe more office work.)

In her book *The Female Brain*, neuropsychiatrist Louann Brizendine makes note of the theory that, "For women, foreplay is everything that happens in the twenty-four hours preceding [intercourse]. For men, it's everything that happens three minutes before." Meaning: A woman who knows the sink is full of dishes, or that she has to pay the bills that are due tomorrow, can't release those and other details from her brain in order to relax enough to want and thoroughly enjoy sex. It also means that if her husband came home that evening and grouched about the dishes in the sink and the unpaid bills, she'll have difficulty turning her feelings of resentment toward him into attraction and lust. Says Brizendine: "A woman can't be angry at her man and want to have sex with him at the same time."

But for some couples, a diminished sex drive is a shared experience.

"We're both so tired by the time the kids are asleep that our sexual intimacy is very limited," reports a thirty-six-year-old New Jersey mother of three. "We talk about it and both seem okay with it."

A Maryland woman said that she and her husband were sometimes so tired when their kids were small, that after they managed to have sex, he would joke, "Well, that takes care of April."

When I asked my fellow Stay-at-Homers, "How do you and your partner keep your sexual and emotional intimacy alive despite the demands of raising children?" a thirty-six-year-old mother of three-year-old twins and a newborn, said: "We don't. Seriously. We don't."

UNEQUAL DESIRE

We'd like to think that if we're not having sex, it's not just because of us—it can't be, right? Surely if a few weeks have gone by with no initiation from either partner, it's just a (mutual) phase. We figure he's just not thinking about it, and we count our blessings since we're not all that into it either. And sometimes, that's true.

It's also sometimes true that a woman can be more into sex than her partner is. A gal I worked with recently shared with me that when she was pregnant, and later when she was nursing, she was horny all the time. She says that at first, her husband thought it was great, but the activity finally reached a point where he had to ask her to back off just a bit. He needed a chance to, uh, recharge.

Both anecdotally and physiologically, though, such stories tend not to be the norm. The brain truly is a sex organ, and because male and female brains are biologically different, so too are male and female sex drives. The part of a man's brain that controls sexual desire is, according to Brizendine, two-and-a-half times larger than the sexually focused part of a woman's brain.

Thoughts about sex can "float through a man's brain many times each day on average," she notes, "and through a woman's only once a day." By way of example, Brizendine cites a study that examined brain scans of both sexes watching a "neutral" scene of a man and woman having a conversation. "The male brains' sexual areas immediately sparked—they saw it as a potential sexual rendezvous," she writes. "The female brains did not have any activation in the sexual areas. The female brains saw the situation as just two people talking."

The hormonal changes of pregnancy, breastfeeding, and even childrearing each have an enormous impact on a woman's sex drive. Compared to men, says Brizendine, women caring for children generally experience "less interest in sex, more worry about kids." Many times breastfeeding women find that the act of nursing, which releases surges of the feel-good brain chemical dopamine and the hormone oxytocin, can be nearly as pleasurable as an orgasm. And when a woman's intimacy needs are met by emotionally bonding with her new baby, physically bonding with her baby's daddy isn't such a priority.

No matter how you look at it, having a baby usually means less booty.

The Bringing Baby Home project, an ongoing study by psychologist John Gottman at his Seattle-based Relationship Research Institute, reports that up to two-thirds of couples experience a significant decline in marital and sexual satisfaction after their first child arrives. Another ongoing study, the National Marriage Project at Rutgers University, has found that many Americans view the years before the arrival of children, and after those children leave the nest, as the most satisfying time of adulthood. Additionally, according to the Rutgers scholars, "One recent review of over 100 research studies found that parents report significantly lower marital satisfaction than nonparents." Yikes!

CHILDPROOFING YOUR LOVE LIFE

Okay. We know what the problem is. But how do we *solve* it? If sex is so important, but we aren't always geared up for it, how do we bridge that gap?

Communicate: This involves talking and paying attention, and therefore some men may bristle at having to discuss their *feelings:* too bad. You can explain that although you *want* to want to have sex, you're exhausted by caring for kids all day and, frankly, you sometimes feel unappreciated. He can then explain that he's exhausted by working all day and sometimes feels unappreciated but,

Indecent Proposals

Among the distressing side effects of the information age is that men (and yes, women) can now be unfaithful from the comfort of their home. Porn, sex chat rooms, and even local liaisons are all available via the Internet. A husband wanting to play out an embarrassing fantasy, or one frustrated by his wife's child-induced exhaustion and sexual indifference, can get his kicks (and ready attention and gratification) by surfing the web. Similarly, a lonely Stay-at-Home mom desperate to feel attractive and alive has more options than to seduce the general contractor who's renovating her kitchen.

One seemingly innocuous source—www.craigslist.com—has become the go-to place for Internet-acquired sex. In fact, a February 2007 appearance on *The Daily Show* by Craig Newmark, the list's founder, was dominated by jokes from host Jon Stewart about the site's sex anywhere, anytime usefulness. While a person can log on to Craigslist to look through local classifieds to find, say, a bicycle, that same person can also peruse an erotic forum of live, local classified ads or postings, by nearby people seeking various immediate encounters.

Now, please don't get paranoid. It's super unlikely that your partner would ever do anything of the sort (or get involved in online gambling or any other inappropriate, trust-betraying, Internet-accessible behavior). And if he did, the fault and responsibility is with him—due to his own immaturity and selfishness—not you. But knowledge is power, so file this tidbit under useful information you should never need.

hey, he still wants to have sex. The point is, talking is better than not talking. And although talking often isn't a turn-on for men, it can be a *big* turn-on for women, so much so that such verbal intimacy can lead to physical intimacy.

Be appreciative: If the name of the game is now quality and not quantity (see page 207 for more about this), take pleasure in the rare moments of sexual intimacy. "If anything, our sexual relationship has improved since we've had kids," says Nicki, a thirty-three-year-old mother of three. "We don't take our intimacy for granted anymore."

Make a date: Since it's harder now to be spontaneous, you and your partner will need to make plans for spending time alone together, somewhere, somehow. It can be an enormous mood lifter to know that the two of you will be getting away for the night in a few days, or that you'll be going to dinner together at a restaurant in a few hours, eating food someone else prepared for you on dishes you won't have to wash. If getting a sitter and leaving the house isn't an option, even knowing that you'll have dedicated time together after the kids go to bed can do the trick. Either way, explains a forty-two-year-old Stay-at-Home mother of three, "My husband and I stay connected by scheduling date nights, which turn into date days, as we tend to be better connected all day when we have intimacy looming in the evening plans."

Take a trip: While a dinner out or quiet time together at home is good, it doesn't have the aphrodisiacal power that can be achieved by a real change of scenery. If you can, get a sitter or grandparents to watch the baby or the kids so you can go away. Do it—"even if it's only for the weekend or an overnight," advises Kellie, an Ohio mother of two. Leaving the kids can be anxiety provoking, especially the first time, but they'll be fine, and you and your spouse will have time to reconnect, which is good for everyone in the family. As Kellie points out: "Kids need to become comfortable with you going away, and learn that when you do, you'll come back. They also need to understand that you and your spouse or partner need time together as a couple."

Put an apron on him: To help with the household chores, not . . . oh, I'm not going there. The point is, if you're feeling bogged down by diapers, dishes, and dust, you're not likely to want to get down and dirty. If your partner isn't already sharing in the chores, ask him for help. If he isn't thrilled by the idea, explain that if you weren't so wiped out, you'd have more energy for "other activities." In addition to saving you some labor, the effort itself can feel like a bouquet of flowers to a Stay-at-Home mom. "There *is* something about seeing your partner do even a little thing around the house, like picking something up off the staircase to bring it upstairs, or helping fold laundry," says survey respondent Robin, a mother of two. "It can make a huge difference in how you feel toward that person." Another tactic is to point out that a man emptying the dishwasher is hot! According to *Porn for Women,* a photography gift book published by the Cambridge Women's Pornography Cooperative, a handsome, sensitive man doing housework is the ultimate turn-on: The book's cover features a studly (fully clothed) guy vacuuming a living room.

Try it, you'll like it: In other words, have sex with your partner, even if you're not totally in the mood, and even if it's no-frills quickie sex. Follow Nike's motivating mantra and "Just do it!"

Sometimes, it takes going through the initial motions to get your mojo to kick in.

Take the long view: The clichés are true—children are only small once. And this too shall pass. Although, by the time it does pass, you will need to have sex covertly so your now-alert-to-their-surroundings children won't know what's going on! On that note: Once your children are old enough that you don't have to listen for every nighttime whimper, make it a routine to keep your bedroom door closed, even when you're doing nothing more than snoring away. Since you and your partner don't intend to become celibate during your golden years (or your forties or fifties), the closed-door rule will save your teenagers the embarrassment of possibly knowing when mom and dad are, *gross*, doing it.

Advice for Keeping Love (and Lust) Alive

Women who answered the survey for this book offered the following "sex tricks":

"Early mornings, since sometimes you're too exhausted at night."

—Kellie

"A phone conversation that always ends with an 'I love you,' a kiss and hug when he comes in the door or before he leaves, occasional date nights, early bedtimes for the kids."

—Colleen

"I never decline his advances, because I know how tired my husband is, and if he's making the effort, I can too."

—Amy

"Middle of the night sex, especially when you have older kids."

—Pat

"Intellectually, sex feels like another task I need to take care of. But if I can shut my brain 'off,' it's a lovely way to let off steam, relax, and be intimate."

—Rachel

"When the children are in school and my husband is off work, we have a date morning. One of our favorite things to do is to go out for brunch and just talk. It makes me feel like when we were first dating, like we're getting to know each other all over again."

—Debbie

"Talk on the phone throughout the day, and try to get out every month or so just to talk over coffee or a beer without the kids."

—Jen

"We go through phases. One phase was date night at home after the children went to bed. Our current phase involves getting into shape. We have a challenge to go to the gym together fifty times in five months."

—Mary

"Every eighteen months, we go away without the children. Getting away helps remind us why we're together."

—Linda

SEXERCISE

One way many moms are reviving their dormant or distracted libidos is with toys—the adult kind. When my friend Brooke asked if I would go with her to a slumber party in her neighborhood, she had to explain that she wasn't talking about a sleepover. (Slumber Parties, for you latest-trend virgins out there, is a nationally franchised, at-home retailer of sex toys for women, perhaps as popular for our generation as Tupperware and Avon were for our moms and grandmothers.)

I wasn't so sure I wanted to go. Finally, I decided to give it a shot, figuring I didn't know the other guests, and Brooke and I would keep each other's secrets. Not only was my husband thrilled for me to leave him with the kids that Friday night, he encouraged me to shop and not be cheap.

The saleswoman at the party I attended, which included two dozen guests in their thirties and forties, was a tall, stunning, vivacious brunette named Dana Barish. She's a Slumber Parties superstar, having been featured in many newspaper and magazine articles, and even on the *Today* show. At our party, Barish claimed that her part-time sales job (evening parties, at-home administration work) was bringing in six figures a year. By the end of the evening, I understood why.

Barish's sales pitch is like foreplay. She starts gently, showing the group the silly novelty items that are available in many malls: Card decks with pictures of sexy men, tasty lip glosses, dirty joke books. She then displays clothing racks of pretty pajamas and sexy lingerie. Again, nothing more embarrassing than what we've all seen in a Victoria's Secret store or catalog. Next come the more sexual items: some gels for stimulating him, others for arousing her. During this part of the evening, Barish asks for two volunteers, gives each woman a small jar of cream and asks her to go into a bathroom and dab the cream on her private parts. By now, most partygoers have consumed at least one glass of wine. Amid giggles, the two sacrificial lambs leave for the bathrooms to do what they've been told. When they emerge, each woman has a surprised look on her face.

"What are you feeling?" Barish asks. One gal says the spot feels tingly and cold; the other tingly and warm. Both wear big smiles. Ladies quickly grab their order forms and start checking off boxes.

Roughly an hour into her presentation, Barish opens a suit-case and begins to build a skyline of colorful dildos, each larger and stranger than the one before. Hoots and guffaws fill the room when the silicone phalluses are passed from guest to guest for closer examination. Next come devices to use on him, handy for when he wants sex and you just aren't up to the task. (Hysterical laughter erupts at Barish's pantomime performance showing how she squirts lubricating gel onto her lustful spouse's "package," slides a rubbery sheath onto it, and pumps away for just a minute or two, hardly having to skip a beat while she watches TV or reads a magazine.)

Lastly, after several glasses of wine and the sharing of sexual intimacies by many in the crowd, Barish unveils her grand finale, the climax, if you will, of her NC-17 performance: The vibrators.

By this point in the evening, women who had arrived at the party thinking they'd politely buy a camisole are now poking each other's arms with throbbing, buzzing vibrators and comparing notes over which one (or several) to buy.

The Stay-at-Home Survival Guide's Sexual Survival Kit

After spending a day caring for children, Stay-at-Home moms often feel there isn't enough time in the day, or energy left, for screwing around. (In any sense of the word.) Because of that, Dana Barish, a sales rep for the "romance products" marketer Slumber Parties, says items that make *him* go faster and put *her* in the mood are essential boudoir supplies for a Stay-at-Home mom. Barish's recommended shopping list:

Lingerie: Barish believes that too many Stay-at-Home moms dismiss sexy lingerie as something they no longer need and, due to the aftereffects of childbirth, can't really wear. Her counterargument: "Lingerie is actually needed *more* now than when you were single. Sexiness comes from within, and it's very hard to feel sexy in grandma panties and a T-shirt with a stain on it. To get in the mood, you need to dress to undress!" She adds that lingerie can actually hide what you want to hide and accentuate what you want to show off.

Vibrators: Because, says Barish, "They're good for your health and well-being." Yes, really. "Moms don't want to take the time to make themselves feel good," explains Barish. "However, one of the best ways to get rid of stress is an orgasm. I've had many doctors and midwives send their patients to me for exactly that reason. When a mom tells me she does not 'need a vibrator,' I explain that vibrators can be used by couples together as a bedroom accessory. A vibrator doesn't replace a partner."

Lotions and potions: So-called "sexual heighteners" that are dabbed onto one's strategic parts to cause feelings of warmth, coolness, and tingling can, Barish claims, "turn good sex into *great* sex. We call them 'foreplay in a jar.'"

A 'boy toy': This squishy, tubular device—one brand name is the "Super Stretch"—is, says Barish, a "time-saving" hand-job tool, manipulated by a woman while worn by a man, although a guy can also use the device by himself. Under both circumstances it's advisable to apply a lubricant.

Barish also advises using colognes and lotions that contain plant-based pheromones, which are said to inspire sexual attraction and excitement when dabbed on pulse points of the body. And, for the very adventurous, she suggests that couples lose their inhibitions and invest in a "swing," which, Barish declares, "allows you to do things you would have to be a gymnast to do during sex!" *My oh my.*

(If you're now feeling the urge to go shopping, privately, you can check out www.slumberpartiesbydana.com.)

While no one at the party I attended shared information that night about exactly what she bought, I later learned that in several of the households, the husband's initial balking at the credit card bill turned to appreciation. One fella, whose wife bought a sort of vibrating ring for him to wear while they made love, reportedly declared, "I feel like the Bionic Man!" The friend who had invited me to the party called a few days later to declare that her Friday night shopping spree may have saved her marriage. "We feel like honeymooners again!" she exclaimed.

About her clients, Barish says: "The Stay-at-Home moms tend to be really pressed for time, so sex is often the last thing on their to-do list." It's also difficult, she says, for women to feel sexy around their partners when they spend most of their time being treated as, and feeling like, a mom. "It's my job to teach women how they can release the inner 'sex kitten' they had when they first started dating," declares Barish.

Whether you attend a sex-toy party or do some discreet shopping online or in a local store, getting creative can be a great way to jump start a stagnant sex life and make time together more exciting for you both.

A Special Message for the Partners of Stay-at-Home Moms

Simply put: If you want some action, you need to woo the mother of your children the same way you did *before* she was the mother of your children. That means instead of pouncing on her when she collapses exhausted into bed, make and take her on a *real* date. Do whatever you did before you had kids: Find a sitter and take your wife (whom you can think of as your girlfriend if it helps), to dinner. Go to a movie. Sneak her off to a hotel for a night. Figure out a way for the kids to sleep elsewhere so the two of you can have the house to yourselves.

You likely get to leave your home on a regular basis, and probably do this unencumbered by offspring. The mother of your children often doesn't get out of the house, and when she does, it's with one or several little human beings attached to her. Imagine if you lived and worked at your office. Imagine if, during the only time you did leave the building, your boss, staff, and colleagues were always there with you. Horrifying, isn't it?

Women who spend their days caring for children need time to reenergize the part of themselves that enabled them to become moms in the first place (i.e., their sex appeal and sex drive). To really get in the mood, a Stay-at-Home mom often needs new scenery and a chance to clean up and dress up. She needs to be complimented. She needs to feel desired and seen, by you at least, as (to use a crude but popular turn of phrase) a MILF. Translation: Mom I'd Like to F***. She also wants help caring for the house and kids and, most of all, she wants to be heard. Remember: This is a person who currently spends her days with children who don't listen, and with whom she surely can't have an adult conversation. Take her out, talk, and *listen*—and you're *in!*

Hey, guys. Don't close the book yet. I'm not done. Even if you don't want to listen to me (the author of a chick book), you should listen to a bit of advice from a man who has walked in your shoes. According to JB Tellez, whose wife, Heidi Raykeil, wrote a book called *Confessions of a Naughty Mommy,* the strategy for "domestic bliss and hot sex" is to follow the "three Cs," which he defines as Chat, Chill, and Chores.

Whereas my "chat" suggestion is to talk about whatever a gal wants to talk about, Tellez's chat recommendation is to talk about sex. "Idle chat about whether a short stepstool in the shower would help parts line up could suddenly lead to the kid getting a playdate at the neighbors' and you getting a midday scrub," he writes in a postscript to his wife's book about the havoc parenthood wreaks on parental sex lives.

Tellez says the "chill" is achieved by not stressing about how many times a week you do or don't get action, because "It's *quality,* not quantity" that now matters. "Rank the quality of your average roll in the hay as X out of ten," he explains. "Then think about if that's as high as you want it, and how often you get that high. If you're like me, you'll find that a ten once a week beats the hell out of two fives."

But the most direct path to passion, says Tellez, is by picking up after the kids, and yourself. "The idea that I might be seen as a misogynist prick just for leaving my dirty socks on the couch just didn't occur to me," he writes. "Needless to say, it has occurred to my wife. So do yourself a sexual favor fellas—share the housework."

Tellez claims that the three C's have done well by him. "Something is working," he writes. "I'm a long-married dad, and I don't stress about sex. In fact, it's hotter than ever."

Motherhood: Who's the Expert?

H ere's a little quiz to see just how good of a mom you are. Give yourself one point for each of the following rules you actually followed or follow:

- Babies should be breastfed for their first year of life.
- Children under age two should not watch television.
- Children ages three and older should watch no more than two hours of television per day.
- Children should start drinking from an open cup at twelve months of age.
- Unless being used at mealtime, sippy cups should *only* be filled with water.
- A baby must weigh twenty pounds *and* be older than twelve months before being placed in a forward-facing car seat.

How did you do? If you scored a six, congratulations! Based on these half-dozen standards, you're a perfect parent—according to the American Academy of Pediatrics and the American Academy of Pediatric Dentistry.

If you didn't score a six, well, join the club—you may not be "perfect," but you fit in perfectly with most American moms. (Unless the mother I am and the mothers I know, have met, have seen, and have spoken with are the rare exceptions.) Here's why we "less than perfect" parents fall short.

The car seat: Many a mother converts her child into a forward-facing car seat before the child meets the precise safety criteria. (Eleven months old, but twenty-two pounds; thirteen months old yet still eighteen pounds. . . .) Why? Because it's a whole lot less nerve-racking to have her child facing forward than to be driving with a screaming kid she can't see because he's facing backward. And the backseat forward-facing mirror she spent twenty bucks on and tried to install at *just the right angle* so she could look into the rearview mirror at *that* mirror, to see what all the fuss is about, has been bumped out of position by either the baby or big brother or by the groceries piled up between the two in the backseat.

The sippy cup: Few one-year-olds (or two- or three- or four-year-olds for that matter) can be trusted not to spill or fling a beverage in an open cup, hence the longer-term use of sippy cups. Regarding the water-only rule for between meals: Yes, as a means of cavity prevention, it absolutely makes sense that kids not nurse a sippy cup of milk or juice for hours on end. But really, bonus points to the mom who actually trains her toddler to either be satisfied drinking only water between meals or else to sit at the table and drink from a regular cup every time he wants milk or juice.

Nursing: Breastfeeding timeframes vary based on each woman—her lactation, her child's nursing patterns and needs, the needs of her other children, and often her return to work. American women are told to breastfeed for a full year, but employed moms are rarely given one-year maternity leaves, nor is every employed mother able to pump and store her breast milk at work.

Television: While many of the women who answered my survey say they try to limit the amount of television their young children watch, and a handful reported not even having a TV in the house, the only woman I've ever met who attempted to block her children from daytime TV entirely—while still having televisions in the house—was not a Stay-at-Home mom. She was an employed mother who delegated the enforcement of the no-TV rule to her nanny.

The standards for such proclamations about television, nutrition, behavior, and safety are often set and promoted by people who, while highly educated and regarded in their field, don't spend days on end home alone with children. There's the ideal world and then there's the real world. Stay-at-Home moms live in the real world, and they work with real children.

"I like to think I have a PhD in common sense, which I think is far more useful," says Erin Z., a mother of an eight- and five-year-old. "Fast food occasionally. Mostly when it's convenient for *me*. They can stay up late when they can sleep in if they're tired. They *never* get out of car seats unless we're just down the street, or I don't have enough for the carpool, in which case I fasten everyone into seatbelts. I think some parents follow rule books verbatim, but don't apply them to the right situations. You need to know your kids and adjust accordingly."

Molly, a Georgia mother of a toddler boy, agrees: "I followed all the 'rules' for the first eighteen months. Then I caved in and let my son eat a french fry. Amazingly enough, the world did not come to an end, and I'm learning to be a more relaxed mom."

L'EXPERT, C'EST MOI

Louis XIV of France is said to have declared, *"L'Etat, c'est moi."* Essentially, "I am the State." When it comes to caring for their children, mothers, particularly Stay-at-Home moms, often declare about themselves, "I am the Expert."

Reports Debbie, a mother of three and a former sixth-grade teacher from upstate New York: "When my daughter was two months old, her pediatrician told me to only nurse her every four hours. I tried to be a good mom and listen to the 'expert.' But my daughter was always hungry. When my boys were born, I nursed them on demand when they were newborns, then about every three hours as they got bigger. I soon realized *I* was the expert!"

Lyn recalls realizing too late that she knew and understood her son's needs better than the experts did. "I think back on my four-month-old first child, and me waving black-and-white cards and mobiles in his face incessantly, playing him classical music, and massaging him daily according to the latest baby-care theories," she says. "This is a child who we now know falls within the Attention Deficit Disorder spectrum, is easily overstimulated, and struggles with auditory and tactile sensory overload. Who knew? Actually, I did. Something just didn't seem right, but all the books pointed me in the wrong direction."

What Lyn's son needed would now be considered a violation of the second rule noted at the beginning of this chapter—no TV. "The only thing that worked was *Sesame Street,*" she says. "In the middle of the night, during the day, anytime all else failed. The books say don't let little children watch TV, but *Sesame Street* was the only thing that would soothe and calm this overtouched, over-stimulated child. So he watched TV, a lot of TV, and I know now it was because of how his brain was wired that he *craved* it. My son is now an A+ student in a strong school. He's a driven athlete. He's kind, compassionate, and extremely polite. Thank goodness for *Sesame Street*."

In an essay published in *Literary Mama,* writer Denise Schipani reveals that to get her babies to actually sleep, she placed them face down in their cribs, in clear defiance of the Back to Sleep guidelines developed over the past generation to prevent Sudden Infant Death Syndrome (SIDS). The reason Schipani broke the rule: Her babies screamed on their backs but slept soundly on their bellies. The experience lead her to conclude that a mother's judgment sometimes needs to trump what she's been told, even by her child's pediatrician. "When we put all our trust in the parenting gurus, listen to them slavishly rather than discriminatingly, we have less trust in our own budding parental wisdom," she writes. "Expert voices shouldn't drown out the inner voice that tells you what your baby wants, what your baby needs."

Before becoming a Stay-at-Home mother of three, Heather was a nanny, and later, a preschool teacher. "Many experts live in ivory towers rather than in the real world. After all, they are working full time," she notes. "When it comes to the occasional Happy Meal and a bit too much TV, I think there's some wiggle room. Stay-at-Home mothers have no breaks and way too much to do, so on occasion, we have to rely on the TV as a 'babysitter' or feed our kids takeout to give us a bit of time to send emails or do the dishes without the kids making a huge mess or fighting over toys."

Veteran mother of four Ginny reports, "All of my children slept on their stomachs as infants, they all had cereal at three weeks, fruit at six weeks, and whole milk by nine months. None were breastfed, they didn't go to preschool, they were allowed to play until they were exhausted. They didn't have forty-five 'activities' that took their time away from just plain old-fashioned being a child. Our family enjoyed being with and entertaining one another." (And, adds Ginny, in reassurance to other less-than-picture-perfect parents: "Although I cuss like a sailor, my children don't curse at all.")

Dixie, who spent two-plus decades as a Stay-at-Home mom, provides some Zen advice to current moms: "Your instincts are not perfect, but they are as valid as many of the child-rearing philosophies that go in and out of style. Read, ask questions, trust those you respect—and trust your instincts."

Now that I'm a Stay-at-Home mom with a half-dozen years under my belt, I'm much more skeptical about the innate infallibility of the many "experts" who spout childcare tips. For instance, while academics, parenting editors, and TV correspondents are certainly informed about their subject, they typically work full time and, if they are parents themselves, have household and childcare help. Because working at a high-level job and physically caring for little children generally can't happen simultaneously, these experts often have less hands-on child care experience than the audience they're advising. So if you're ever feeling inadequate because you aren't looking as good as those advice-touting experts on TV, or if you're not doing what the amorphous "They" say you should be doing, remember that "They" are on television or in an office *talking* about children, while you are actually at home *with* children. You're a parenting expert too—albeit one without a fat paycheck, fabulous wardrobe, and corner office.

ELMO VS. SPONGEBOB

While we're on the subject of mass media influences, unrealistic advice and expectations sometimes emanate from celebrity moms, whose extra boost of star power seems to elevate their advice above the opinions of us mere mortals. TV star Kelly Ripa, in lamenting her own TV-addicted childhood, has been quoted as saying about her three children: "I want the kids to develop good habits. They're allowed to watch an hour of TV on weekends." During a television interview, Madonna, then a mother of two, explained that the televisions in her home are only for watching movies, which are generally rationed to one a week. Adhering to such hard and fast anti-TV rules is probably quite doable for Ripa, Madonna, and other celeb moms, who more than likely have employees to keep their children entertained, occupied, and transported, as well as their houses clean, refrigerators stocked, and meals on the table. Superstar moms don't need the daily break from hands-on parenting a kids' TV show can provide while a regular old mom makes dinner.

But the message all moms get (even, apparently, superstar moms who've made millions from TV) is that it's better to not let your children watch television. I know I'm embarrassed to admit how much television my kids sometimes watch. But should I be?

When my preschoolers are watching TV, they're tuned into *Sesame Street, Blue's Clues, Hi-5, Super WHY!,* or *Little Einsteins.*

Each is an educational program that really does educate and inspire kids to interact with the lessons. I don't let them watch the violent, hyperspastic programs that make up the Cartoon Network lineup (I've blocked the channel). We watch Nickelodeon in the morning, when the little-kid shows are on, and try to avoid it in the afternoon, when the screeching big-kid programs, such as *SpongeBob SquarePants* and *The Fairly OddParents,* take over.

Thanks to the pioneering efforts of *Sesame Street* (on the air since 1969), plenty of shows today are specifically created for little eyes and ears and growing brains. Parents today also have access to commercial-free channels, which are handy for keeping marketing madness at bay. While there's still too much trashy children's programming on the airwaves, cartoons have come a long way since the smack'em-in-the-face-with-an-anvil humor of Bugs Bunny and *Looney Tunes.* And Disney movies, which can be very violent and upsetting (dead moms, dead dads), are no longer the only film entertainment options for children.

No parent or caregiver should be sticking a child in a room with a TV and calling it a day. Nor should parents be allowing a television—or for that matter, a computer—in a child's bedroom. (Although according to a study published in 2007 in the journal *Pediatrics,* 43 percent of three- to four-years olds, and 20 percent of kids under age two, do have a television in their rooms.) But failing to follow to a tee the rigid TV guidelines doesn't make you a bad mom.

Before feeling beaten down—or worse, like a failure—consider where the childrearing tips and standards are coming from. It's also important to be realistic about what practices are essential to your child's well-being and what you can actually achieve. The most practical bit of parenting advice I've heard lately was related to me by survey respondent Elizabeth, who writes: "Before my first child was born, I had asked my mom, 'How am I going to know what to do?' She told me, 'All you have to do is love him. He won't know that you've never done this before. You'll learn together.'"

HIGH ANXIETY

While many of us grew up being able to roam our neighborhoods from dawn til dusk, we now live in an age when children generally can't move about in public unsupervised. Although some people believe today's parents are overprotective, and that the dangers moms fear are little more than hype, a fear is a fear: Whether the risk is real almost doesn't matter. Because the family is fearful of the possible danger, it has an impact, regardless of its likelihood.

While car seats and seatbelts and bicycle helmets have made childhood safer than a generation ago, many aspects of daily life are more dangerous (or seemingly dangerous). There are more cars on the road today than a generation ago, and those cars are moving at higher speeds than in the past. There are also more people, both good and bad. In 1967, the U.S. population reached 200 million. In 2006, the headcount topped 300 million.

Main Streets and small downtowns where shop owners and beat cops know the residents they serve are now outnumbered by shopping centers, big-box retailers, and strip malls. (Until moving to Maryland, I always lived in a town or neighborhood that revolved around an actual Main Street or center of town. I have a hard time explaining to folks here why the local strip malls that are called

Main Street and Town Center are neither a real Main Street nor town center.) It's one thing for a child to walk a few blocks along a sidewalk on a two-lane, tree-lined road past other homes and local businesses to the Main Street ice-cream shop. It's another for a child to venture alongside a six-lane commercial thoroughfare with no sidewalks or crosswalks and then walk through a vast, treeless, as-phalt parking lot to an ice-cream freezer in a gas station mini-mart.

For many children, playing kickball or riding bikes or playing catch in the street is not an option because of traffic. While a mother might allow her own kids to horse around in their fenced backyard while she's inside, it's harder to do when other children are visit-ing. In an age of liability, few moms would want to be caught not watching the children playing in her yard (particularly if it has a swing set, trampoline, or pool).

And then there's the greatest parental fear: the sexual preda-tor. Although the odds are quite low that your child will ever be snatched by a kidnapper or sexually assaulted by a stranger, such crimes do occur. Pedophiles and sexual deviants do exist. Additionally, many adults can look back to inappropriate incidents experienced in their own childhoods. As a young teen in the late 1970s, I was approached on two occasions—once while walking to school, another when a friend and I were in a shopping center park-ing lot—by a man in a car flashing his genitals. Other people have experienced much worse.

But unlike in my youth, when parents didn't seem to worry much about sexual predators, pedophile priests, or even date rape, parents today aren't as clueless (or in as much denial). Unlike in the past, Boy Scout activities now require that a boy's parent always be present. And unlike in the past, one of the key lessons children are taught about "stranger danger" is that if they become separated from their parent or caregiver, they should seek help from a woman who has children with her: "Find another mommy, and ask her to help you find your mommy." It's good advice. Few mothers would deny comfort and protection to a child in need. As police officers aren't on every corner, it's generally useless to tell a child to look for one to help. Giving a child the once common instruction to find "someone in a uniform" may not be the safest strategy.

Heather, a former nanny who is now a mother of three, articulated the fear parents have today, and the consequences of it, when she told me, "It's important to remember that during the *Leave It to Beaver*–era of Stay-at-Home motherhood, mothers generally sent their children outside unsupervised to play with neighbor kids for half of the afternoon. Although outside play is obviously better than watching TV, we all need some time to do other things without having to supervise our kids. So where another generation went out to play, we have our kids watch (hopefully educational) television."

ALPHA, BETA, MOMMA

As if the "Mommy Wars" between Stay-at-Home and employed mothers weren't enough, according to media sources and marketers, tensions are now brewing between so-called Alpha Moms and Beta Moms. "This newest skirmish," *USA Today* reported in 2007, "is more about personal parenting styles."

Alpha Moms are bent on turning their offspring into Harvard-ready, karate black belts who play center on the basketball team, speak Chinese, and dance the lead (male or female) in *The Nutcracker*. Such mothers, the theory goes, are formerly high-achieving career women who consider motherhood their new career and, accordingly, set measurable goals and lofty ambitions. These are the women who play office via their involvement in the PTA and channel Martha Stewart when giving their child a birthday party. Refreshments matching the party theme made? Yes. Invitations designed? Yes. Entertainment scheduled? Yes? Favors assembled? Not yet. Grandma bought the wrong shade of pink tulle for the two-dozen gift totes she's been commissioned to produce.

On the flip side (as one extreme must be balanced by another) are the Beta Moms, also referred to as the Slacker Moms. These are the women who forget to send the check for junior's karate enrollment, lose the school permission forms, and feed the kids in the car on the way to school. They are either intentionally disorganized (*My time is better spent with my kids than sorting through that pile of mail*), or sadly disorganized because motherhood is truly overwhelming (*I intended to open the mail, but haven't been able to*), or hopelessly disorganized because they're truly oblivious. (*Mail? We get mail?*).

Each side in this new war supposedly thinks the other is either too controlling or flakey, nearly obsessive or neglectful. About themselves, the women believe good moms are perfectionists or playful, cautious or casual, focused or flexible. How stressed, satisfied, or nonplussed each type of mother is by the control or chaos that surrounds her is open for discussion and debate. Regardless, the last thing this world needs is another war, even one as silly as the Alphas versus the Betas.

I suspect that there is, or perhaps should be, a bit of both types in each of us. I'm mostly an Alpha person. I'm ambitious, organized, and task-oriented. But as the mother of twins, and now with a total brood of three, I've had to become a Beta person as well, by lowering my expectations a bit and learning to go with the flow. With one child, my house and car were always clean and orderly. With three, I can't keep ahead of the cyclones that touch down throughout the day. I can no longer enter a bathroom in my home without having to clean a mess left by a child. (Actually, that's not a good example. The messes irritate the hell out of the Alpha in me.) However, I have learned to be very Beta regarding my children's clothing. When my daughters dress themselves for school wearing stained T-shirts, pajama shorts, and scuffed shoes on the wrong feet—and refuse to let me change their outfits—I just say, *whatever,* and I mean it. I'm trusting that the preschool teachers and the other moms will understand why I chose not to fight that battle. If they don't? *Whatever.*

Shhh . . . Don't Tell!

Or rather, scratch that. Tell *everyone* you know that this is what real moms, especially real Stay-at-Home moms, do! Let's stop being ashamed of not being "perfect," kick the stigma that goes with it, and stop being so hard on ourselves.

We let our children watch TV: We have to. It's often the only way we can shower, go to the bathroom, prepare meals, clean, or do anything not directly related to caring for a small child or children. "I've always believed that if *Mister Rogers' Neighborhood* hadn't come on TV at 4:00 PM, I'd be drinking sherry," says Dixie, whose children are now in college. Praise and appreciation also comes from mother of three Sarah B., who says, "Never underestimate the value of TV. It can make the difference between insanity and sanity for both you and your kids."

Our children eat junk food: For moms in the car much of the day, shuttling to schools and activities, sometimes the best way to quiet and feed a hungry child who's strapped into a car seat is with french fries procured from any of the countless drive-thru windows suburban mothers pass each day. We're not proud of this, but a child's Cheerio fascination only lasts so long.

We're not flipping flashcards all day: We have them. We just don't do flashcards or read picture books nearly as often as we believed we would (or others think we do or should) while being home full time with our children. An exception: Mothers who homeschool. Kudos to those gals.

Our kids listen to our music: There's only so much of "The Wheels on the Bus" a gal can take. Sometimes, instead of popping in a sing-along CD, we put on the radio or play our own music—which, according to Pat, a licensed social worker who has been a Stay-at-Home mom for eleven years, is a very good thing. "The kids who can sing Ramones and REM songs are more interesting to be around," she declares.

We go days without showering: When you have active, preschool children in the house, it can be hard to let down your guard long enough to get naked and climb into a shower. Not only can't you see or hear what your children are up to when you're getting clean, sometimes you're forced to bolt like a soaked streaker should a crisis arise. Yes, showering very early in the morning or at night would make sense, if you had the energy at those hours. (On your showerless days, just wash your hair in the sink, sponge off the essential parts, or think of not showering as a form of environmental activism—all that water you're saving!)

Our wardrobes are outdated: Keeping fashionable and *au currant* requires having money to spend, the time to spend it, and the freedom to shop and try on clothes. Instead of being bummed by that, look at the benefits: You save money by not being a slave to fashion and, if your measurements have grown due to motherhood, you don't have to stare at the new you in a cruelly lighted fitting room. All that said, there is a happy middle ground between trendy couture and tired T-shirts paired with sweats.

Our kids dress oddly: When a four-year-old insists on wearing Batman pajamas to school, is it really worth the emotional and physical confrontation required to remove the pajamas from her body and put on actual day clothes? Some days, no. Another strategy for avoiding the dressing at daybreak tug-of-war: Put your children to bed in their next-day clothes. "It's not like they get dirty in their sleep," explains an employed mom who does this so she and her girls can get out of the house on time in the morning. Her backup plan: Bring clothing in the car and dress the girls at or before going into preschool. "Because they want to play with their friends, they're motivated to get dressed quickly," she says.

We don't have nightly sit-down family meals: It's a lovely idea—a family gathered at a table to eat and talk about the events of the day. But the touching image is often shattered by babies and toddlers who need to be fed early, young children who need help with homework, and an employed parent coming home after 6:00 or 7:00 PM, when mom and kids are strung out (and little ones may already be in the tub). If family dinners don't work for you, don't sweat it. They'll be much more practical—and far more enjoyable!—when the kids are older.

We get sick of our kids: We do. And it's okay to admit it. (While I say as much in the preface, I repeat it here, because this is an important point.) There are times we feel pawed at rather than loved. There are moments when our children's cries give us splitting headaches. Being a Stay-at-Home mom is a job that doesn't end at day's end. It's not realistic for you, or anyone, to think you should enjoy the work all the time. It is realistic to occasionally want to be where children aren't. Acknowledging as much doesn't mean we don't love our kids (we *love* 'em), or that we're not grateful to be home with them. And it doesn't mean we want to lock our children in a closet. If anything, it means we sometimes want to lock *ourselves* in a closet—with a reading light, a good book (like this one), a peaceful CD, some comfy pillows, and a cozy blanket. Wow, doesn't that sound like a great thing to do, *right now?*

TEN

The Mommy Brain
(or, Why We Often Can't Think Straight)

Women often joke about how pregnancy makes their brains turn to mush. At a certain stage of pregnancy, the joke is biologically true. But after the babe arrives, a woman's brain bounces back—unless her postpartum hormones go wildly askew, or she finds herself feeling trapped by the routines and expectations of her new Stay-at-Home mom career.

While *Sesame Street* and flashcards are considered beneficial to a developing toddler's brain, endless days of PBS Kids and Candyland can make a mother batty. For some women, Stay-at-Home motherhood can be so intellectually stifling that it leads to depression, anger, and serious self-image problems. "I really miss the intellectual stimulation of working and being financially independent," says mother-of-two Laura P., a social worker with an Ivy League master's degree. "Those feelings impact my self-esteem no matter how strongly I believe I should be home."

Laura P.'s mixed feelings aren't unusual, or unexpected. We live in a society that both pushes women toward staying home and chastises them for doing so. But being a Stay-at-Home mother doesn't have to mean boring days and endless chores (most days, perhaps, but not every day). Women can do hands-on parenting while also staying engaged with themselves and the world beyond their homes. It takes effort, but there are ways to keep from becoming depressed or, no offense, dumb.

Looking to current events for a positive example, consider that U.S. Representative Nancy Pelosi, current Speaker of the House and second in line to the presidency, is a former Stay-at-Home mother of five. Although she was a political volunteer for years, Pelosi didn't run for office until her youngest child was finishing high school. So try to think of Stay-at-Home motherhood this way: It's entirely possible that a future president of the United States is right now reading this book—while she's sitting on a couch with her child watching *Blue's Clues*.

THE HORMONES MADE ME DO IT (WELL, SOME OF IT)

We all know that during pregnancy and immediately after birth a woman's hormones can be out of control. A formerly rational, intelligent, capable person can become a whimpering, sniveling couch potato who weeps at TV commercials and can't muster the energy or focus to read a newspaper. In the bedroom, the former vixen who liked to model slinky lingerie is more inclined to snuggle into flannel pajamas and hunger for sleep, any sleep, than for a long night of lovemaking. Women's bodies and brains change with motherhood. Problem is, when it happens, neither we nor our partners truly understand the changes or how to deal with them.

"The female brain is so deeply affected by hormones that their influence can be said to create a woman's reality. They can shape a

woman's values and desires, and tell her, day to day, what's important," writes neuropsychiatrist Louann Brizendine in *The Female
Brain*. Hormonal influences start at birth and change throughout
a woman's life, sort of like, says Brizendine, "the weather itself—
constantly changing and hard to predict." By comparison, male
hormones are more constant. But, and I stress, constant *doesn't*
mean better. A man can be constantly aggressive, which isn't a good
thing. The point of Brizendine's book is that the male and female
brains are *different*; neither is better nor worse.

Among the differences is that a woman's hormones (oxytocin,
progesterone, estrogen, and even testosterone) go through enormous changes during pregnancy, while breastfeeding, and continuing on into caring for older children. These hormones can inspire
great clarity (about what matters and doesn't matter in life) and
bring great pleasure. But swirling postpartum hormones can also
lead to absentmindedness, depression, and anxiety, each of which
can have dire consequences if left unchecked.

I have a friend who is convinced that his wife's unrecognized
postpartum depression after the birth of their second child started
the downward spiral that ultimately ended in a nasty divorce.
Because a person often can't see what's happening to herself, it may
take a spouse, partner, close friend, or relative to convince a mom
she might benefit from help. Various coping mechanisms, including a larger discussion about medication and therapy, are noted in
Chapter Thirteen. That said, the physical and emotional problems
experienced while being a Stay-at-Home mom are not all medically
related or managed. Nor is becoming a Stepford Wife the solution
to dissatisfaction.

IT'S NOT ALL IN OUR HEADS

Hormones and biochemistry aside, there are numerous daily life experiences that can make Stay-at-Home women feel, well, a little crazy.

Do I have ADHD?

Probably not. But it's a thought that does cross many women's minds. Why? Because they think about the number of things they want to do but don't, or the projects they start but don't finish, or the chores they actually do but don't do well, or the tasks they do, only to have to do them again.

Says Erin S: "I miss having projects that have definitive endings." Adds Sarah B.: "I love to make lists and be able to cross tasks off as I accomplish them, but there are some days when I'm lucky to get the breakfast dishes in the sink before dinnertime." On survey respondent Joni's list of her Stay-at-Home challenges: "Constantly being interrupted. When I do create something mentally stimulating to do, I can't do it without having to stop at least once a minute."

The distraction problem led an MBA–holding Stay-at-Home mother of three (an infant, preschooler, and first grader) to post the following comment on a chat room for San Francisco Bay Area moms: "I can't quite figure out how to balance being a quality parent, [being a] wife, and finding time for myself. I am feeling especially bad because my mother keeps making comments about how she was able to raise a large family *and* work. She can't quite understand why I seem frazzled at times."

On the one hand, as a Stay-at-Home mom you may think, *I don't have a job. I'm home all day,* and, consequently, you believe you should be able to complete a simple task like changing out the kids' summer clothing to fall, or culling through the bags of hand-me-downs your neighbor dropped off, or replacing the torn shelf liners in the kitchen. But you can't get to those things. Or you actually do start sorting the clothes, but by day's end your bedroom is filled with piles of clothing, which the kids then find and jump in, scattering them throughout the room. Since you now have to start sorting all over again, you either move the clothes into one large pile or shove them into a trash bag for dealing with on another day.

When your husband sees the mess and asks, "Why did you start this if you weren't going to finish it?" or "What's so hard about sorting clothes?" you either get really angry or you can't answer, because you can't think of a good reason why you didn't finish the job. You didn't leave the house all day, except to drive the three-year-old to and from preschool, and later to meet your kindergartner at the bus stop. You haven't even made dinner yet, because you've been so busy sorting the clothes. What happened?

What happened is that instead of accomplishing a big task, you've spent the day performing dozens of tiny, uninspiring, seemingly meaningless tasks and chores and errands, each of which took a little bit of time but, when added together, consumed the entire day. Each runny nose wiped, each search for a shoe, each request from a child for a drink interrupts your flow and takes time from doing something else.

For instance, imagine you're sitting in your kitchen at your computer, trying to pay bills online while your toddler is entertaining herself nearby with toys. About five minutes into your task, your child approaches you with a runny nose:

- You see your child has a runny nose.
- Before she can wipe her runny nose on your pants, you get up from your chair to get a tissue.
- You return to the child and wipe her nose.
- Now you see that the child's shirt is wet and messy, as are your fingers.
- You remove the child's shirt.
- You go to the kitchen sink to wash your hands.
- The sink has dishes in it, so you rinse the dishes to put them in the dishwasher.
- But the dishwasher is full of clean dishes. You empty the dishwasher and then fill it with dishes from the sink.
- You tell your child to play with her toys while you go upstairs to get her another shirt.
- When you get upstairs you toss the shirt into the laundry room.
- Passing the bathroom on your way to your daughter's closet, you realize you actually need to use the bathroom. You do, and you use up the toilet paper.
- You go to the hall closet and get more toilet paper.
- You return to the bathroom to replace the roll.
- The bathroom trash is full, so you grab the bag and replace it with another.
- You go into your child's room to find a new shirt.
- While there, you see that a sippy cup, full of milk, is in her bed, and that she's left her wet overnight diaper on the floor.
- You put the diaper in the trash bag you're carrying. (Wow, that was efficient!)
- You make your daughter's bed and gather the sippy cup.
- On the way back downstairs, you catch another glimpse of the laundry room and realize you have enough dirty clothing to do a load of wash.
- You open the washing machine to discover there's already a wet load inside.
- You start to put those wet clothes into the dryer, but the dryer is full.

- You pull the clean clothes out of the dryer and put them in a basket.
- You put the wet clothes in the dryer.
- You put the dirty clothes, including the yucky shirt, in the washing machine and start the washer.
- Since you really don't have time now to sort the clean clothes, you leave the basket of clean laundry on your bed.
- You return downstairs and search for your shirtless child.
- You pass the sink, so you rinse the sippy cup and put it into the dishwasher.
- You try to shove the bathroom trash into the kitchen trash container, but it's full.
- You take the trash out to the garbage cans in the garage.
- You come back into the house and put another bag in the trash container.
- You find your child.
- Her nose is running again, her face and chest now need to be cleaned, she has gotten into the bills and papers you were working with, she needs a diaper change, and it's lunchtime.

How much time did it take to wipe that child's nose? Fifteen minutes? Twenty minutes? A half-hour? Imagine variations on this scenario playing out dozens of times a day. (By the way, your on-line banking site has logged you off by now.) Imagine that same scene, except with additional offspring in the house. You don't have ADHD. You have children!

WHY COULDN'T I HAVE IT ALL?

When I was a magazine editor I worked with a writer, a mother of three, who did her job entirely from home. As Marilyn had no regular childcare, she wrote at night, and as her editor, I could only work with her by phone in the morning when all of her children were in school. She was crazed juggling kids and her part-time, home-based job; I was crazed juggling my office-based job, a bad commute, and a toddler back at home. As we griped about the demands on our time, she said something I've never forgotten:

"Women like us are always stressed," she said. "We want a career, but we also want to be home with our kids. The mothers who are happy are the ones who've made a clear choice: Either to work and pay for a great nanny, or give up on a career and raise their kids themselves. You and I want to do both, and that's our problem."

Ouch. The truth hurts. But we're not alone in not being sure about which road, or roads, to take.

"I question my decision every day," says Beth, a Dartmouth MBA and former asset manager who's now home with two children. "The answer to that question, thus far, has always been, 'Yes, it was the right decision.' But it's definitely hard to stay at home with children all day, especially knowing I have the credentials to have a very successful career."

Says Joni, a former sales strategist, now a Stay-at-Home mother of two in Colorado: "I always knew I would stay home with my children, but I had no idea how hard it would be emotionally. I miss work. I miss showing off my big brain."

Another mom who wanted to complete the survey emailed to say she'd do so later: "Can't fill it out right now because it would be way too negative. I'm currently attempting to remove black crayon from my home office wall as my many framed diplomas mock me from above." I never did hear from her.

So many women struggle with the pros and cons of wanting to live two lives at once—to be both a "working" woman and

Stay-at-Home mom. Marilyn and I were attempting to raise children while also being gainfully employed and intellectually challenged, but for us, doing both was the challenge. Stay-at-Home moms don't have the same type of juggling to do as employed moms, but because of that, they often feel they have little intellectual stimulation, or they see their diplomas as wasted paper.

When that happens, it's important to mitigate those feelings. While going back into the workforce is a solution, at the moment, doing so may actually cause, rather than relieve, stress. Intellectual challenges *other than* returning to full-time work can suffice, especially if you remind yourself that being home caring for small children is what you're doing right now, but not necessarily forever. Reducing the number of balls you have in the air at the moment can be a choice to celebrate rather than lament.

WHO AM I?

Once the dust settled from leaving my career, having twins, and relocating to a new state, I found myself asking that exact question. When my efforts at freelance writing and editing were subsumed by the needs of my children, and contact with friends and colleagues from my "past life" had reduced to a trickle, I felt I had essentially disappeared.

As mere observers of the world beyond our homes, women whose daily lives revolve around children can be left feeling disconnected from society and themselves.

"In the beginning, I had trouble letting go of who I was. I wanted to make sure everyone knew what I used to do," says Kellie, an Ohio mother of two who had been an assistant to an NBA sports agent. "I'm past that now, but I see it in so many moms who are new to staying home and haven't yet made peace with their choice."

Adds Joni: "I've forgotten what I like to do during daytime hours. I don't get more than a few minutes at a time to do anything I like, so I'm limited to doing only things that can be done in small time allotments. I don't have time to read a book, so I stock up on magazines and often just read the short articles."

"I have now been home for more than four years, and I'm feeling the strain of it on my psyche," says Laura, a mother of two preschoolers. "I don't have a weekend. I don't get in a car and leave my job. I don't have time for myself. I feel very constricted and dissatisfied. There are times I feel like I'm ceasing to exist as an individual."

Dixie's two children are now in college, but she well remembers her own struggles when she could no longer say she was a biostatistician and hospice worker. "I missed the 'respectable' answer to 'What do you do?'" she says. "I missed the ready identity."

It may be an American convention to assess people by what they "do." However, a woman I know has come up with a wise, and sensitive, solution to the sometimes loaded question by instead asking, "What do you do with your time?" Some people "answer with their paid work, others with hobbies, some with their parenting," she reports.

Earlier in this book, on page 167, several women explain how they answer the "What do you do?" question. But mastering that answer is only a small part of accepting and describing the new you. When you're really feeling as if you've disappeared, it may be time to think about how you can reappear—preferably in a productive, positive manner, as discussed in the next chapter, and not in a Britney Spears sort of way, which, alas, does occur among even noncelebrity moms.

YOU'RE SMART—AND SUCCESSFUL!

There are times I've been very frustrated living as an outsider looking in. Now that I'm out of the paid workforce, I've become very attuned to the incompetence of many people who are in it, and I think I'm even more irritated than I used to be by shoddy or late work done by businesses and service people I wind up having to pay. For a while after I left my job, I would lament the unfairness of how my intelligence and skills were not being fully used or financially rewarded now that I was "just a mom." Then, during a series of discussions with similarly capable women who left careers to be at-home moms, one conversation focused on the idea that women like us are smart and successful—perhaps even *smarter,* and *more successful,* than all those folks who do go to work, which we'll define for this purpose as going to a paid job every day.

Here's the logic of this theory: Most employed people would love not to work. Most would likely prefer to have more time at home, more time with their children. Most would also probably prefer to be financially sound without having to produce an income. Now continue that line of thinking. Those of us who are "smart and successful" found partners who would love and support a family, or we financed our own motherhood careers by busting our butts in the workforce prior to having kids. Those of us who are "smart and successful" are able to run a house and care for a family while living within a budget.

So when you're feeling down about the value of your intelligence and achievements, try to spin the situation. A woman who actually manages to become a Stay-at-Home mom *is so damn smart and successful,* because she doesn't *have to* go to work. Hey, that's you!

HELLO? I STILL HAVE A BRAIN!

Most men these days are accustomed to working with women. Many have women as colleagues or bosses. But since becoming a Stay-at-Home mom, I've noticed that the social disconnect between the sexes often has more to do with *what* you do than with what gender you are.

On the occasions I attended parties in New York or its suburbs when I worked in publishing, I spent as much time talking with the men at the party as I did with the women. My job, the experience of my train commute to work, and my high-level community involvement gave me common ground with many men I knew. It also made me different from the wives who stayed home with children. When I moved to Maryland as a Stay-at-Home mom and started attending neighborhood gatherings or functions for my husband's job, I was no longer a magazine editor or community leader. I was "Brian's wife" or the "baby twins' mother." For most people, "Brian's wife" isn't as interesting as "the magazine editor who's also on the commuter commission."

Knowing that I am so much more than just his wife, Brian would kindly try to introduce my past experiences into conversations. I often did too. But it always felt so desperate. While men I knew when I worked can still relate to the person I used to be, men

I meet anew generally see me as a wife and Stay-at-Home mom. During a conversation with my friend Ben, a man who knows about my education and career past, he said he could tell I needed to be intellectually busy, not just kid busy. "You're the kind of person who needs to keep her brain active," he said.

I know Ben is right about me, but I think the same is true of many women, as articulated by *New York Times* reader Nancy Dziedzic. In May of 2007, Dziedzic posted the following comment on the newspaper's website, in response to a column by *Times* writer Judith Warner about public attitudes regarding "working" versus Stay-at-Home moms:

> I don't understand why everyone—including and perhaps especially women—assumes that Stay-at-Home motherhood automatically means you become a stupid, unengaged zombie. I mean, of course I know that motherhood makes you feel stupid, unengaged, and zombie-like at times, because a mother has to tap into unparalleled reserves of mental and emotional energy just to get through the day with young kids. It's incredibly hard, no question. But why do we think a woman can't possibly have a fulfilling intellectual and social life if she's at home with kids? Just because I'm a mother doesn't mean I've lost the ability to read and think, for Pete's sake. I do manage to keep up with world events and even—gasp!—have interests outside of my kids. . . . I've had enough of everybody assuming women necessarily have to lose their brains with their placentas.

Several women who answered my survey felt the same way.

"I tend to feel less 'needed' by the world as a Stay-at-Home mom, other than to my kids, of course," says Annabel. "When someone calls me for advice related to my former career, or about anything, really, that always gives me a bit of a pick-me-up. Stay-at-Home moms can be great resources."

Adds Kellie: "I know I'm a smart, successful woman, but I sometimes wonder if my husband remembers that. He and I were recently helping my brother with his résumé. I have a journalism degree, but my husband was surprised by how knowledgeable and helpful I was. It was as if he'd forgotten I do have a mind for business."

In such instances, it often behooves a Stay-at-Home woman to stand her ground and remind the person who's underestimating her, "I know I'm working as a mom now, but I did spend more than a decade as a . . ." (And if the belittler is your spouse, perhaps remind him, "Hello. Before I quit my job to care for *your* children . . .") At parties, instead of feeling excluded from work-related conversations, or becoming sucked into more potty-training talk, introduce a new subject: "Hey, what about those Yankees?" Well, you get the point.

But there will be times when, no matter what you do or say, you will be treated and judged based on 1) being female and 2) being a mother or potential mother. There's little to do about those types of people, other than to not let them get you down. My friend Lyn tells a story of how, when she was in law school, she went home to South Carolina to see her parents. While there, she and her father visited with a family friend who was a local judge. "The conversation ended," Lyn recalls, "with this jovial but frank Southern gentleman asserting, 'What a shame it is that girls like you feel it *necessary* to take a law school spot that could go to a man who will someday need to support a family. You girls eventually stay home anyway.' I was floored. I resolved then to never give up my career in favor of a family."

However, years later, when faced with a first born who had severe allergies and some difficulties, Lyn struggled with her decision to stick with her career. When her second child arrived, she quit her job. It was Lyn's father who proved immensely supportive in helping her make peace with that decision. "He told me I could put my vast education to no better use in the world than raising my two little boys," she explains. "I have no reservations about the choice I made. I believe that well-educated, accomplished moms can help raise a generation of young men who will respect and value women who have personal goals."

Smart women shouldn't be made to feel that they're wasting their intelligence by working as mothers. As a society, we should want smart women (and for that matter, men) at home raising children. As women who are home caring for children, it's up to each of us to carry ourselves, and think of ourselves, as the intelligent, capable, hard-working people that we are.

Staying Sharp, Staying Informed, Getting Involved

After publishing her anti–Stay-at-Home manifesto *Get to Work,* author Linda R. Hirshman wrote an op-ed piece in *The Washington Post* asserting that Stay-at-Home women were politically uninformed, and that when it comes to making choices in elections, they vote as their husbands do. I really hope that's not the case. If it is in your household, there are many ways to reverse the situation and stay informed about—and even involved in—current events:

Read a newspaper: You can have the paper delivered, make it a daily routine to get out of the house and buy one, or read the news online. The nice thing about the online edition is that if it isn't free, it's usually much less expensive than having a paper delivered to your door. Another plus is that online reading doesn't result in a pile of newspapers transforming themselves into a homework assignment—for you. When you read online, you can scan the headlines and invest time in only the stories you want to read, when you have the time to read them.

Regularly check or subscribe to informational websites: There are all sorts of website-based newsletters or news summary pages these days, most of which can email you with daily updates or become the home page you see when you log onto your computer. Such web-based newsletters include political sites, women-oriented sites, and sites sponsored by trade or industry journals. The latter are an excellent way for you to keep informed about your former business or profession, which is a good thing to do in case you someday go back into the workforce. (See Chapter Fifteen for more on making a career comeback.)

Tune in to a TV news or documentary channel: You'll learn more from CNN or PBS than from Jerry Springer or any of the other confrontational daytime talk shows. If you keep a television on for background noise, select a news channel over one broadcasting sitcoms, cooking shows, or soap operas. Two irreverent and fun sources of news are the Comedy Central "fake news" programs *The Daily Show* and *The Colbert Report.* Each spins comedy from actual news events, sometimes with more accurate commentary and context than the real news channels. Both shows also feature interviews with newsmakers and newswatchers, such as politicians, celebrities, journalists, and authors.

Listen to news radio: Flip the dial at the top of the hour to a local news channel for a report of the latest happenings; keep tuned to National Public Radio (NPR)—which has intelligent, news-oriented broadcasting all day—via radio or the Internet; or subscribe to a satellite radio network for a large selection of talk and news programming.

Read smart magazines: Everyone loves to escape into the gossip rags and celebrity magazines, but Brad Pitt and Angelina Jolie aren't headed for the White House. Many of the women's service, home, and fashion magazines are interchangeable, so there isn't much reason to read more than one. Instead, include a newsweekly (*Time, Newsweek, U.S. News & World Report,* etc.) among your routine magazine reads. The newsweeklies are a good resource and news summary when you can't read a daily newspaper or watch the news on a regular basis.

Be selective about the books you read: Stay-at-Home moms don't have a lot of free time for reading, which is often our reason for not joining a book group or even daring to pick up a book. However, since any reading you get to do can be for pleasure (as opposed to being for school or work), your Stay-at-Home time can be an opportunity to read the books you always wanted to read. For instance, I was deeply involved in first work, and then babies, when the *Harry Potter* series began, but I've since been able to read all seven books. A history book I wanted to read took me a full year to finish, but I eventually completed it. Another option is listening to books on tape or CD, which you can do while driving, or taking a baby for a walk, or even cleaning your house. While trashy romance novels and thrillers have their place, your precious reading time can also expand your horizons and keep you informed.

The multimedia approach: Do a bit of everything. "I read two newspapers a day, five to eight magazines a month, and listen to National Public Radio all day," says Gerri, a former corporate human resources director. "It helps me feel I'm part of the world."

Politics and activism: To really feel a part of the world at large, a Stay-at-Home mom can go beyond staying abreast of events to actually advocating for a cause—including doing so as a mom. For instance, Seattle-area members of the national advocacy organization MomsRising (www.momsrising.org) brought their kids along when they met with the Speaker of Washington State's House of Representatives. Their cause: To advocate for paid family leave. (The legislation passed.) Women who can't attend meetings or marches are still able to help by writing letters and emails to legislators, by phone banking, or hosting house parties for causes, and even by knocking on doors for candidates (with babes in tow). And remember, Stay-at-Home moms are a highly courted voting demographic. Your opinions, desires, and votes do matter.

Get Me Out of Here!

The nineteenth-century French novelist Honoré de Balzac said, "A mother who is really a mother is never free." Yes, we know. But once in a while, we'd like to interact with the world as if we were. We don't want to be rid of our children completely, we just want an occasional, *little tiny bit* of freedom, so we're not entirely consumed by being full-time Stay-at-Home moms.

When a mother's group I belong to issued a call for volunteers, one member responded with a question and request of her own. "How does anyone have the energy and time to volunteer when they have young children?" she asked. "Those of us who feel we're struggling from crisis to crisis sometimes wish we knew the secrets of those happy-looking moms who seem to sail through it all so effortlessly."

"Seem to" is the key phrase, since few women sail through motherhood effortlessly. But having some time for yourself—or for getting involved in activities beyond motherhood—will help you stay happy, sane, and could be, as per the title of this book, even a matter of your very survival. While this chapter will explore ways Stay-at-Home moms can pursue non–child related interests outside of their homes, if what you find here doesn't quite save you, the upcoming chapters focus on the importance of interacting with friends, and on how not to let depression and solitude (or a lack of *any* solitude) get the better of you. After that, "Where's My Stand-In?" looks at options for getting the childcare help you need, so you can take a short (or even a weekend) break from your day (and night) job.

So let's get started at getting you out and about!

VOLUNTEER WORK: DO WHAT YOU WANT TO DO, ON YOUR OWN TERMS

A common theme among Stay-at-Home moms is that once they've gotten over the hump of new motherhood, and perhaps past the tumultuous toddler years, they often find something to do beyond diapers, dishes, carpools, and cooking. Many women take charge of managing the family's finances. Some coordinate and supervise home repairs and major renovations. And some get *very* involved in charitable organizations, homeowner or neighborhood associations, and school PTAs and PTOs.

For many years, Lyn, a former trusts and estates attorney, led the parent teacher organization at the school her three children attend. She successfully cochaired a fundraising effort to raise several million dollars for a new high school. She also ran three benefit auctions for the elementary school that, all told, netted more than $200,000. Event planners and development directors get paid big bucks to do what Lyn does for free.

Karen, a former community health educator and mother of three, was the volunteer chair of a county commission on the status of women. Nanette, a mother of two and a former fitness club manager, leads a women's service organization and orchestrates its annual charity gala. An ob-gyn I know turned Stay-at-Home mom of two school-age children works a few shifts a month at a nonprofit women's health clinic to keep her skills current and her license valid.

From my time in the volunteer sphere of Stay-at-Home motherhood, I've found that it's easy to see which women once had a career at which they excelled. While it's true that some frustrated career women turned at-home moms do become the Bitches of the Bake Sale and Volunteers from Hell, most I've met haven't. In fact, these women are so good as volunteers, they often put the paid staffers to shame.

Linda, a former systems analyst and Manhattan mother of four kids under the age of eight says, "I volunteer to keep myself challenged and to provide an outlet away from my children." Among her assignments: Cochairing the preschool book fair, as well as serving as the treasurer on her church council.

Andrea, a former Stay-at-Home mom who writes about her divorce on page 140 of this book, credits her "loads of volunteer work" with "filling my otherwise blank résumé." Because her volunteer jobs included several years of professional-level assignments, such as chairing and planning large-scale fundraisers and various community outreach efforts, Andrea's Stay-at-Home career was filled with examples of how she gained and used her managerial and organizational talents.

For many reasons—the desire to stay active or be involved in the community, to keep a résumé alive, to pursue an interest and, of course, pure altruism—Stay-at-Home women often give away their hard-earned professional talents for free. Volunteering to help a truly needy cause, or for your own personal fulfillment, is a wonderful thing. But be warned: Volunteering to save an organization from its own incompetence is another.

I often wonder, if the tables were turned, would Stay-at-Home men do the same? I have a hard time imagining a bunch of dads decorating the teachers' lounge for a staff luncheon, or slaving, without any compensation, over every detail of the Fall Harvest Fun Fest. The occasional inequity of the expectations—and the assumption that moms can work gratis at both mindful and mindless tasks—is a reason some Stay-at-Home women purposely don't volunteer, or when they do volunteer, they make sure they volunteer *smart*.

"There are forces out there who apparently believe that the reason you gave up paid work was to work for them for free," asserts survey respondent Sandra, a former trial lawyer. "Hence they don't organize themselves and get their act together to function like the for-profit or nonprofit business they are. They trust that you have internalized that staying at home to rear children is akin to slacking off, and that you need to do 'real, adult work.' My advice is don't volunteer willy-nilly, or just because someone asks you, or, especially, just because it's a good cause. Is it *your* cause? Does it make sense for you to be away from your kids to do the work? A lot of things balance on the backs of women in our society as it is. Volunteer work balances on the backs of women who are unpaid to boot!"

Sarah G., a former museum administrator in New York City, is a frequent volunteer in the Virginia town where she now lives, but she's also a cautious volunteer. "The best thing I've found for me to combat loneliness is to get involved with something," she says. "I do a lot at my kids' school, but since I'm not interested in the politics of the PTA, I don't sit on committees. Instead, I work in the library, in the gardens, help the teachers, work in the cafeteria, decorate for parties. I'm the scorekeeper for my son's baseball team and the director of our neighborhood swim team, which is the closest I'll get to neighborhood politics."

"I felt like I had a job," says Andrea, about the volunteer work she started once both of her children were in school full-day, "because I could easily log in more than thirty hours a week doing community volunteer service or working at the kids' school, where I became extremely involved with the PTO." But in addition to using her skills in a way that later benefited her in finding a paid job, these volunteer activities also helped her as a parent. "I wouldn't trade that experience for anything. I felt I had a finger on the pulse of everything happening at my children's school. That was very important to me."

YOUR OTHER LIFE: CLUBS, HOBBIES, GIGGLE JOBS

A mother needn't have a nanny or go back to work full time in order to do things to "improve" herself, or pursue personal interests or passions that, unlike volunteer work, aren't done in the service of anyone but the woman herself. As survey respondent Aoife says, "Have your own gig, be it a calligraphy class once a week, a very part-time job, or singing in a choir." Adds Nancy, a

Stay-at-Home veteran: "Having hobbies and a passion for things besides your children can help you maintain your sanity and show your kids that life does not revolve around them. I think children need to see this."

When Nancy's children were very small, she worked one morning a week at a friend's flower shop. "I love flowers and being around flowers. The work was emotionally beneficial to me," she says.

Ginny, whose youngest child is in high school, is a volunteer extraordinaire, but also a member of a book group, a knitting group, and several local organizations, including a Toastmaker's Club, which has helped her develop impressive public speaking skills. (For more about Ginny's many activities see page 345.)

Many Stay-at-Home moms join volunteer-run organizations such as Moms Inc. (www.momsinc.org) and Mothers & More (www.mothersandmore.org), each a nationally reaching, volunteer-run support group for mothers or, in my area, Professional Moms at Home (www.professionalmomsathome.org). These organizations help mothers meet each other, and they are usually a good source for playgroups, Mommy & Me–type activities and, just as importantly, "girls' night out" social events. Depending on where you live, you can seek out and join a newcomers club, which is typically a local, volunteer-run organization that welcomes women who are new to town or are new moms. Such clubs sponsor events for women, couples, families, and moms and kids (www.newcomers club.com has a directory of newcomers groups nationwide).

Great (Little) Escapes

Many of us remember the television commercial for Calgon in which a harried woman pleads, "Calgon, take me away!" As requested, the Calgon bath powder whisks her into a large soaking tub surrounded by candles, with demanding kids, husband, and barking dog all left behind. It sounds cheesy, but when you can't get away *away*, taking a warm, fragrant bath can be a rejuvenating escape from the demands of children and home.

Several survey respondents said that when their husbands arrive home, they make themselves scarce. "If I've had a rotten day, I will go up to my room with a book or take a drive while he takes over managing the kids," says Maura, a mother of five. Julie C. does the same with her husband and two toddlers. "He rough-houses with the girls when he gets home from work," she says, "and I slip away behind a closed door to read a book and decompress."

At-home escapes can also be found via the Internet, by participating in a chat room, social network, or, for real escapism, an online game. "I play a multiplayer, online role-playing game called World of Warcraft," says Anne, who has a PhD in biology and is now home with a toddler. "I've made a number of friends online through the game, and I've risen to the level of officer in a 500-person guild. My playtime has decreased as my child has grown older, but I still find the game to be a welcome source of escape, entertainment, community, and non–child centered activity."

Here are a few other tried-and-true suggestions from Stay-at-Home moms for escape and relaxation when Dad or someone else takes charge of the kids:

▶

- Leave the house and get your hair done (or your nails or your toes).
- Watch *Oprah*. (As a mom I know once told me: "I feel like she's my best friend!")
- Sit in a coffee shop and enjoy a latte.
- Read a book, newspaper, or magazine.
- Take yourself to a movie.
- Shop for yourself, by yourself.
- Take a long nap or crawl into bed early.
- Run an errand (alone).
- Sit on the couch and watch a DVD or primetime TV show of your choice.
- Lock yourself in your room, home office, or wherever you can hide undisturbed.
- Email friends or family.
- Surf the Internet, visit or join an online community, or read or write a blog.
- Have a phone date with a distant friend.
- Meet a nearby friend for a childless, spouseless meal.
- Enjoy a glass of wine—or, within reason, a really strong drink!

My Giggle Job

The company I worked for during my first pregnancy allowed parents (both mothers and fathers) to take up to twelve months of unpaid leave to care for a new child. It's a wonderful benefit for people who can afford to take it. And after much agonizing about finances and my career viability, I decided that I would. But as every mother knows, not going to work doesn't mean not working. And very soon into my leave, I realized that while going to a job five days a week is hard, it's often not as hard as having a baby attached to you everyday—all day—when you're on the phone, when you're sitting, when you're standing, when you're walking, when you're eating, when you're using the bathroom. I started to miss my "real" job simply because it allowed me to do all those things alone.

Several of my friends were on maternity leave when I was. We shared the same lament: We like to work, and for various reasons (ranging from economic to emotional) we *need* to work, but with new babies to care for, we just weren't up to working at a job that had major responsibilities, long hours, or required a long commute. (For instance: At the time, my roundtrip commute between suburban New Jersey and Manhattan took three hours a day—more when the trains or subways were delayed.)

It turned out that my maternity leave ennui was well timed. Shortly after I gave birth, Williams-Sonoma, the elegant kitchenware chain, opened a shop one mile from my home. When the store started hiring temporary help for the winter holidays, my son was four months old, and I was becoming desperate for some semblance of independence. I decided that for my mental health (my sanity!) I *needed* to work at Williams-Sonoma.

I knew the manager, so I asked her if she would consider letting me work extremely part-time. She agreed to hire me for one weekday evening and one weekend day a week. My salary: $6.50 an hour. I was thrilled.

As a holiday sales associate, my uniform was the Williams-Sonoma's signature apron, which covered whatever outfit I slapped together, so dressing for work was simple. As I wandered around the store's stockroom (imagine a fabulous, well-equipped pantry) and stood behind the checkout counter, I felt like I was playing store. I found it fun, *and* I relished the fact that for at least eight hours a week for six full weeks, I was able to leave my house without my child in tow. At Williams-Sonoma I got to talk to adults, spend hours in a festive place, sample good food, do my Christmas shopping, and shop vicariously through customers who needed my help spending their money. Best of all, I had a job that truly stayed at the office. I frequently daydreamed about never returning to my magazine job in New York City. I imagined a new career working retail, minutes from home, at Williams-Sonoma.

My mom friends were envious. The Stay-at-Homes wished their husbands, like mine, would take care of the baby (or kids) so they could go to work for fun. The mothers with demanding full-time jobs outside the home fantasized about, as my friend Carol put it, being able to have a "widget" job, which she characterized as a nonmanagerial job that starts and ends at set times, asks that you just move your "widgets" as told, and doesn't require bringing home work. While I thought of the gig as my "sanity" job, another friend, a Stay-at-Home mother of two who joined me in pursuing a temporary retail career, dubbed her Williams-Sonoma stint her "giggle" job. After all, my friend Jen and I (and it turns out some other part-timers) were working for fun (giggles) in order to escape from our daily lives. Any of the three names would fit.

Considering what many of us spent saving money with our 40 percent employee discount, we were *paying* Williams-Sonoma to let us work in its store. I knew I was lucky not to be dependent on the job for my livelihood, or even for extra cash. If that were the case, working day after day on my feet on retail's frontlines, especially during the holidays, would have been neither relaxing nor giggle-inducing. Separate from providing me with a refuge, part of the enjoyment of the job for me was probably that it was new, temporary, and optional.

But I did have fun. I liked arranging merchandise on the store's shelves and using the register. I even got a kick out of selecting the perfectly sized box or bag for a customer's purchase. The variety kept me energized, and while my body ached after a full day on my feet at the store, it wasn't the same draining type of exhaustion I felt after a nonstop day with an infant. Being away from my son for even those few hours recharged me and helped me better enjoy my time with him. (It also allowed my husband time alone with the baby and gave him a taste of the good and the bad that comes with being the primary caregiver.) But when the holidays were over, so was the job.

My Widget Job

Fast forward three years: Before quitting my Manhattan-based magazine career (the details for why I did are explained in this book's Introduction), I lined-up a thirty-hour-per-week sales job at a different Williams-Sonoma store about twenty minutes from my house. At this point in my life, the retail job would serve three purposes: As my husband had taken a consulting position in a city far from our home, I needed to be more available to our son.

The job helped with my transition from full-time career woman to mother who works family friendlier hours. And, once I left the staff of *People,* we'd need new health insurance. At the store, I worked only evenings and weekends, which allowed me to leave my son in the care of my mother, husband, or an occasional sitter, rather than with a regular nanny. Whereas I used to be away from my home and child for as much as sixty hours a week, I could now be around more often than not. And because the job didn't form the basis for my livelihood or ultimate career path, neither nasty customers nor inept staff stressed me out.

To the full-time staff, I was a curiosity. ("Why would she leave a glamorous magazine job to work here?") Some were threatened by my competence; others were thankful for it. I didn't care. After working my way up the corporate ladder, while navigating a brutal commute, financial challenges, and juggling either nighttime grad school or parenting, it was such a relief to have all that behind me. Those first few postcareer months were like a vacation to me. Even though I wasn't intending to make retail a career per se, I was quickly bumped up from a regular sales associate to a lead, with managerial duties and responsibilities.

However, within seven months of starting the job, pregnancy complications forced me to quit. On the plus side, my short-lived retail career enabled me to collect disability, from both the state of New Jersey and my privately funded policy, and retain health insurance by paying for the premiums via COBRA (the federally mandated health insurance retention program by which former employees are eligible to keep their employer-sponsored insurance for up to eighteen months).

The Pros and Cons of Working in the Widget World

In the years since that last Williams-Sonoma gig, I've considered other sanity jobs, and even attempted one (at a Super Suppers franchise), but I've been stopped in my tracks by the distances I'd need to travel and the difficulties of coordinating a work-for-fun schedule with the needs of three kids and the responsibilities of a spouse with a demanding job. Like finding and keeping any job, sanity jobs are highly dependent on your circumstances and needs. Pursuing such work is also dependent on your state of mind and where you are in your life. As a new mom, a small get-me-out-of-the-house job was just what I needed. As a veteran mom with several Stay-at-Home years under my belt, I've found I need something more. (Thank you for reading the results of my latest "sanity job.")

However, if you can swing it in terms of childcare coverage, working a few hours here and there at a nice eatery, or at a salon or a store you like, can be good for your mental health, in addition to providing you with other perks. Ginny, mentioned earlier, did shifts at a fancy gardening center and, later, a decorative housewares boutique—both to get out of her house and to furnish it using her employee discounts.

Other women I know have taught fitness classes (free gym membership and babysitting in the childcare room) or become a preschool teacher's aide (free or discounted tuition, and your child comes with you). My girls took a tumbling class taught once a week by a mom who brought her two-year-old along. If leaving the house truly isn't an option due to problems finding childcare, taking in small projects (paid or not), like editing a newsletter, reviewing legal documents, or keeping the books for a very small business can keep your professional skills sharp and keep you connected with the world beyond your motherhood.

The benefit of such efforts isn't the income (which in many cases can't even pay for a tank of gas) but what it can do for your mind, body, and soul. Although, over time, even tiny paychecks can add up. My friend Karen figures that the money she earned as a birthday party coordinator at her local YMCA by working a few hours every weekend had, over two years, netted enough to pay for her flight to Paris, which is where she and her college roommate took themselves for their fortieth birthdays. Their spouses remained behind, and each stayed home from work to care for his respective kids. What a gift!

Finding a Club or Activity Just for You

One benefit of not having to hold down a paid job is that when (yes, *when*, not *if*, we're thinking positively) you do have time away from the kids and your job as a caregiver and homemaker, you can attempt to focus the time on yourself. Women use such times to veg out and indulge (*I'm getting a pedicure and reading a trashy magazine for an hour, and I don't care what anyone thinks!*), and also to pursue interests that have been on the shelf for a while, due to work, work and kids, kids. So how can you find something fun for *you*?

• Read local parenting magazines to locate clubs and activities.
• Check your newspaper's community or events pages.

▶

- Enroll in a continuing education class at a community college or adult school.
- If you have the time, and money for tuition, take classes toward earning a degree.
- Attend a library- or club-sponsored book group discussion.
- Visit your local bookstores and coffeehouses to see if they're hosting any interest-oriented events. (For example, a gelato store I once lived near hosted a weekly Italian-conversation class, open to all.)
- Participate in a crafts or do-it-yourself workshop at an art-supply or home-improvement store.
- Join a fitness center.
- Pursue either paid or volunteer freelance projects you can do from home, at your pace and on your schedule, and that do not require regular childcare.
- Volunteer at your child's school or attend PTA or PTO events.
- Commit to a cause or project you feel passionate about, such as helping on a political campaign, an advocacy effort, or a community board.

You Gotta Have Friends!

M y first-born child was five weeks old before I managed to get the two of us successfully out of the house on my own. I'd had a difficult cesarean recovery, and the summer had been too hot to even want to go outdoors. At the time I lived in Westfield, New Jersey, a great colonial town that is both lively and walkable. It was less than a mile from my house into town, so, with my son in his stroller, I started on my way.

As I walked, I remembered that the town's mayor, with whom I had occasionally worked, also had a new baby. I'd met his wife, Karen, in passing a few times, and she had seemed nice. I decided to take a chance and knock on her door. Karen answered while nursing her daughter. Before I could even open my mouth to explain my presence, she exclaimed, "Thank God you're here!" Karen and I have been great friends ever since.

Like me, Karen was a first-time mom who spent her initial postpartum weeks overwhelmed and alone in her house with a newborn. We both had jobs waiting back in Manhattan, and we both welcomed the break maternity leave was giving us from our offices and tiresome train commutes. But neither of us was ready for the isolation of being home with an infant. Karen and I spent the rest of our respective maternity leaves in each other's homes. We went on day trips, hosted playgroups, and took our babies to Mommy & Me classes together.

Karen wasn't my only Stay-at-Home mom friend, nor was I hers. We both found that being a new mother in Westfield, population 30,000, made us veritable friend magnets. There were new moms in the park, at the library, at the YMCA, and at the local Starbucks, all desperate for adult company during the day. With such a bounty of riches, however, can come false starts.

At first, *every* woman with a child the same age as yours is a potential best friend. Over time, the infatuation wears off and you realize the *only* thing you and your new best friend have in common is that your children are the same age. Those relationships fade away. But the mom friends that stick help each other immensely. As I discuss at length in Chapter Fourteen, it was my Westfield girlfriends who took care of me and my preschool-age son while I was on bed rest during my second pregnancy.

Linda, a Manhattan mother of four, had a similar experience with her girlfriends. "I ended up with an emergency appendectomy when my youngest was just four months old," she reports. "One of my best friends came to pick me up at the hospital. Another friend sent dinner. Yet another took my boys for the afternoon and so on. The network really responds when you need it to. And I would do the same for them."

Survey respondent Andrea observes that, "A day can be a million times less stressful if you and a girlfriend spend a few hours of it chatting while policing your kids at the park or in your basement playroom." Indeed, but I believe Nancy, a Connecticut mother of three, captures the sentiment best when she says: "Without friends, I would be paying for expensive therapy."

MAKING NEW FRIENDS

The friends you're likely to have in your Stay-at-Home life can differ greatly from the friends you had before. When I was a new Stay-at-Home mother, it seemed that only a handful of the moms I met or spent time with were "career women" turned at-home moms. Most didn't mourn the life they'd left behind. Some were married to well-to-do men so, unlike me, their Stay-at-Home motherhood came with a nanny or frequent babysitter, a weekly housekeeper, a vacation home, and the freedom to shop, lunch, work out, or get their toes done whenever the urge hit. For a long time I felt I didn't really fit in. Over time, and with effort, I found my place.

"It's not unlike going to college," observes Pat, a licensed clinical social worker now home with two school-age children. "You no longer get to see, as often, your old friends, and you're having to choose friends from the people you see as a result of your child. My advice is to keep yourself open to the whole lot of them. You may find that the women you might not have opted to hang with initially may in fact be the ones you remain friendly with for the long term."

While motherhood may lead you to become friends with gals who are very different from yourself, you do need to have *some* common ground. "You want to connect with a mum who's on your wavelength, has some of the same approaches as you do," advises

Aoife. "I hear some women talking about tracking down an 'academic' preschool or daycare for their two- and three-year-olds. I'm more interested in preschools that are about play-play-play, so I find I hook up with mums who feel the same way."

Where the Moms Are

Places you might just make a new friend—or at least find a grown-up to talk to:

- Parks, playgrounds, and pools
- Newcomers clubs
- New-mom and other types of parenting clubs
- Local women's and civic organizations
- Preschools
- School volunteer events
- School-bus stops
- A nail salon, hair salon, or day spa
- Doctor's office waiting rooms
- Mommy & Me classes
- Bookstore or library story times
- Exercise classes
- The sidelines at kids' sporting events
- At a religious function
- Sales and vendor parties
- Social events you're invited to (friends help friends make friends)

WAYS YOU CAN BREAK THE ICE

So now that you've been convinced you need to get out and about and connect with other moms (in truth, you didn't need convincing as much as encouragement), here are ways you can break the ice and start playing the friend-making game:

Hand out your "business" card: Men pick up women in bars. Mothers pick up other mothers in playgrounds. If you and a mom hit it off, and you'd like to get the two of you and the kids together again, you'll want to exchange contact information. Avoid searching for a pen and scribbling a number on a scrap of paper by taking a page from the business world and creating a personal card with your name, phone number, and email address. (If you don't make the card mommy specific, you can hand it out to nonmom grown-ups as well.) Says survey respondent Nicki, a mother of three: "Don't wait for people to engage you. *You* need to make plans with *them.* Every Stay-at-Home mom is dying for adult company, but few are willing or able to make the first move."

Host a playgroup: If you belong to a group (such as a preschool, or newcomers club or a homeowner's association) that publishes a directory, and the book lists the names and birthdays of children, call the moms who have kids the same age as yours and invite them to a playdate. You can host at your house or, if you'd rather not invite strangers into your home, at a park. Nearly a decade ago I flipped through the directory of the Westfield Newcomers Club and called a woman named Daryl with the suggestion that, since our children were born two weeks apart, we have a playdate. Daryl and I now live 200 miles from one another, but we remain such good friends that last year I got to be part of her fortieth-birthday trip to

Paris! Also on that adventure was Daryl's good friend Krista, whom she met through me. (I had brought Krista into our playgroup after meeting her at a YMCA "strollercise" class.)

Host a no-kids gathering: While playgroups and playdates are great and oftentimes essential, they don't solve the immediate problem of a mom needing a break from her children or having an outlet that has nothing to do with kids. A great way to meet other women is to host a wine tasting party, or a Bunco evening, or a book group. What often happens is that one gal hosts the initial gathering, and those who want to stick with it offer to hold the follow-up events at their houses. "I now play Bunco once a month with my neighbors," reports Johanna, a mother of two grown sons and a teenage daughter still at home. "The group was started by a neighbor whose adult children live in another state. She had the same problem as new Stay-at-Home moms. How do you meet people if there are no children to take to the bus stop, or if you're not working outside the home?"

Host an outing: If you know of moms you never get to see, other than in the carpool lane at preschool or while waiting for your children outside karate class, send out a note or email announcing, for instance, "A Mom's Movie Night Out." You pick the movie, the date, and the time and ask women to RSVP to you or just meet you at a specified place. A gathering like this works on several levels: Women don't like to go to movies by themselves. Men don't always like going to chick flicks. Compared with other activities, a movie ticket for one is affordable. It's often hard for a couple to find a sitter or leave young children at bedtime (in this plan, Dad stays home). And if you and the women don't click, you can go your separate ways. If you do get along, the ladies can go out for dessert or coffee or drinks after the movie. You can offer to arrange another outing, or perhaps someone else will do it.

Host a clothes jumble: This is a gathering, suggested by survey respondent Aoife, in which you invite friends and neighbors to bring clothing items they and their kids no longer wear. (We all know kids outgrow clothes, but moms do too.) The clothes are placed in piles around the room, and everyone has a chance to rummage for items that suit them. Says Aofie: "You may find you don't have as much time to go clothes shopping for yourself anymore, and this is a great way to get rid of your own stuff and get new things." And perhaps meet new people.

Host an open house: When my husband and I moved into our current home, which is in a rural area where residents generally interact by waving at each other from afar, we realized the only way we'd actually get to meet our neighbors would be to invite them over. So we popped cards into the mailboxes of about two-dozen nearby homes, inviting each household to stop over during our holiday open house, which we planned for a Sunday afternoon in December. Nearly twenty households attended. We met neighbors we can now call on in emergencies, whose preteens have become my helpers, whose yards we can go in to visit farm animals. Our holiday party is now an annual event, as is the summer block party our gathering inspired the veteran residents to resurrect.

Strange bedfellows: Sometimes your best friends are the people most unlike you. My friend Karen and I are examples of the opposite extremes of contemporary childbirth. She gave birth to three children without any painkillers while being cared for by midwives. I gave birth to three children by cesarean section, with extra drugs pumped in by request. Karen nursed each of her children for more than a year. I attempted to nurse and gave up after a couple of weeks. But we never judge one another, and we always support each other's choices.

Erin Z. says she met her best friend, who lives down the street, during a rainy-day garage sale: "She had just moved into the neighborhood and needed to get out of a house full of boxes. Because of the rain, she was my only customer. We sat on my front steps and talked for two hours. That was three years ago. Our children are the same age and gender. We now vacation together, barbeque, have mom and kid sleepovers. We come from very different backgrounds—mine strict Catholic, hers more liberal Jewish—but we learn so much from each other. I joke that God put us together to teach us that the grass isn't always greener."

Ways Stay-at-Home Moms Can (and Do) Help One Another

Showering: No, not together! But it's perfectly acceptable to say to a visiting mom friend, "Hey, can you keep an eye on the kids so I can take a shower?"

Chores: My friend Karen and I made a pact to help each other accomplish a task in each of our fixer-upper homes. I agreed to take her nine-month-old daughter for three hours so she could paint some furniture. The following week, she cared for my son so I could paint my dining room. Although Stay-at-Home moms feel disorganized and inefficient, when freed of children, it's amazing what we can accomplish in a short amount of time.

Errands: Rather than struggle with loading kids into and out of the car for every quick errand, my friend Pam and I hopped into one car, with our babies in the back, and did our collective errands. While she ran into her dry cleaner, I stayed in the car with the kids. We did this at drug stores, the post office, the video store. After our errands, we had lunch at a diner (where we could each use the ladies room while the other stayed at the table with the children). Friends are also essential when moms are, for a variety of reasons, housebound. Says Annabel: "They are the people I call on when I can't get out of the house, such as when I have a sick kid, to bring medication or pick up milk."

Drop-off childcare: Girlfriends help girlfriends go to the doctor (especially the ob-gyn) without their kids tagging along. While it's tacky to ask a friend to watch your child so you can go to lunch with another friend, it's perfectly appropriate to ask for help in order to get medical care. And it's also nice for one mom to offer another a chance to simply have time on her own. "When you can, just give a friend the treat of taking her kids for a couple of hours," suggests Liz R., a mother of three boys. "The biggest surprise in doing this for the first time is that it's often easier to have more children in your house than fewer. They distract each other and break up the sibling rivalries that erupt when it's just your own kids. Keep the time short when you're first trying it out, maybe an hour or so, just enough time for the other mom to run an errand or get dinner started by herself."

Fun outings with the kids: It can be unnerving to travel alone—such as to a beach or zoo or museum—with your child or, especially, children. But when moms take field trips together, the adult-to-child ratio improves. "My friends help out by simply meeting us at the park with their children or going to the beach," reports Debbie. "We help each other so we can be Stay-at-Home moms who go fun places!"

Date night: This one usually requires the assistance of your husband or partner. How it works is that while Dad is home caring for your children, you go to your friend's house to care for her children while she and her husband go out for dinner—or, if you're really good friends, dinner *and* a movie. The following week, the roles reverse. Fathers experience some evening alone time with their kids, whether they want it or not. And although the moms are still caring for children, they're not in their own homes. When her friend's crew goes to sleep, the babysitting mom can veg out, watch TV, or read a magazine. If she were home, she'd probably do a household chore. (When the child needing care is a portable newborn, the babysitting duo can stay home together.) Says survey respondent Tracy, who has a toddler and a newborn: "We swap babysitting monthly with two other families, so my husband and I get at least two evenings a month to do something together. The arrangement allows each couple a night out without the cost or anxiety of a babysitter."

Surrogate sisters: Having friends who you know will come to your rescue, should you ever need rescuing, is priceless. "I have been blessed with a few friends who have become like family, and they always have my back," says Stacey, a New Jersey mother of two. "They bring my kids home from school if I need them to, have them for sleepovers when I can't find a sitter, and basically do what my sisters would do for me if they lived in this state."

OUR "WORKING MOM" AND NON-MOM FRIENDS

While Stay-at-Home motherhood can bring new friends, it can also be the wedge that causes you to drift from old pals and the people with whom you once spent most of your waking hours. When I quit my job at *People* magazine, the folks I worked with were neither supportive nor unsupportive. The grind of the job required them to move forward, unsentimentally. I had left their lives, and they didn't have much curiosity about (or commonality with) mine. I didn't know it at the time, but I had crossed a line. Working people, especially working mothers, no longer had as much interest in me.

On the home front, I started to notice that my employed mom friends mainly gravitated toward one another or to the women in our circle who had, in their experience, always been Stay-at-Home moms. It was as if my team didn't know what to make of me now that I had put myself on the bench. Had the employed women and I become repelling magnets? Like me, leaving the workforce was financially possible for them. But did they now see in me what they were unwilling to do, which was choose their children over their careers? Or perhaps I was sending the bad vibes their way. Perhaps they sensed my envy at how they were emotionally and logistically able to have it all, when I couldn't.

At the time I felt particularly abandoned by one friend, who was actually a Stay-at-Home mom during the years I was an employed mom. I didn't work Fridays then, and I would make a particular effort to take her son off her hands so she could get a break. She would call me at work or in the evening, and I'd make time to talk. By coincidence, she returned to the workforce at the same time

I quit. Our paths had crossed going in the opposite direction. She was now extremely busy and instead seemed to focus her friendship energies on other employed moms.

Survey respondent Erin Z. makes an astute observation about the world of motherhood friendships. "The rules are completely different than during any other time in your life," she explains. "You will be hanging out with people you never would have hung with in college, and you'll realize there were so many wasted friendships in your past. Motherhood makes you raw. Because you become so exposed, you find people who *really get it,* and that's such a great connection."

Friends are truly essential to the survival of every mother, whether she works outside the home or not. It's best to stay connected to as many as you can. When I went back to work after my one-year maternity leave, I made a big effort to stay involved with my Stay-at-Home friends. When I quit my job two years later, they welcomed me back into the fold, and I am forever grateful that they did.

Ideally, the friends you have as a woman who happens to also be a mother shouldn't fall into a she's-either-with-me-or-against-me sorter. For so many reasons, ranging from each of us individually to society-at-large, it is important that friendships exist between Stay-at-Home moms and employed moms (and, for that matter, people who have children and those who don't).

For instance, a Stay-at-Home mom can be an employed mom's eyes and ears while she's at work. In case of an emergency, a Stay-at-Home neighbor may be able to relieve a babysitter or pick up sick kids at a daycare center before an employed mom can arrive. The volunteer efforts of Stay-at-Home mothers greatly benefit schools, children's sports programs, and community activities.

Stay-at-Home mothers benefit from having female friends in the workforce by having a resource to go to when professional services are needed (e.g. medical, financial, legal). And if the time ever comes when a Stay-at-Home mom wants or needs to return to the workforce, it's her working friends who will be a network for job leads and a source of recommendations. Also, adds Gerri, a Stay-at-Home mother of two girls, "It's important for children to know women who are professionals as well as moms."

Although media depictions often pit employed and Stay-at-Home moms against each other, it is possible for such women to be supportive of one another. Says Megan: "A good friend of mine who works full time, but whose husband is a Stay-at-Home dad, has often complimented me on my children's abilities, saying she knows it's a direct result of the one-on-one time they have with their mom."

Observes Lyn: "I have a very good friend who works an insane schedule yet still does a very good job parenting her three boys. My kids benefit from knowing hers and being in her home, where the values are the same but the procedures are different. And her kids benefit from being in my home and experiencing our environment."

Regardless of the shared positives and examples of differently engaged moms playing nice, the most important reason for women to support each other's choices—to work, to have children, to not have children, to stay home with their children, to be employed mothers—is so women can *continue* to have choices.

But to bridge what may seem like an unbridgeable gap with a friend who can't fully relate to your new, at-home world, both parties need to recognize the roadblocks and want to work around them. One simple example is to consider the logistical challenge of two people connecting by telephone.

Stay-at-Home moms usually can't chat during the kid demand–heavy mornings or early evenings, but those commuting hours are often the ideal phone and catch-up times for an employed person who's traveling by car or public transportation. A Stay-at-Home mom can sometimes make calls during a child's nap, but an employed friend may not be able to hang on the phone right after she arrives at work (the morning-nap phone window) or when she's in the midst of her day (the afternoon-nap window). The same disconnect occurs between new moms and their friends who have no children. The friend shops, travels, and goes to restaurants and bars, while your scene doesn't get any hipper than the swings at the park or another mom's house for playgroup.

If the friendship is important to you and your friend, the two of you can negotiate the obstacles by making phone dates, staying in touch by email, scheduling a regular outing (even with your respective kids) or, for the friend who has no children, alternating times between when the friend accompanies you on a kid-centered activity and occasions you leave the child with your spouse or a sitter. Such nonmom friends can also provide you, a Stay-at-Home mom, with safe haven when you want and need a break from all things family. My best friend from college, the woman who set me up on a blind date with the man who became my husband, has not married and has no children. After I had a child, we'd meet for occasional restaurant dinners. Now that we live far from each other, our visits have to be overnights, which allows me, and sometimes a former roommate who also has kids, a child-free evening away, typically at the single gal's place in Manhattan or at a fun destination between our homes.

LETTING GO OF OLD FRIENDS

Some friends are friends forever, but many aren't. It's likely nothing you or they did. People just grow apart, due to distance, schedules, family situations, job demands, various activities, and interests. It is odd, though, looking back on your life, to think of the girls you were so tight with in high school, the guys you hung out with in college, the people you worked with day after day, with whom you now have little or no contact.

"I definitely feel disconnected from friends who don't have kids and are working full time," says Jennifer D., who is newly home with her first child. "We don't have the same everyday life and things to talk about. And some of the activities we used to enjoy together—going out for drinks, dinners—take a lot more effort to arrange on my part, effort I don't feel is necessarily appreciated on theirs."

When your child is young, other moms with babies can be your lifeline. But as your children grow, you may become friends with their friend's moms or with women you meet through school activities. While you may still be friendly with your "baby friends," there's a good chance you'll look at old playgroup photos and not be able to identify many of the women and children who, for a time, were an integral part of your life. It's hard to believe, but it happens.

In fact, relationships can change to the point that you end up drifting away from a friend who at times was almost like a sister. Lyn tells of how she and a law school classmate became such close friends that the woman is the godmother of one of her sons. But as the years passed, their ability to connect diminished, in large part because Lyn had three children and the friend had none. When a child's illness caused Lyn to forget and miss a scheduled outing, the woman never forgave her. To this day, Lyn wonders if there was more she could have done to heal the friendship, and whether there's more she can do now.

"My mom says that some friends are just too much effort," says Lyn. "They're what she calls 'toxic,' and nothing will ever be enough for them. I'm not so sure this is the case with my friend. I think it may be that the reality of my kids was toxic to our friendship. In a way, I just didn't have the time or emotional energy to give to her at the level that she anticipated or expected. Now that my children are older, and I have a little more time for my own personal interactions, I wonder if I should extend the olive branch and make an effort to reestablish our connection. But then I think about the fifty things on my to-do list, and I wonder if that friend and I will simply end up in the same situation all over again."

When looking at the friend turnover in your life it may also help to remember that life is fluid and changing, and we do our best when we are able to ride those waves. That lesson was reinforced to me by a professional organizer named Jodie Watson, whom I met while interviewing entertainer Sherri Shepherd, one of the co-hosts on the daytime TV talk show *The View*, for a magazine called *Organize*. (After finishing the manuscript for this book, that freelance assignment and a few others unexpectedly landed in my lap.) While helping Shepherd get control of the physical clutter that had been consuming her life, Watkins told her, "When you let go of what you have but don't need, God can come in and bless you. But when you hold on to everything, there's no room for new blessings." The same theory can apply to friends. Some will leave your life, but in doing so, they'll provide you with room for new friends, new blessings.

BEING A GOOD FRIEND . . . OR, YOU'RE NOT PERFECT, AND NEITHER ARE YOUR KIDS

Self-esteem is a good thing, within reason. Nothing turns off other moms (i.e., your friends and potential friends) than a woman who openly judges other women's parenting skills, is a busybody, or doesn't recognize that her own children aren't adorable angels come to Earth.

To each her own: In your career as a Stay-at-Home mom, you will encounter women from throughout the expansive universe of motherhood. Some will parent just like you do. Some will do things you would never do. You'll meet moms who bribe their children with dessert to get them to finish their meal, and others who won't let their kids leave the table until they've eaten every last vegetable. You'll meet moms who stick a lollipop in their child's mouth to stop a tantrum, and others who won't allow even a taste of sugar. You'll meet moms who will leave their kids in dodgy childcare rooms filled with runny-nosed toddlers, and others who won't trust the care of her child to anyone.

No matter the situation, unless you feel a child is truly being abused or neglected, you will need to bite your tongue. As an example, some of my friends swore by a family daycare provider who took several children into her home. On their recommendation, I checked the place out. What I saw was too many children corralled into too small a room with an enormous big-screen TV, and I chose not to leave my son there. When my friends asked why I wasn't using their sitter, I said it just wasn't going to work out. As I was polite and didn't slam their choice, they politely didn't interrogate me about mine.

The other trap to avoid is superiority, which is a tone and attitude (perhaps unintentional) emitted by some mothers. Years ago, I spent time with a woman who, during her pregnancy, had dismissive words for women who chose bottles over nursing. Only after breastfeeding failed to work for her, and she turned to formula, did she become sympathetic to the choices of bottle-feeding moms.

All children get sick, and all children misbehave: While other babies in our circle of friends had runny noses and ear infections, that same mom claimed her daughter "never gets sick." While our children were sometimes whiney and cranky and miserable to be around, when her daughter acted whiney and cranky and miserable in our presence, we were told, "I don't know what's wrong. She's never like this." While our toddlers were dynamos from whom we had to protect our homes and belongings, her daughter "never gets into anything."

The truth of course was that her child *did* get sick. While it's possible her daughter didn't touch things she shouldn't, and was only whiney and cranky and miserable around us, that's hard to believe. It's also possible that the mom's behavior was more representative of her own insecurity than any actual arrogance. Regardless, putting down other people's kids while you place your own on a pediatric pedestal isn't cool. Neither is being in denial of your own child's bad, inappropriate, or difficult behavior. Mothers can and will empathize with the woman who needs reassurance or is trying to keep her wild child under control. Less goodwill flows toward a mom who turns a blind eye, especially while her youngster wreaks havoc on everyone and everything in sight.

I like the mom, it's her kid I can do without: I know of a playgroup that broke up due to the roughness of two children. One little boy had biting and other unsociable behaviors. A second child, whose family fancied him a Major League Baseball player in training, would throw balls and swing at pitches during even our indoor gatherings. As a result, the moms (and some babysitters) spent much of every playdate protecting their charges from the biting of one boy and the bat-swinging and ball-tossing of another. Ultimately, the mothers of the calmer children decided they couldn't take the risk. In dribs and drabs, the playgroup dissolved.

Sometimes a group of women can really enjoy one another's company, so long as their kids aren't round. That's important to remember, even if in the day-to-day of motherhood it's hard to put into action. For instance, over time, the mom of the biter stayed away from mother-and-tot gatherings, because it was hard to control her child, who later turned out to be on the autism spectrum. (See page 75 for more about parenting a special-needs child.) The baseball player and his mom stopped being included in mom-and-tot group activities. The women in the playgroup had been both brought together and, for some, pushed apart by their children.

When the second generation doesn't mix as well as the first, the inclination can be to either force the kids to play together or for each mom to go her separate way. The latter may be what happens, but the better solution could be to keep the friend as an adult-time friend. After all, as life goes on, your child won't hit it off with every one of your friends' kids, and similarly, you won't be best pals with every playmate's parent. No one likes to be forced into a relationship with a person they don't enjoy being with. However, when together time is desired or necessary, it's useful to think of ways you can enjoy your friends and tolerate their kids, as mother-of-two Leslie notes: "Sometimes my friends' children are better in my house than in their own, because when they're here, my house rules govern."

In some cases, poor or eyes-wide-shut parenting can be the cause of tense or lost friendships. "A couple friends of mine have very unruly, mouthy kids," notes Amy. "I don't enjoy being around those kids at all, so those friends and I don't see each other very often, even without the kids, because I think it's the parents' fault the children are like that in the first place." In some situations, speaking up and pointing out the bad behavior to the parent or directly to the child can result in an angry "No one tells me how to raise my kids; no one yells at my kids except me" response, which is an assertion I've heard from otherwise pleasant mothers upset by the harshness of a sitter or a school teacher. Is the teacher being unfairly strict? Is the child truly a brat? Maybe, maybe not. What is a certainty is that as parents, it's our job to raise our children to be the kind of people other people (i.e., those who don't innately love them like we do) will want to be around.

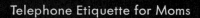

Telephone Etiquette for Moms

Mothers with children at home typically don't have the time to hang on the phone and shoot the breeze. (Although some observers might argue that minivan-driving moms seem to always have a cell phone at their ear.) Mom friends in sync with one another know how to communicate without imposing.

"I have several girlfriends I can call when I need someone to talk to or vent to or ask an opinion of," says Amy, a mother of two. "We don't get to talk in depth as often as we'd like, but we all know that we can call each other out of the blue to ask one quick question and then get on with our day. There's no pressure to have a long, involved, 'catch-up' conversation when we only have time for getting the answer we're looking for right then."

Julie C. finds that as a mother home with two toddlers, she avoids calling old friends who don't yet have children. "I remember pre-kids how annoying those phone calls were when a screaming child was in the background," she says. "I don't want to burden my friends with the same thing." (My screaming-child pet peeve: Calling a mom friend and having to negotiate with the two-year-old who commandeers the phone to "Please, *please,* let me speak with Mommy.")

When telephoning a mom, it's always best to ask, "Is this a good time?" "Are you in the middle of something?" "Can you talk now?" If you don't, and you take up a lot of your friend's time, your future calls might be screened. And no one wants to be the person about whom other people say, "Let the machine get it. I don't have time for her now." Stay-at-Home moms need other

▶

Stay-at-Home moms to take their calls, which can sometimes be of immediate importance for you or the care of your child.

However, the "I'm thinking of you" call or email can be a welcome intrusion. Annabel says she is grateful for "the friends who call from time to time just to say hello or check in. I always appreciate knowing that someone is thinking of me."

BE A GOOD NEIGHBOR

A pothole that's wise to avoid is the nosy neighbor syndrome, which can be tough to do, since, as Stay-at-Home moms, our work, family, and social life revolves entirely around where we live.

I once had a neighbor who, it seemed, telephoned me whenever she saw a work truck or a delivery vehicle at my house. The woman, a Stay-at-Home mom, would call to say hi, but also to ask what we bought, what we were having done, where, and by whom. I was new to the neighborhood and initially appreciated her interest in me. Since I was home with three children under five, I was also thankful to have a conversation with an adult. But after a while, I realized that although the woman was trying for us to become friends, she was nosy—as were many of the people in that new home development, which although it wasn't a gated or country club community, was just as insular and self-involved as many members-only clubs can be. Despite all the surface pleasantries, the subdivision was populated with simmering Hatfield and McCoy–like feuds between groups of women and among couples.

The lesson I learned from those in and near the crossfire was that it can be super to become best friends with your immediate neighbor or neighbors, to become like sisters, able to pop into each other's homes at will. But if things go sour, the situation can be awful. As Kara, a Stay-at-Home mother of two in Colorado warns: "Just because someone has kids and lives near you doesn't mean you *have* to be friends." (Friendly, absolutely. Best friends, maybe.)

While immediate neighbors can be hard to steer clear of, you *can* remove yourself from a group of moms you just don't feel comfortable spending time with. Within the Stay-at-Home mom world are all sorts of subcultures—Suzy Homemaker Moms, Fitness Moms, Take Charge Moms, Princess Bride Moms, Diva Moms, Home-Schooling Moms, Partying Moms, the legendary Soccer Moms—that may or may not be the right fit for you. "Several mothers I knew were making gourmet, organic baby food, while my son still wasn't sleeping and I was about to jump off a bridge," recalls Molly. "I knew jarred food was fine. I didn't enjoy being with those moms much. They were quite pushy. I had to develop a thick skin and some other friends."

In a case like the one Molly describes, moving on is the thing to do. Dixie, a veteran Stay-at-Home mom, speaks from experience when she says, "Friends are so important that choosing them wisely is vital. Don't waste your time on 'friends' who are competitive or make you feel bad about yourself."

Voices: On Being a Good Friend

"Reach out to a mom if you think you'd like to know her better. You've got nothing to lose and everything to gain. Also, do a favor for another mom. It may make you a friend for life. Someday she or someone else will be there when you need help."

—Kellie

"Try really hard to make friends with other moms, even if they're not exactly like you. I struggled for a long time trying to force myself to stay a part of some mom groups, but now I'm glad I did. Even though I'm very different from them in many ways, we now have a lot in common that we can share with each other."

—Whitney

"The friendship needs to work both ways. If you ask your neighbor to watch your kids, make sure she knows the offer is always open on your side."

—Jill

"Making friends takes time, and while your babies give you one point of connection, it's not enough to sustain a true friendship if you don't have similar interests."

—Jennifer D.

"Don't give advice unless asked. Just listen. Parenting can be frustrating, and sometimes a person just needs to vent."

—Sheriene

"Be honest with your friends, but don't be mean. You may agree on 90 percent of your parenting styles, and not on the remaining

▶

10 percent. That's okay. Support each other. This is a tough job, with lots of little developing personalities that may not always fall into groove with your own."

—Rachel

"Mostly what Stay-at-Home moms need is someone to listen to them. If I'm venting about how my child doesn't sleep well, I don't want to hear about how your child is an even worse sleeper than mine, or that he has been the perfect sleeper since birth. Listening, listening, listening is what helps moms stay friends."

—Amy

"It's important to calibrate expectations. It's often difficult to find time for anyone besides your kids."

—Gerri

"Make sure you can talk about nonmotherhood things with mom friends and nonmom friends. Only grandma wants to hear all the kid details!"

—Molly

"If you have friends without children, talk to them about how your life has changed. When I had friends who had children before I did, it was impossible for me to understand why they were so bad at keeping in touch. It seemed to me that if they weren't working, they should have loads more free time. It would have made me more understanding and not feel hurt if those friends had been more open about how overwhelmed they were feeling, and how difficult it was for them to find time for their friendships."

—Laura P.

THIRTEEN

Surviving (and Seeking)
Solitary Confinement, and Other
Strategies for Staying Sane

The words are well meaning but often impractical and more than a little infuriating.

"Nap when the baby naps."

"You need time for yourself."

"You should get a sitter to help you."

"Count to ten."

"If the kids get on your nerves, leave the room."

"Just ignore the crying."

"Set aside a night a week to go out with your husband."

Great advice, really. But how can a mom clean her house when the baby is awake? Who, precisely, is going to watch the kids so a woman can have time to herself? How can a family on a tight, one-income budget afford a day at the salon, or Mom's gym membership, or a babysitter and a dinner out? Even teenage sitters in my area make $10 an hour, nearly twice the federal minimum wage. (Somehow families with children are expected to pay a higher wage than profit-making employers.)

I can still remember my panic the first time I was left home alone all day with my infant son. As my husband left the house at 7:00 AM to catch his train, I sat in the kitchen, still aching from a cesarean while cradling a ten-day-old infant in my arms. I had no idea how I would fill the twelve or more hours until Brian returned, and I was terrified of having to spend the entire day by myself. Nearly a decade later, I face the similarly difficult yet very different challenges presented by three very active, demanding preschool and school-age children.

Both motherhood scenarios—home with an infant or corralling older children—can be isolating and frustrating. Like Stay-at-Home mothers everywhere, my days are spent almost entirely in the company of children while my opportunities for speaking with adults are either limited or nonexistent. And when I do manage to spend time with another adult, it's usually with a mom, and either her kids or mine keep us from really being able to talk, or talk about anything other than kids! As Johanna, a mom living in upstate New York, admits, "I miss having conversations that don't revolve around school, sports, and the PTA."

Sarah B., who became a Stay-at-Home mom at age twenty-six, reveals, "I felt extremely lonely after I had my first son. Almost as if I didn't have any friends. I even felt I wouldn't know how to make a friend if one was standing in front of my face. Fortunately, an old acquaintance asked me to join a book club she was starting. Most of the other women she invited belonged to the same moms' club. I asked if I could join and they said yes. I'm still friends with most of these women. That first interaction with other Stay-at-Home moms gave me the confidence and know-how to make other female friends."

Kara, now a Colorado mother of two, recalls that, as a first-time mom, "I was often lonely. My daughter nursed so much, and I would always leave the room if people were around. Finally, I just got over my embarrassment and started nursing anywhere and everywhere. My sister yelled at me for nursing at the dinner table. Oh well. I nursed my daughter until she was fifteen months old. It would have been a very lonely fifteen months if I didn't start nursing in public."

Although as Stay-at-Home moms we don't go to work, we still experience those start-of-the-workweek anxiety pangs. "Every Monday morning, and often during the mornings in between, I find myself in a bit of a mood," says Megan, who's home with two little boys. "After a weekend of the whole family being together, I realize how nice it is to have my husband home. As he's walking out the door, I experience a feeling of betrayal. Something in me cries out, 'You're not just going to leave me here alone with them, are you?' It's silly, but it happens often, despite the great love I have for my children. I miss the extra help and freedom my husband provides. But I also miss having a place to go."

Working people generally have colleagues to shoot the breeze with, or they interact somehow with the outside world. Stay-at-Home moms, especially ones who find it hard to get out of the house with the kids, often have few or fleeting daily encounters with other human beings and find the change palpable. "Aside from my husband, I never have a conversation with men anymore," notes

Emily. "In the beginning of staying home, I really missed having that male exposure. Now I feel like I have nothing in common with men, unless one happens to be a Stay-at-Home dad!"

And as much as we appreciate our husbands and partners, as discussed elsewhere in this book, husbands and partners often can't or don't provide the intellectual or emotional interaction a Stay-at-Home woman seeks. Actual or perceived isolation can have a serious psychological impact on a person's health and overall well-being. "Isolation is devastating to the human psyche," writes marriage counselor Gary Chapman in his self-help book *The Five Love Languages*. "That is why solitary confinement is considered the cruelest of punishments."

CITY MOUSE, COUNTRY MOUSE

Where a family resides can also affect a woman's Stay-at-Home state of mind. With my first child, I lived in a colonial New Jersey town. I could pop my son into the stroller and walk to parks, the library, great shops and restaurants, and to the homes of my friends. When I was going batty, all I had to do was take the baby for a walk, and I'd find someone out in the community to talk to.

Since that time, I've lived in first a suburban subdivision and now a rural area. While I enjoy my pseudo farm-living, the location, like the subdivision's, requires a car to get anywhere. Instead of gathering at the park gazebo in town, moms here congregate at a play area inside the local mall, which I find to be loud, airless, and depressing. Due to my kids' schedules, I spend most of my day driving to and fro, with only passing adult contact. While couples often flee cities when they have children, urban living can have its benefits for Stay-at-Home moms.

Laura P., a social worker, spent her career in Manhattan and the first years as a new mother living in London, where her husband had taken a job. "Being alone to care for my child felt much easier in London than it has in the suburbs of California, where I now live," she says. "In a big city, it's very easy to walk out the door and be surrounded by adults. In the suburbs, people live farther away from each other, and as the children get older, their schedules become more complicated. It seems much more difficult to get together with other moms and kids. Having to get in a car to go anywhere makes it harder to get out than it did in a city."

I VANT TO BE LEFT ALONE

Greta Garbo wasn't a Stay-at-Home mom. But with that oft-quoted line, lifted from the 1932 film *Grand Hotel,* the actress could have been speaking for Stay-at-Home moms everywhere. Even though you may feel alone as a Stay-at-Home mom, the reality is, you're neither alone nor left alone. A time will come, if it hasn't already, that you may desire both.

"The thing I miss the most about work is the ability to decompress," reports Jen, an attorney and mother of two. "Before I left my last job, I had a forty-five minute commute home. While grueling, the trip allowed me time to shake off the workday and relax. I don't get that opportunity as easily anymore. Many times, I'm counting the seconds until the children are asleep so I can attend to the things I need to do, like balancing the checkbook or cleaning the bathroom, which aren't necessarily things I *want* to do. The demands can be unrelenting."

Rachel, a Seattle mother of three, laments, "I miss home being a place of quiet refuge."

The maternal desire to be left alone is poignantly described in *Tell Me a Riddle,* written by Tillie Olsen and published in 1961. I felt understood when I heard about the short story, considered a literary classic, while listening to a book talk on National Public Radio (NPR). In the story, an elderly man wants to move into a retirement community with lots of social activities, but his wife refuses. Olsen writes that after a lifetime consumed by the demands of raising seven children, the wife, Eva, "would not exchange her solitude for anything." Her house is "no longer an enemy, for it stayed clean—not as in the days when it was her family, the life in it, that had seemed to be the enemy: tracking, smudging, littering, dirtying, engaging her in endless defeating battle." Eva cherished, writes Olsen, "being able at last to live within, and not move to the rhythm of others, as life had forced her to."

I found it reassuring to know that the maternal desire for time alone was the subject of an acclaimed piece of literature. The story made me feel that there's some universality to what I was (and still often am) feeling. It wasn't until I became a mother that I ever had the desire, like the fictional Eva, to be left entirely alone. In the past, like many young women, I panicked at the thought of not having weekend plans, or of spending a full day by myself or, dread upon dread, sitting alone at a restaurant. As teenagers, girls shop together and go to the movies together, although both of those activities are just fine to do alone.

"I would love to be alone more," admits Sandra, who home-schools the elder of her two children. "One problem with being a Stay-at-Home mom is that there isn't enough alone time."

Adds Cindy, who is home with two children: "While my husband and I need time alone as a couple, I also need time by myself. Because we can't leave our kids for any length of time, we either vacation as a family, or each of us goes off on our own. It's my only way to have a break, and I look forward to it each year."

A mother's group I belong to, Professional Moms at Home, asks a question of the membership every month. One question offered the following scenario:

Pretend you've won a contest. Your two prize choices are:

1) $1,000 cash. (Tax-free, no strings attached.)

2) Twenty-four hours of "Me/Alone" time. (Assume that, in your absence, your kids would be cared for by someone you trust completely.)

Which would you choose, and what would you do with the cash or "Me" time?

Of the women who answered, all but one chose Option 2, either directly or by changing the rules slightly. Several smart gals said they'd take the $1,000, then cash in a babysitting voucher from grandma and use the money to disappear on a vacation with their spouse or go someplace alone. I agreed with the mom who said she'd take Option 2 and stay home alone all day to, in her case, "sleep, eat, read magazines, scrapbook" and simply enjoy having her home to herself. Since my first child was born a decade ago, I've never had even twenty-four hours of alone time in my home—but I do have an itinerary in my mind of what I would do if I got it.

It's not that Stay-at-Home moms want to be rid of their family or ever truly *be* alone. It's just that spending some time at home on one's own can be rejuvenating, by either providing a woman with the opportunity to rest or to get projects done without interruption. More than flowers or jewelry or a fancy dinner, time to oneself can be the greatest gift a husband, partner, or family member can give a Stay-at-Home mother. As the novelist Pearl S. Buck wrote, "I love people. I love my family, my children . . . but inside myself is a place where I live all alone, and that's where you renew your springs that never dry up."

DESPERATELY SEEKING . . . SOMETHING

Having a child and leaving a job are major life transitions. It's the rare woman who doesn't have moments of feeling overwhelmed, terrified, or downright depressed while navigating such life changes. Sometimes newly learned or focused coping skills can help us manage. Other times, such as when feelings of depression, anxiety, or worse take hold, professional help may be needed. For instance, a few days of postpartum "baby blues" might come and go, but postpartum depression (PPD) is a serious illness that requires medical intervention.

How a woman copes as a person who is a Stay-at-Home mom will vary with the woman and her situation, but it's important to take yourself and your feelings seriously—and to not be shy or ashamed to seek help when you need it. Whatever coping mechanism you use, be it one described in this chapter or a remedy you devise on your own, remember that even though you may sometimes feel more alone or uncertain than you ever have, you are sharing an emotional experience with an incredible number of women, present and past.

Back in the 1950s and '60s, overwhelmed or unhappy home-makers took to their beds with depression, hit the liquor cabinet, smoked like fiends, or popped Valium and other sedatives to dull their nerves and soldier through their uninspired domestic lives. Despite the collective nostalgia that '50s style family life is the archetype we should aspire to, the era's Stay-at-Home moms are not entirely good role models. Although drug, alcohol, and nicotine abuse certainly hasn't disappeared, today's Stay-at-Home mothers report battling the blues and feelings of isolation with more positive methods that range from meditation and exercise to support groups and book clubs to, in certain cases, therapy and physician-managed anti-anxiety or antidepressant medications.

Short of going back to work to address the isolation, or hiring a nanny to lend support, following are some of the many coping mechanisms shared among my friends and with me from the women who answered questions for this book. "If you don't take care of yourself, you can't take care of anyone else," writes survey respondent Joni, a Colorado mother of two preschoolers. "By taking care of your own emotional, spiritual, physical, and other needs, you'll have much more genuine energy, interest, and love to give to your children."

GETTING FIT, FEELING FIT

For some women, jogging and crunches aren't torturous means of burning off baby flab but are instead endorphin-inducing activities that keep them healthy and on an even keel.

My friend Booie, a star soccer player in college who's now a Stay-at-Home mother of two and an occasional tennis teacher, moans and groans about feeling depressed and sluggish when she can't get to the gym. If my friend Nanette, a former fitness instructor, misses a week at the gym, she'll look as svelte and fit as she always does. However, she'll feel like crap. When her two children were small, she'd run around town (literally) with one or both seated in a jogger, or she'd sign them in to the childcare room at the gym while she worked out on machines. Exercise is so good for her body and her mind that at age thirty-three, just a year after giving birth to her second child, Nanette ran and finished the 2001 New York City marathon. "Running that marathon, and others, challenged me and gave me goals to aspire to, which I think have helped me be a better Stay-at-Home mom," she says.

In addition to helping you be healthy and motivated and get or stay in shape, exercise naturally produces serotonin, a powerful mood-lifting endorphin. Researchers who've studied the effects of exercise and physical activity on depression have found that it can reduce anxiety and sleep disruptions while increasing self-esteem and the ability to handle stress.

You can exercise with your children by going for walks, bike rides, or swims together in a backyard or community pool. You can also use exercise as your alone time, without kids, or as a way to spend time with friends—either by really working out or just walking and talking as you do laps around your neighborhood. If you're an athletic person and exercising makes you feel good, by all means figure out a way to fit workouts into your Stay-at-Home mom routine, whether you exercise at home (such as on a stationary bike in your basement or by stretching on the floor with your baby) or at an actual club. Fitness centers these days run the gamut from basic to posh, as do fitness-center childcare rooms. While I have experienced a couple of fitness center childcare rooms that made me not return, that needn't be the case. A gym with great childcare might be more expensive or further away from your home, but for the benefits, the time and money could be worth it.

It's also worth remembering that exercise doesn't need to be a formal activity, involving spandex and going to a gym. Depending on where you live, good exercise can be organic, in that it can happen naturally as you go about your daily life. When I worked in Manhattan, my weekday commute involved long stretches of walking and stair climbing, usually while carrying heavy bags. Traveling to and from work was the workout that helped me stay fit. (Fun fact: New Yorkers are among the longest-lived people in the United States, in large part because they walk so much—and they walk so fast!) Now, like many Americans, I live in car country. I have to make an effort and decision to walk. But when I do take a walk (accompanied by an iPod or cell phone but not kids), I feel better.

EAT RIGHT, EAT LIGHT

One of the most insulting comments made about women who stay home is that we lounge around in our robes with our feet up, eating bonbons. Here's the reality: If we're in our robes or pajamas, it's because our kids won't let us out of their sights long enough for us to shower and dress. Our feet are never up—they're moving across the floor and up and down stairs. If we do eat bonbons, it's because a piece of candy is easy to grab and pop in our mouths before we pass out from a sugar low due to not eating.

Mothers are so busy feeding children, and cleaning up after feeding children, that we often fail to feed ourselves, or at least feed ourselves properly. Many a mom lives on the kiddie meal leftovers—or worse, fast food—and coffee or diet soda. Motherly caffeine addictions are so common that a group of Mormon women I'm friends with, ladies who don't drink coffee due to their religion, live on Diet Coke, which they've dubbed "crack for Mormon moms."

Poor nutrition can leave you feeling tired, depressed, faint, and more. It's easily overlooked, but having some cereal or yogurt for breakfast, or packing healthy snacks for yourself to eat on the go when you pack them for your kids, can make a difference, as can drinking lots of water instead of soda, lattes, or sugary sports drinks. And if you're breastfeeding, it's essential for your own health, and your baby's, that you eat well and often, and stay hydrated. From an emotional as well as physical perspective, it's also important to have at least one meal a day during which you can actually sit at the table, eat slowly, and enjoy the food on your plate. (Okay, doing that *every day* can be tough to achieve. Start with trying to have a sit-down meal every once in a while.) Wolfing down food on the go or while you fend off children isn't good for your body, belly, or mind.

Also not good for our bodies are the games we play in our minds about food. We think if we don't eat, we'll lose weight, or keep it off. Or we decide that since we're already heavier than we want to be, we might as well eat as much as we want of the leftover birthday cake. Body image and the pressure we put on ourselves about food, or feel from external forces, can get the better of us if we let it.

WHEN YOU LOOK GOOD, YOU FEEL GOOD

We can all envision the archetypal homemaker of the 1950s with a silhouette figure (aided by a girdle and padded bra) keeping house in a pretty dress and stylish heels. Things could not be more different now. The archetype of the modern Stay-at-Home mom is a woman in sweats or jeans and running shoes with her hair pulled back in a ponytail. Gone are the dresses and pumps of the '50s as everyday wear. Even office wear has come to reflect our country's new casual standard. Yet for most women, going to work outside the home does, in some respect, still represent getting "dressed up," and staying home can be a tough transition. Several Stay-at-Home women echoed the sentiments of mother-of-four Colleen, who is pregnant with her fifth and says, "I miss having a work wardrobe."

When you're home all day, it's easy to think, *Why bother? Why bother getting dressed up? Coloring my roots? Shaving my legs? I spend the day being drooled on, and the only people I see are children and other moms.* Besides, as a Stay-at-Home mom living on one income, you're probably saving both time and money by paring down your primping. Nice clothes and salon highlights may have been a habit when you worked. Now they're an expense you might not easily afford.

While economizing and simplifying is good, feeling attractive, put-together, and even pretty helps many women feel better and more confident about themselves. Putting on some makeup and a decent outfit can also help a gal manage her transition from dressing for the office or going out into the world every day. "I've seen too many mums who are so wiped out by taking care of wee ones, they just slob around in sweats and let themselves go," says Aoife, a mother of two toddlers who makes it a point *not* to get into the sweats slump. "I squeeze in a shower every day, even if it means bringing both kids in there with me. I'm no fashion plate, but I wear the same kind of clothes I did pre-babes. For me, even that small thing makes me feel good."

As many of us know, looking and feeling good in our post-pregnancy bodies can be a challenge. My full-term twins did such a number on my midsection that I cried the first time I saw my unclothed body after their birth, and I was demoralized every morning as I squeezed my former size-one self into support undergarments to contain a belly that had lost all muscle and skin tone. Unable to fit into my former clothes but not wanting to buy new ones, I slobbed around in baggy and early-maternity clothes for much of the girls' first year until I accepted that, short of reconstructive surgery (which these days is an available and often chosen option), I'd never again have the body I once did. The pregnancy even increased my shoe size! Childbirth and age change a woman's overall shape and figure—even if she gets all the pregnancy weight off. For all but the truly lucky ones, who return to their already perfect pre-pregnancy shape and size, most women who have given birth will need to cull and refurbish their wardrobes. That's right—I just said shopping was important for your mental health!

STICKING TO A SCHEDULE

It's often said that children find comfort in having a routine. Sometimes the same is true for a mom.

From her days working full time as a writer and editor, Megan is accustomed to having a schedule and meeting deadlines. She says following a schedule as the Stay-at-Home mother of two small boys helps her manage the day and enjoy her new job.

"Having a schedule keeps me from feeling overwhelmed and indecisive about what to do when," says Megan, who organizes her daily and weekly activities using an Excel spreadsheet. "Having a schedule to guide me ensures that the kids get quality time with me every day doing specific things, such as reading or playing outside. It also ensures that I get 'me' time. I can tell the kids, 'No, it's Mommy time now,' without feeling guilty, because they also have a scheduled time." Since Megan began organizing her day at home in the same way she had done for her paid workday, "I am so much happier. We all are," she says. "Most of my bad feelings seem to have disappeared, and I've discovered I have more time than I thought. I've also found that going to bed and getting up at the same time as my husband helps too. It puts us on the same page and gives us more time for each other."

While Julie C.'s schedule isn't on a spreadsheet, she has a daily routine that, she says, "is crucial to my mental health." When her baby is napping, she exercises in her garage for an hour while her three-year-old keeps busy coloring and watching a video. "I also try to slip in a TV show when my one-year-old is taking her afternoon nap and my other child is at preschool," she says.

Andrea's routine takes place before dawn: "I try to get up early in the morning, before the kids are awake, if to do nothing more than come downstairs and sit on the couch in the quiet darkness and pull my thoughts together for the day."

YOUR NIGHT OUT

It really is essential for a woman who's home all day to have regular appointments on her calendar marking her activities or evenings out. Now these aren't boozing, bar-dancing, party-girl events (although, if that's your thing, they could be). Instead, these are outings during which a woman leaves her kids at home and enjoys the chance to do something she wants to do, such as enjoying the company of friends or a nice meal (that she is actually able to eat in peace).

A Girl's Night Out group of gals can develop from long-established friendships, or it can evolve from moms who know one another through playgroups but rarely see each other without children present. Some neighborhoods or social or community organizations have Ladies Only events, such as a monthly restaurant dinner or a book discussion or a game night, held either at a public place or in someone's home. When you have access or invitations to these kinds of outings, it can be worth trying to attend. Even if you have to walk in the door alone, the great thing about such opportunities is that, unlike in high school or college, when you wouldn't dare join a table of girls you don't know, the women attending these types of social functions are also going out to meet new people. Similarly, you may be invited to a party by someone selling franchise items (cosmetics, kitchen gadgets, baskets, purses). Four years ago, I reluctantly attended a candle party. I bought one candle (you feel like you have to buy *something* at these events) and found a wonderful friend. Booie's daughter and my twins are the same age. We continue to help each other with our kids.

By taking part in gatherings you're invited to, you'll get to better know your community, and you might become friends with women who will introduce you to other women and things to do—all of which will help you prevent or combat any feelings of loneliness and isolation. (For more on how to find mom-friendly organizations, activities and support groups, see Chapter Eleven.)

My monthly calendar now includes two regular nights out each month. The first is a board meeting for a mom's organization, which has introduced me to dozens of women I would have never otherwise met. My other outing is a monthly book group, hosted in the homes of its fifteen members. The added benefit of this group, which I was invited to join by a member, is that once a year we go away for a weekend. During my first year as a member, we went to another member's beach house. Most recently, we went to a spa resort in Virginia. And as I've explained to my husband, since I was invited to join a group that has been together for a decade, it would be *rude* of me not to participate in their trips!

Unless she's out of town, Maura, who has five children, rarely misses a book group meeting. "It's important for me to have my 'adult' time," she says, "and I don't feel guilty about leaving the kids and my husband home on their own for a while." Some husbands, however, aren't as supportive as Maura's or mine. There are women whose spouses refuse to do a solo shift of kid duty, which means the mom can't leave the house until the children are asleep. This is the gal who misses the restaurant dinner and arrives in time for dessert, if she's lucky. If I've just described you (and I hope I haven't), try borrowing a quip reported to me by a fed-up Stay-at-Home mom who, announcing she was going to a mother's club party, declared to her spouse: "I've had a tough day, so I'm going out for drinks with my coworkers!"

YOUR ALONE CONE

I despise the children's show *Dragon Tales,* largely because I can't stand Wheezie, who is the shrieking half of the show's two-headed dragon. But I do appreciate a term coined by her and her better half, Zack, who each occasionally retreats into a dunce cap–like "Alone Cone" to get a break from the other. Every mother needs an Alone Cone. For a mom who can't easily get out of the house, the Alone Cone is sometimes the only peace and quiet she has.

My Alone Cone involves sitting at my laptop writing or emailing. I've become so adept at tuning out the chaos around me—when I'm not in charge of managing it—that so long as my husband can be the go-to parent for the kids, I can sit at my desk in the kitchen and be in the room, yet it's like I'm locked away in a private study. (Me to Family: "I know you see me, but I'm not *really* here.") Your Alone Cone might require that you leave the house and do something to relax your mind and body (such as getting a massage or spa treatment), or it may simply be you having some physical distance from your loved ones (such as behind a closed door). Or perhaps all you need are your earbuds and your iPod, with the volume pumped up loud.

YOUR DAY NEEDS TO END

In *A Woman's Guide to Sleep*, Joyce Walsleben, PhD, then-director of the New York University School of Medicine's Sleep Disorders Center, notes that a mother typically loses 700 hours of sleep during the first year of her child's life. Since many women have more than one child, that sleep deficit just increases with time. Says Walsleben: "Women are probably the most sleep-deprived creatures on Earth."

As a Stay-at-Home mother, you're on duty 24/7. (And you really are, since you sleep where you work.) But there needs to be an end to your working day, or at least an end to your day working as a mother.

I know that if I'm not off the kid shift by 8:00 PM, by which time my husband is usually fully in charge of the crew, I'm a very unhappy camper. Although I'm still busy at work after eight, my night work is brain work (the banking, the household paperwork, my email correspondence, this book) and not hands-on mothering work. When the kids make demands on me after I clock out, I tell them to find their father. When they don't, or if he's not home and they're fighting bedtime, I have implored, and sometimes screamed, "Please, my day needs to *end!*"

You can't be an on-duty mother every waking minute of your day. Yes, your partner worked all day too. But he didn't work all day as the hands-on father of his children. Parenting is work, and both partners are often exhausted by day's end. You and your partner will likely both work a sixteen- or eighteen-hour day while raising your children. You can do it, but a few of your work hours need to involve tasks that differ from your routine.

In an article in *Parenting* magazine titled "Quirky Rules That Work," writer Barbara Rowley says that when her kids were small, she used the rule, "I don't work past 8:00 PM." Her children and husband learned that if they wanted mom involved in bath time and bedtime stories, they'd best get the process in motion so she could go off-duty by eight. Rowley says the lesson taught her family that mom is "not endlessly available" for everyone's needs.

PRAYER AND REFLECTION

Of the women who answered my survey in depth, a few spoke of how religion helped them in their jobs as Stay-at-Home moms. "I have a strong religious belief that helps me find meaning and satisfaction in what I am doing," says Sarah B., who is home with three children.

Megan, who is mentioned a few pages earlier about establishing a daily schedule, says she sets time aside during her day to read scripture. "While reading fiction lets me escape, when I read scripture, I find a spiritual wisdom that changes my perspective and brings much-needed comfort," she says. "The only time I really feel I've failed at being a good mom is when I let myself get too angry with my kids and thus handle a discipline situation poorly. Instead, when I ask God for help, I can usually remain patient, maintain my composure, and keep my self-respect in those heated moments."

Faith also helps Megan combat the loneliness she sometimes experiences as a Stay-at-Home mom. "I find when I'm feeling the most alone, I ask for help, and He shows me someone who truly needs me," she explains. "Reaching out to others forces me to look beyond myself, and I quickly realize how easy I have it and how fortunate I am. If loneliness is my biggest problem, I'm pretty blessed."

In a similar vein, many women find comfort by having some quiet time to reflect, which they do with the assistance of calm music or sounds, incense, or meditation, the latter of which two of my friends have successfully pursued for spiritual solace. One mom, who finally has time to breathe and think now that her three children are in school full day, has sought out a coach to teach her how to meditate. The other friend, who has three younger children, tries to visit a Quaker meetinghouse on Sundays. She leaves her kids at home with her spouse and participates in the service, most of which involves the congregants sitting quietly in silent prayer and meditation. She admits that, in the beginning, it was hard not to nod off (she's a busy mom, after all), but says, "you get used to it, and besides, the chairs aren't comfortable for falling asleep."

NEW-AGE TECHNIQUES

Enhanced inner peace and calm can also be achieved by harnessing some of your body's own healing power through non-Western techniques and practices, including acupuncture, massage, yoga, and relaxation training like biofeedback.

In biofeedback, for example, you train yourself to not react to everyday stresses with a physical "fight or flight" response—shallow breathing, fast heart rate, clenched fists and jaws. During an office visit, technicians monitor your heart rate, breathing, and hand temperature as indicators of stress (cold hands equal stress), then instruct you in breathing and visualization techniques that allow you to lower your stress response naturally. Biofeedback can be used to help you stay calm, or to fight without medication symptoms of stress, including headaches, high blood pressure, and sleeplessness.

Another body-based technique for reducing stress and discomfort is acupuncture, the ancient Chinese medical tradition of placing needles into pressure points on the skin as a means of treating disease, relieving pain, and promoting well-being. Many people use acupuncture, which is painless, to relieve stress and achieve relaxation. Although it is a standard medical technique in many countries, in the United States, acupuncture is still considered an alternative medicine procedure, albeit one that is now covered by some health insurance companies.

A less physically tangible coping technique that some find useful is called visualization or creative visualization, which, in essence, involves the use of imagination and positive thinking to make goals and objectives come true. This technique, which can be learned from a coach, therapist, or even a self-help book, typically involves picturing and articulating one's goals, and repeating mantras or affirmations.

COUNSELING

Becoming a mother is a huge change in a woman's life. If at the same time a woman leaves her job and friends in order to stay home to care for her child, she can feel as if the person she was has disappeared. It's not uncommon for a mom's feelings of isolation and depression or anxiety to become so disruptive and worrisome that seeking professional assistance from a therapist or physician is the best (and sometimes essential) solution. The following email details how professional counseling helped a woman interviewed for this book.

> I started seeing a counselor a few weeks ago to help me work through some of the anger and frustration I've felt in the past year, going from having one child to two. She's been great. She's helping me see what a huge transition I've been in for the past three or four years, going from being a self-employed woman who had tons of time to herself and made a lot of money, to being a mom who has no time to herself and made just $5,000 last year. Before therapy, I had never really thought about how much my life has changed in the past few years. In addition to the kids and not working, I also moved from the West Coast to the East Coast during that same time. It's been nice to be able to think about all that has happened and honor what a significant transition it has been.

Sometimes what an overwhelmed woman needs, what *any* person needs, is someone to talk to. Friends and family can be great sounding boards, but there are times when what's required is someone who won't take personal offense at what you may say, who won't interrupt you with his or her own stories, and who you can be fully confident won't blab your business around the neighborhood. The key to seeking out professional therapy is finding the right person and appointment time, and a price you can afford.

To find a therapist, you can ask your doctor for recommendations, check the yellow pages, or contact your insurance company for in-network providers. You can also seek leads from a local women's clinic, a nearby university or teaching hospital, your religious institution, or friends who have been in therapy.

As for actually being able to arrive at an appointment, see if a provider can schedule you when your child is at school or during a time you can find a sitter. Or try for an evening, weekend, or early-morning appointment, which could enable your husband or partner to be home with the kids. Other options: If you have an infant, see if you can bring the baby with you. Also, some therapists, after having met with you in person for a few sessions, will allow for telephone appointments, which could perhaps be scheduled during your child's nap or at a time you can count on him being occupied by a TV show or toy.

Therapy typically costs about $100 for a forty-five-minute to one-hour session. If you are insured, investigate whether your insurance plan covers outpatient mental health counseling. If you have no counseling coverage, look for a free or low-cost clinic or counselor, an organized support group, or a provider with a sliding scale. In order to bill an insurance company, the practitioner—be she a psychiatrist, psychologist, or licensed clinical social worker—will have to make a clinical diagnosis and often detail a treatment plan. So as not to put a label on their clients, which some patients fear could have later repercussions or embarrassment if revealed, many service providers are specific yet vague. For example: A diagnosis of "adjustment disorder" can be explained as you simply needing assistance to get through a change in your life. (You may be clinically depressed, but no one needs to know that.) A treatment plan of "weekly one-hour individual therapy sessions over the course of eight weeks" can get the treatments covered while not revealing the details of what you're talking about.

Professional therapy can help identify specific problems affecting you, and it can help you formulate concrete solutions and action plans. Unfortunately, many people who could benefit from counseling don't pursue the help they need. If you think therapy may help you, investigate your options.

MEDICATION

A time came in my mid-thirties during which I was enormously stressed about juggling a demanding job, a long commute, a child at home, and plans to have another. I was also facing my husband's layoff from an Internet company gone bust and his acceptance of a lucrative offer in another city, which I knew would eventually require us to move. By chance, during this time, two friends made casual mention of having similar feelings during periods of extreme transition and stress. Both got control of their feelings, and regained their coping mechanisms, by taking a medication called Paxil, which is one of a number of SSRI medications, short for Selective Serotonin Reuptake Inhibitors, that are used to combat depression and anxiety.

One friend was prescribed an SSRI after the building in which he worked, directly adjacent to the World Trade Center, was destroyed before his eyes on 9/11. The medication helped him manage his increasingly debilitating fear, anxiety, and sadness. Another friend, a woman, took medication while dealing with the devastating illness and ultimate death of her beloved father.

At about the time I thought I would lose my mind, a third friend called. When I described my feelings of overwhelming stress and anxiety, she said, "I know exactly what you're going through." Chloe then proceeded to explain how she had become a bundle of nerves after having two children within eighteen months, and then leaving her career to care for them while her husband finished graduate school and pursued his internships. She was then uprooted twice so her spouse could continue his training in different cities.

Chloe said her moods swung from despair to fury and back. While her feelings and reactions to all the changes in her life were understandable, she was frightened by what was happening to her and mentioned her stress and anxiety to her doctor. She felt relieved to learn that her symptoms are common among people going through times of difficult change, and the doctor confirmed that because women are often hit with many transitions at once—marriage, pregnancy, balancing work and family, leaving a career, caring for everyone except herself—many find themselves suddenly unable to manage. Often added to the mix are the assorted hormones swirling around women's bodies from pregnancy, breastfeeding, even changing menstrual cycles due to age and later peri-menopause. All of these forces can combine to form a tornado of emotions, thoughts and desires that make daily life, even getting out of bed, a challenge due to physical reactions in your brain chemistry.

Chloe revealed to me that once she started taking an SSRI, she found herself better able to cope with all the changes, transitions, and demands put upon her. (As only an MD can order prescription medications, a woman considering such drug intervention needs to see an ob-gyn, internist, family practitioner, or psychiatrist.)

When I described my own building anxiety, confusion, and despair, my doctor agreed that medication would help make my thought processes clearer by taking the edge off my overwhelming feelings and helping me to function. And it did. After a few zombie-like days, I emerged to being able to think rationally and not simply emotionally. I was able to identify the causes of my stress and what I had control to change. The most positive effect of the medication was that it helped me handle sad situations without bawling, and I could once again take on difficult tasks without feeling overwhelmed. On the flip side, these medications can make some users numb to expressions of great joy, humor, or fun. I noticed a personality change in one friend taking the same medication as I. She turned from the expressive, quick-witted, easily riled, over-the-top girl I knew into someone so even-tempered and calm her blood didn't boil about anything. Part of her appeal, to me, was how she would call bullshit on bullshit, and I missed the fight in her.

While not considered to be physically addictive, these medications can be psychologically addictive, in that the user can become afraid to stop taking them. "If I stop, will I crack up?" "Am I feeling better because of the medicine, or because my situation has improved, or because I have more experience now and can better handle my new life?" It can be hard to know. When using SSRIs, it's important to educate yourself about possible side effects and stay in the care of a doctor who can manage your prescription (and change medications or make adjustments if necessary).

People who use antidepressant and anti-anxiety medications are often embarrassed to admit their reliance on them. And some insensitive people may judge those who use prescription remedies as weak or, worse, unstable. I think that's both simplistic and unfair. The truth is that many people "self-medicate" their depression, insecurities, stress, and anxiety by overindulging in booze, cigarettes, and illegal or misused prescription drugs. When I was on medication, I found it odd that I kept quiet about my use, fearful of being judged, but my friends who admitted to putting away a bottle of wine most nights had no such concerns.

What's also important to keep in mind is that Stay-at-Home moms are only one of many subgroups of adults needing and seeking help to manage stress and crises or even behavioral challenges. I know a couple of women who struggled for years with interpersonal and organizational problems because they weren't properly diagnosed with, respectively, bipolar syndrome and attention deficit disorder, until after they had children. For these individuals, and for those affected by chronic anxiety or depression, medications often need to be taken for life. For others, the prescriptions can help in getting through a rough patch. Actress Brooke Shields is very open about her use of Paxil to recover from a debilitating postpartum depression, which she detailed in her memoir *Down Came the Rain*. In such cases, when the depression or crisis or hormonal imbalance has passed, so does the need for any medication.

Several of the women who answered questions for this book said medical management is what helped them cope with sadness, stress, and various anxieties, including the demands of motherhood and domesticity. "I fought *so* long to not take any medication," wrote a survey respondent about using an SSRI called Lexapro. "But I finally gave in, and I feel so much better."

Voices: Strategies for Staying Sane

"Sometimes I just give myself the day off. A 'day off' means I'm still with my kids, but I decide I'm not going to get anything accomplished that day. I take the pressure off to clean anything or catch-up on anything or do anything other than feed and monitor my children."

—Laura

"If things are going terribly wrong with the kids, I try to change the environment. Go for a walk, go to McDonald's or to the store for a special treat, go to the park, the library, or bookstore. I suggest that a mom invite a friend over or go on an outing at least once a week to change the monotony in her schedule."

—Sarah B.

"You have to get yourself out of the house, if even to go to Target, and just talk to other people. You might not meet your new best friend, but at least you'll have practiced an adult conversation. As far as maintaining both existing and new friendships, you have to be flexible and remember that you're you, not just someone's mother or wife."

—Jen

"I really like watching TV by myself at the end of the day and just vegging out."

—Liz R.

"Email! What a boon for mothers."

—Sandra

"Going out with my girlfriends to vent helps. And my husband and I often sit and talk after the kids go to bed. He has a calm approach to life, which helps put everything in perspective."

—Erin Z.

"A telephone headset when you have babies. With your hands free, you can stay in touch with people while you fold laundry or carry an infant."

—Diane A.

"I put my daughter in a babyproof play area and I do something in another room, just to get some space. She might scream with anger, but she usually settles down in a few minutes, and I have some peace to recharge my batteries. An added benefit is that my daughter is learning to entertain herself, which is an important skill to have."

—Anne

"My neighbor and I will often get together in the yard, while the kids play, and have our own happy hour until our husbands get home."

—Kellie

"Coffee in the morning and wine at night."

—Denise

Where's My Stand-In?

When a Broadway star twists her ankle, her understudy ensures that the show will go on. When the president of the United States is incapacitated, the vice president takes charge. When a Stay-at-Home mom is sick, unavailable or in desperate need of a day off, she's generally out of luck. "That's one of the hardest parts of motherhood for me," says Diane A., who's home with two preschool girls. "No sick days."

The inability to move about freely and control one's own schedule is among the most frustrating and, at times, frightening aspects of being a Stay-at-Home mom. We don't get sick days (even though being around little kids exposes us to germs galore). Going to the doctor for a basic maintenance check like a physical, a mammogram, or a dental cleaning requires extensive planning to secure childcare coverage. For some gals, even going to the hospital to give birth doesn't garner a break.

"When my daughter was born, I stayed in the hospital, and my husband was home with our two sons," reports a California mom. "It was a complete disaster. The house looked like a tornado had come through. There were pizza delivery boxes everywhere, and our three-year-old son took the keys and left our home to find me. My husband had a few scary minutes searching the apartment complex for him."

We all have emergencies, activities, and obligations that require we find someone to care for our children when we can't. On those occasions, a Stay-at-Home mom needs to rely on her husband or partner, family, friends, neighbors, or babysitters. We also have times, *many times,* when we just need a break. As René, a Stay-at-Home mother of three, points out (repeating wise counsel from another mom): "While you'll always love your kids, you won't always *like* them." It's during those moments that a Stay-at-Home mom really needs a few hours or a full day off. That's when we depend on our husbands or partners, or upon those same family members, friends, or sitters, but also such places as preschools, drop-in child-care programs (like a church-sponsored Mother's Morning Out), and babysitting co-ops.

Ideally, when schedules do allow, we hand the kid(s) to our partner. Most modern dads are more than capable of caring for their children, especially as compared to the fathers going back one or two generations. Although a dad can't breastfeed a baby, he can do everything else, and he should be able to pinch-hit for mom when she's out for the count, or give her time off by taking sole charge of the kids on a Saturday, for example. Few "working" folks would be happy about spending seven days a week at the office or on the job, yet Stay-at-Home moms are expected to be on duty, or, at the very least, on call, around-the-clock. I know too many women who can only get a break on the weekend by hiring a sitter, and too many men who actually believe they can't (or shouldn't) be left alone to care for their three-year-olds. You care for the children all day on your own without help. A father should be able to do the same.

To: All Men with Children
c/o: The Mother of Your Child(ren)

1. Fathers *care for* their children, they don't *babysit* them. (Terminology matters.)
2. And guys, when the kids are yours for the day, always taking them to visit your mom, where she entertains the gang, isn't the same as you taking care of your kids. Yes, the outing gives your partner a break, but if you run to Mommy every time you have the kids on your own, your mother might come to resent your wife handing the kids to you, because you, in turn, hand them off to her.

As children grow, the responsibilities of both parents can and should change. Some men truly are fearful of caring for infants, yet they're thrilled to throw a ball around with older kids. (Similarly, some moms love the baby stage but grow weary of pushing a toddler on a park swing day after day.) Laura, a Stay-at-Home mother of two preschoolers, recommends that you "revisit your 'agreement' with your husband on a regular basis. When you can have a little more freedom from the little ones," she says, "make sure your spouse can give that to you." Asking for time off isn't asking for a favor. Time off isn't a great "gift" (for which you are beholden). Stay-at-Home moms need and deserve breaks from their duties, for everyone's sake—theirs, their partner's, and even the kids'.

THE VILLAGE PEOPLE

In olden days, or so we're told, families lived near one another, enabling a Stay-at-Home mom to have a mother, aunts, sisters, or cousins nearby to help. In many cultures, the birth of a child still brings the new mom's mother, aunts, sisters, or cousins for an extended, helpful visit. Yet for many of us today, that ready support simply isn't available.

Several survey respondents reported having to fly in their mothers from other states or cities for help during such routine illnesses as the flu. Most respondents said their husband was their primary—and sometimes only—childcare backup. Pilar, who has a toddler, explains that with her husband stationed in Iraq and her mother back home in Mexico, "I have no backup or family here in Maryland. There have been times I've been sick with a fever and couldn't get out of bed. But since there was one else to watch my son, I had to care for him myself."

In 1996, then First Lady Hillary Clinton adapted the proverb "it takes a village to raise a child" into the title of her book, *It Takes a Village*, which discusses the responsibilities of society toward children. Critics (most notably Republican presidential nominee Bob Dole) railed that "it take a family to raise a child." Nearly a decade later, U.S. Sen. Rick Santorum, a conservative from Pennsylvania, produced his own manifesto, *It Takes a Family*. The reality is, it takes both a village and a family. Assuming that, at a minimum, having family support of some sort is a given, unless every family can care for every medical, educational, emotional, and physical need experienced by their children, a "village" of caregivers is essential—including doctors, teachers, babysitters, police, and even a parent's employer.

And when that child's grandma or aunt doesn't live right around the corner, it's nonfamily, such as friends and neighbors, from whom a parent seeks and receives assistance. Both Stay-at-Home women and mothers who are employed outside the home know this.

As I've noted elsewhere in the book, when I was living in New Jersey and on bed rest with my twins, it was my girlfriends who cared for me and my preschool-age son while my husband was working in Maryland. These women drove my son to nursery school in the morning, arranged for him to take the same after school classes as their kids, and essentially kept him occupied and cared for until the late afternoon. Toward the end of the pregnancy, the other Brian in my life (a friend of my spouse, Brian), called me whenever he was going to the supermarket on his way home from work. Armed with one grocery list from his wife and a smaller one from me, that Brian would shop for two families—and deliver my order. Although I never asked for his help, he knew I needed it.

At the time, my mother lived twenty minutes from me, but she worked full time. So after the girls were born, my most consistent weekday helper for the seven months I was on my own with three kids was "Auntie Fran," a recently widowed woman who lived in my town. She was recommended to me by her daughter, a recent college grad and occasional babysitter who in turn had been sent my way by another mom who had also struggled through a difficult pregnancy. Fran came to my house for an hour in the morning, to stay with the babies while I drove my son to preschool and did a couple of errands. She returned for two hours in the evening so I could feed and bathe the gang, and myself, before bedtime. At least once a week, one of several girlfriends would leave her husband—and, if she had any, children—at home and do an over-night shift with the twins at my house. Because my own mother and husband couldn't be on hand, Fran, the other Brian, and my girlfriends—all local villagers—served in their stead. A collection of other villagers, who I knew peripherally through friends or my son's preschool, came forward and assisted as well.

Family and Medical Leave Policies

Signed by President Bill Clinton, the federal Family and Medical Leave Act of 1993 (FMLA) protects an employee's job if that person needs to take a break from work due to his or her own medical emergency, or in order to care for an immediate family member (such as after the birth or adoption of a child, or a spousal or parental illness). The break, which is unpaid, can extend for as much as twelve weeks during a twelve-month period. Eligibility varies based on the size of the business the employee works for and the person's specific job. In theory, if your household can afford an unpaid leave, this act would enable your spouse or parent to take time off to care for you (and, as a result, your kids) during a difficult pregnancy, after a complicated delivery, or during an extended illness or recovery. To learn about FMLA, go to the Department of Labor's website at www.dol.gov.

However, many (dare I assume, most) households can't afford to have a breadwinner take an unpaid leave. With that in mind, three states—Minnesota, California and Washington—have enacted paid family medical leave policies. For more information, see the website for the National Conference of State Legislatures at www.ncsl.org.

Kara, who relocated a few years ago from the New York area to Colorado, knows she may someday have to rely on her village for help. "We have no family here, so my husband would have to work from home," she says, contemplating her backup plan should she ever be unable to care for her two preschoolers. "But he travels quite a bit. I do have a few really great friends here, and a good neighbor who would help."

It's possible that you'll someday need to look to your village for help. And sometimes, if people can't see your need—or if they don't know exactly what to do or how to best offer assistance—you may actually have to ask for help. Observes Leslie, a mother of two, whose friends came to her rescue when she was on a pre-eclampsia–induced bed rest with her second son: "I didn't have to ask my girlfriends for help, but several later said they knew I never would have come right out and asked for it. I think woman often don't want to 'bother' anyone, but the truth is, people are usually glad to be able to help."

BEING IN TWO (OR MORE) PLACES AT ONCE

There are many times when a mother of multiple children finds herself needed in two or more places at the same time. For a moment, put on your exam-taking hat and consider this true problem:

> A mother has twin girls who, due to academic necessity, attend different preschools located ten miles apart, in an area about twenty miles south of their home. Her son attends school fifteen miles north of the home. The boy's school begins at 8:10 AM. The girls' schools are about thirty-five miles south of the boy's. One of the girls attends school

> five mornings a week, starting at 8:30. The other twin at-
> tends two preschools: One school holds classes on Mondays,
> Wednesdays, and Fridays at a church ten miles west of her
> sister's school and also begins at 8:30; the other program,
> located ten miles east of her sister's school, is in session on
> Tuesdays and Thursdays, beginning at 8:45. How can this
> mother get her three children to school on time?

Confused? I still am. The scenario is true. It described my week-day mornings for the academic year 2006–07.

The solution to the problem was for my husband to drive our son to school during his commute north (which required understanding from his colleagues and boss as to why he'd be in the office by nine rather than before eight). Although I didn't like asking for special treatment, I did, and one of the preschools eventually allowed me to drop off a twin ten minutes early three mornings a week. On the two mornings that child attended a different preschool, I delivered her to school late or swapped carpooling duties with a classmate's mom.

People will help you, and institutions will sometimes bend the rules. You just need to figure out what you need, be creative about the possible solutions, and ask nicely.

WHO (OR WHAT) WILL BE YOUR UNDERSTUDY?

Following are some options:

Make it possible for your partner to (occasionally) work from home: Back-up number one for most Stay-at-Home moms is dad. If your partner has a job that enables him to work from home rather than taking the whole day off, he may be able to help out more often and with less stress should you fall sick or have another un-planned event. While not every employed person can actually do his or her job from home, many now can—with the right equipment. If there's a possibility you might need your spouse at home frequently, or for occasional chunks of time, it may be worth equipping your home with a high-speed Internet connection, a reliable computer, printer, scanner, and fax machine, as well as a telephone answering machine or voicemail service. To facilitate uninterrupted business conversations and concentration, a dedicated home office is ideal, if you have the space. If not, any room with a computer, phone, Internet service—and preferably a door—will do.

All that said, if dad is staying at home in order to care for the kids, he needs to understand that he likely won't have a super pro-ductive workday, at least while the children are awake and need to be fed, entertained, and supervised; simply being an adult present (somewhere) in the house is not enough.

Mother's Morning Out: Knowing that Stay-at-Home moms need a break, some churches and community service groups offer low-cost, drop-off childcare programs in which a mother can leave her child(ren) with sitters at a church or community center for a couple of hours, so she can run errands or simply have a few hours to herself. I used a Mother's Morning Out in Westfield, New Jersey, during my son's first year. Preregistration was required, and each mom was allowed a single two-and-one-half hour session per week. It was worth doing, even though in the beginning it was traumatic for both of us: My son would cry about being left. I was exhausted by the time I had packed his supplies, rushed out of the house, loaded him into the car, drove a mile to the center, hoisted him out of the car, and carried him in his infant carrier through the church parking lot and up the stairs.

Because I lived close to the church, I'd often drop off my son, then race home to shower, pay bills, or check email, or else run errands in town. However, in comparing notes with a mother of two children, I found that she spent her two hours sitting in the local Starbucks, enjoying her coffee and reading. Her reasoning: "Sitting and reading is something I can't do when I have the kids around. Out of necessity I have to take them food shopping and on other errands anyway, so this time is for me to do things I can *only* do on my own."

Babysitting co-ops: When these arrangements work, they can be a huge help, as it is to survey respondent Julie C., a Silicon Valley mother of two. "We take turns watching each other's kids so we can run errands, go to doctor's appointments, etc.," she explains. Generally, a co-op is formed by a group of moms who are friends or who know each other through an organized mothers' club. When a woman needs daytime babysitting, she can call another member of the group for help. (The kids are usually dropped off at that woman's house.) When the no-cost service is used, the user then owes the co-op (or in some cases the particular member) the same number of hours. You can of course use this same sort of barter system with your girlfriends and neighbors without being as formal.

Another option, which is useful for nighttime outings, is for you and your partner to establish an arrangement with another couple. "We have close neighbors with whom we trade having our kids spend the night at each others' houses," says Leslie, whose children are five- and three years old. "One night we have four kids, but then the next time we have none!"

Babysitters and mother's helpers: It's worth keeping in mind that there are different kinds of babysitters and helpers for different needs. Depending on the duration of time you need coverage and the ages of your children, potential helpers can range in age from eight to eighty and can do everything from take the kids off your hands completely to cuddle a new baby while you escape to take a shower. The best source for sitters is by knowing the young (or older) people in your neighborhood, by seeking out referrals from other moms (who are willing to share) and, when that doesn't work, by putting an ad in a local newspaper or on a community board at a church or job board at a nearby college. Nanny or childcare agencies generally aren't a good source for finding part-time or occasional babysitters, and the finder's fees can be quite costly. Success with website resources such as www.sittercity.com, which charges a membership fee, can vary greatly depending on your location.

Here's a general guide as to the benefits and potential drawbacks of different age groups of sitters:

• **Ages 8–10:** Kids of this age love babies. While an eight-year-old surely can't be left on her own with a small child, she can entertain a baby (or several little kids) while you're home and allow you freedom to do other tasks. Preteen boys or girls can sit on a couch and give a bottle or spoonfeed a baby in a high chair. They can crawl on the floor with a baby and sit on a blanket and play blocks. They can push a baby up and down the sidewalk in a stroller. All the while, mom can be making dinner, returning phone calls, cleaning the house, gardening in the yard. A mother can even take a shower *and* dry her hair! When my son was born, I was blessed by the assistance of two ten-year-old neighbors, Mary and Thomas. Each was a youngest child, forever desperate to have a younger sibling. Mary and Thomas were careful with my son, and were so appreciative of having a "job." They showed up (as a team) at their appointed time. They took turns giving him bottles and even changing diapers.

Survey respondent Florida reports that her eight-year-old neighbor, K.C., helped her survive the early years of caring for three baby boys—a one-year-old and twins that arrived three days after his first birthday. If Florida had to go to the supermarket, K.C. came along to push an extra cart. If she took the boys to a park, K.C. was an extra set of useful arms and legs. K.C. fed the babies, wiped noses, and when the babies napped, K.C. would watch TV while listening for baby murmurings or cries so Florida could take a nap as well.

The agreement I had with my young helpers (and their parents) was that if I asked Mary and Thomas to come over and work, I paid them. (Typically $1 each for an hour.) If they visited the baby on their own because they wanted to play with him, they didn't get paid. As an added benefit, my Mary and Thomas, and Florida's K.C., each matured into a full-fledged sitter.

• **Ages 11–13:** Count yourself lucky if you live near a "tween"; babysitters of these ages are often the easiest to get, and they may be even better than their older schoolmates. Because these tweens can't get a paid job in a business establishment, babysitting (and possibly an allowance) is their bread and butter. Eleven-, twelve-, and thirteen-year-olds are useful for daytime help and as a way of keeping babies and preschoolers occupied while mom tries to get something accomplished, even if all she does is fold laundry in her bedroom while watching an hour of *Oprah*.

Only Illinois and Maryland currently have laws about when a minor can be left alone or in charge of younger children. (The minimum ages are essentially ages fourteen and thirteen, respectively, with some caveats.) Otherwise, when a youngster is mature enough to babysit is up to the adults involved. If their mom or dad is home nearby, or if your errand destination is close, a tween can probably be left in charge of, say, a preschooler. Or they can be asked to take your children out into the yard, or for a walk, so you can get your house in order. These kids are also helpful hires for evenings when you'll be just two doors down at a neighbor's house, or during birthday parties or other events during which you need to concentrate on being the hostess, not the parent.

• **Ages 14–15:** These kids can do all basic childcare tasks, plus they're usually confident and responsible enough to handle a short day or evening shift on their own. The other great thing about these youngsters is that, like the preteens, they're generally available, since they can't yet drive or legally work in a business. Since little children can be a handful, and being in a house at night without an adult can be scary, it may be useful to have a sitter this age bring a friend along to help.

• **Ages 16–18:** These are the sitters who, in theory, you want. They can often drive themselves to and from your house and, since they're older, they should (in theory) be more responsible. Problem is, these kids have a social life! And at certain socioeconomic levels, because they don't need to work to have money, they're not interested in giving up a Friday or Saturday night so you can go out.

• **College-aged sitters:** Many college students need to work part time to pay their tuition, personal expenses, or car costs, making them more likely than a teenager to say yes to babysitting work. Plus, if they're in college, you can figure they have a somewhat good head on their shoulders. If you live near a university or college, especially a community college with a large part-time enrollment, there are opportunities to secure semi-regular help from a young person who is an actual adult. While some of these students may pursue babysitting work purely for the relatively high, off-the-books income, many choose babysitting because they truly enjoy being with kids. Every college girl I've found to help me for a few hours a week in the summer was either an education or nursing major.

• **Adult sitters:** Adults who baby- and kid-sit part time may be working at regular jobs but need to supplement their incomes (as is often the case with new teachers). They are often women who have teenage children and miss being around babies, or they might be retired or underemployed and looking to make some pocket change. While it's nice to have the help of an adult, grown-up sitters can sometimes be a mixed bag. Some older people who choose to baby-sit may do so by default, because they're not legally allowed to work, or because they have a string of unsuccessful workplace experiences. As a Stay-at-Home mom in need of an occasional sitter, you have the ability to spend time with a prospective sitter and really get a good sense of her personality and abilities.

- **Very senior citizens:** My friend Karen made use of a lonely octogenarian neighbor by having the woman come to her house and either read books to her two preschool girls or sit on the couch cradling their baby brother. While Helen was too frail to be left alone with the children, when she was in the house, Karen could make dinner, clean, take a shower, or focus her efforts on one child instead of the full trio. Although Helen wasn't paid, she often stayed for meals, was included in family activities, and gained the friendship of a young couple who in turn helped her when she needed a hand.

- **Emergency nanny services:** The availability and effectiveness of these services vary. Most operate by having a family preregister (generally paying a fee or co-pay at that time or upon use). When an emergency situation arises, you call the agency, and they send a caregiver to your home. It's a great idea, although the success of using the service can be very specific to the parents and children involved. This option likely won't work with a child who screams for hours at the sight of new people. Nor would such a service work for parents who'd be extremely uncomfortable about leaving their kids in the care of someone they hadn't met prior to the event. (These services often only allow arrangements to be made a day or so in advance.) My former employer provided access to such a service, and it could be that your partner's employer does too. It might be worth you doing the research, before you're in a jam, to evaluate the emergency nanny options in your area.

YOUR TIME OFF REALLY NEEDS TO BE TIME OFF

It's rare and challenging enough for a Stay-at-Home mother to get time to herself away from her kids. Since such freedom is so precious, your time off shouldn't be spoiled by the person left in charge in your place. As much as possible, try to protect yourself from the spouse or grandparent who takes charge of the kid(s), but then calls during your time away to ask . . .

- simple (dare I say *stupid*) questions, such as, "Where should I throw away a poopy diaper?"
- that you get on the phone and say hello to the kids.
- for ideas of what he or she can do to keep the children busy.
- what to feed the kids since they won't eat what you left.
- when you'll be home (even though you provided that information before you left the house).
- "Can't you come home early?"

To head off such questions, try the following:

- Don't hedge with comments such as, "Call if you have any questions."
- Ensure that the person in charge has everything he or she needs in order to care for the children, and make sure they are capable enough to be able to wing it a little.
- Speaking of which, you need to allow your stand-in to do his or her own thing with the kids. Your mom or partner isn't you, and they can't be expected to do everything exactly the way you would. Sometimes a woman who is the primary caregiver of her children takes ownership of her job, as anyone does, and gets a little territorial. Such behavior can make a man think he doesn't have what it takes to take care of the kids— or lead a wife to not let her husband care for the kids because he won't do it "right."

Now if, despite your great preparations and positive attitude, your stand-in does call while you are out, don't reward him or her by answering their nonurgent questions (e.g. "The baby won't nap.

What should I do?"). Gently but firmly tell your partner or parent that you have complete trust in them and that you're sure they'll figure it out. You can remind the assigned caregiver that you're happy to be called if a child is bleeding or they're on the way to the hospital.

Remember, you work hard on a daily basis taking care of your little ones. Your few hours, or even day or days away from home, shouldn't require that you exhaust yourself with preparations before your departure. Nor should your respite result in you having to put your house back together after your return. Make sure your husband or partner understands that your time off is for you to recuperate from your daily life, and not from the crazed days leading up to your absence. And the renewed you must not be immediately depleted by cleaning the messes and solving the problems created while you were gone. The energy you gain from your much-deserved break is needed to keep you going when you return to your routine.

Quiz: Can Your Partner Handle Being You for a Day?

Any incorrect answers mean you should plan to educate your partner and provide detailed instructions before you disappear. The questions are addressed here to a parent with one child. Change the wording appropriately when more than one child needs care. (The first question is a freebie point every guy should get. If he doesn't . . . well, we trust that won't happen.)

1. Does he know the child's name and birthday?
2. Does he know how to change diapers or manage the child's bathroom routine?
3. Does he know how to dress the child?
4. Does he know the child's daytime schedule and any daily variations?
5. Does he know what foods the child eats and how to prepare them?
6. Does he know the child's allergies, if any?
7. Does he know how to get the child into a car seat, stroller, etc.?
8. Does he know how to get to the places you take the child: school, a play center, a park, library, soccer practice, dance lessons, karate, etc.?
9. Does he know the name of your child's teacher? Friends?
10. Does he know how to reach and get to the child's doctor? Dentist? Any other medical or educational service provider?
11. Does he know and understand the child's health insurance information and coverage?
12. Does he know, or know where to locate, the child's Social Security number?
13. Does he know how to get a prescription filled for the child?
14. Does he know how to keep the child occupied?
15. Does he know which TV programs, videos, or DVDs are appropriate for the child to watch?
16. Does he know how to reach friends or neighbors who can help him, if necessary?
17. Does he know which household chores need to be performed, and when and how to do them?
18. Does he know where to find the supplies he'll need (for the child and for the house)?

> Bonus Question: Does he know how to control his frustration with cranky kids and not being able to accomplish the tasks he needs or wants to do? (If so, give the man an extra point. This *is* a tough one.)

If there were any No answers, and handing him written instructions might not suffice, try to spend a day together as a dry run. If possible, mimic the day(s) of the week he'll be covering, since Monday's events can differ greatly from Wednesday's. Come to think of it, you might *need* to perform such Stay-at-Home mom Boot Camp drills annually, semi-annually, or even bimonthly. The intensity of your partner's Stay-at-Home training is up to you. And if after a day of being you he says the work was easy, emphasize that one day as a stand-in isn't *anything* like doing the job day after day. (You can also claim to have bribed the kids to be well behaved, or that you instructed them to help Daddy be Mommy.)

Making Your Comeback (or Not)

"**A** comeback?" you may be thinking. "The ability to actually go to work and earn money? I can't even answer an email without a baby banging on my keyboard!"

As a Stay-at-Home mom, it can be difficult to envision a future in which you'll be able to move about freely. "It's hard to imagine," says Sarah B., who has three children under five, "that your kids will not always be young and dependent on you."

Although I can now see light at the end of the tunnel (full-day kindergarten is approaching), I'm still not sure how, when, or if I'll be able to make my own career comeback. I'm hopeful that writing this book, and taking on other work-from-home projects that have since found me, are steps in the right direction toward finding a balance that works for me and my family.

Because women who leave careers to care for children rarely leave the workforce forever, a new term has entered the American lexicon: The Comeback Mom. The existence of such a phrase *must* (yes?) mean it's possible for career women turned Stay-at-Home moms to return for a second act in the workforce. In fact, more than 80 percent of American women have children, and some 80 percent of *those* women are in the workforce by the time their children are twelve years old. (Like you, many of those women were once Stay-at-Home moms.)

But any woman who spends a significant amount of time out of the workforce will worry about her desirability as a candidate if or when she decides to return to it. "Women aren't taught how to structure their careers so a break to raise children has a minimal impact," observes survey respondent Diane D., a business development specialist who is home with one child and expecting another. "So many incredible women are in the same boat, all troubled by their choices if they take a break for their families. It's not only a brain drain, but it will impact the ability of women to reach positions where they can have a greater impact and ability to help more women, such as at the executive level of companies and as politicians establishing policy." Diane D.'s main uncertainty about her own career future is the reception she'll get when or if she tries to return to her profession. "Everyone I know who stays out of work has done so because going back comes with such a high penalty on her former wages," she says. "I don't think I researched opt-out penalties well enough before opting out."

Diane D.'s worries are warranted. As syndicated columnist Ellen Goodman wrote in her Mother's Day column in 2007: "Mothers are still treated as if they were a third gender in the workplace." That statement was inspired by a study, published in the *American Journal of Sociology,* in which Cornell University sociologist Shelley Correll proved there is a "motherhood penalty" in the job market. In her research, female job applicants who were assumed to have children, based on tidbits of information in a résumé (such as mention of being an officer in the PTA), were perceived as being less competent and less committed employees. Compared to men (with or without children) and childless women, female applicants with children were half as likely to be hired. If they did get the job, they were offered salaries lower than those given the men and nonmoms. To add insult to injury, the "moms" were also at greater risk for getting into trouble if they missed or were late for work. Faced with those obstacles, no wonder many women become too terrified to go back into the workforce, or can't find jobs worthy of their experience and expertise.

The assumption that a man or childless woman will automatically make for a better employee than a mother is, of course, unfair. Such "maternal profiling" is discriminatory and, frankly, stupid, for so many reasons. Here are two: More women than men go to college, so unless employers plan to hire men who are less educated and less qualified than their better educated and more qualified female applicants, the workforce needs to accept and accommodate the reality that women have brains and give birth to babies. (At this writing, men can't do the latter and, it can be argued, many behave as if they don't have much of the former.) Secondly, just because someone is available to spend countless hours at the office, or chooses to prioritize time at work over time with family, doesn't mean he's a great employee. One of the smartest, most efficient and personable bosses I ever worked for was a hardworking mother of two who wanted to have dinner with her children every night. While her male colleagues spent much of their workday socializing, chest-thumping, taking long lunches, and playing computer games, Suzie stayed focused on completing her daily to-do list so she could leave the office before six.

Notable "Comeback Moms"

Each of these women either quit, curtailed, or postponed a career in order to care for their children.

Meredith Viera left the television news program *60 Minutes* in 1991 when, as a mother of very young children, she was denied her request for a reduced schedule. Although Viera was never fully out of the workforce, family considerations lead her to take on less high-profile jobs. She regained her stature in 1997 as a co-host on ABC's *The View*, which she left in 2006 to replace Katie Couric on *Today*.

A Stay-at-Home mother of five who was actively involved in Democratic politics in Northern California, **Nancy Pelosi** ran for and won a congressional seat from the San Francisco area at age forty-seven (when her youngest child was finishing high school). In 2003, Pelosi became the House Democratic leader. Four years later, she was named Speaker of the House of Representatives, second in line to the U.S. presidency.

In 1998, **Brenda Barnes** quit a top job at PepsiCo in order to be home with her kids. In 2006, she was named CEO of the Sara Lee Corporation. She is, says *Forbes* magazine, "the most oft-cited example in the business press of a woman who ditched her corporate career to spend time with her family, only to regain corporate power."

To combat feelings of boredom and depression while at home caring for two children, in 1973 **Diane Rehm** began volunteering

▶

> at a Washington D.C. radio station. Several years of working at the station for free lead to a paid career in TV and radio broadcasting, most prominently on National Public Radio as host of *The Diane Rehm Show,* a nationally syndicated interview program about news and newsmakers.

Another barrier to a Stay-at-Home mom going out and getting a job can pop up closer to home, when a husband or partner, having gotten used to being cared for by a full-time homemaker, objects to her going back to work. Some may object directly in a caveman-like manner ("You can't go back to work!") or more maturely during a calm, reasoned discussion ("I understand why you want to get a job, but it would be easier for all of us if you didn't"). Other objectors are more subtle, such as by publicly supporting a wife's comeback efforts while passive-aggressively grumbling about them. And then there are the breadwinners who have, intentionally or not, demoralized the mothers of their children into believing they couldn't hack it in the working world, or that their return to it would undermine the happiness of the family.

In a way, you can't blame such guys. Anyone who lives with a fabulous woman (like any one of us) would want to hang on to the perks of having a wife and mother available to manage all things domestic. After all, don't you wish you had a wife? Or, if you're a kid, wouldn't you want a mom at your beck and call? My children accept and understand that my husband has to work and goes to work. But this past year, when I've had to tune out some of their demands or devote my nights and weekends to writing, I was accused of "always working." ("Yes," I countered, "I'm always working, as your and Daddy's personal assistant!") In the eyes of children, Dad's work makes sense, Mom's "nonmom" work doesn't.

Hiring discrimination and forlorn partners and children aside, some women are able to leave the workforce and move back into it as needed or desired. Economist Sylvia Ann Hewitt, PhD, founding president of the Center for Work-Life Policy, dubbed such "nonlinear careers" as a series of "off-ramps and on-ramps" that are used, primarily by women, in order to care for children, elderly parents, and life beyond the workplace. Toward the end of my career in New York I worked for an editor-in-chief who had moved in and out of the workforce, leaving increasingly higher-level positions and returning to top-level jobs as well, depending on her and her family's needs. Having adopted a child, she has newly off-ramped again—from a top post at the nation's largest magazine company. She's an incredible success story, even if she is an anomaly.

FORMER STAY-AT-HOME MOMS ARE GOOD FOR BUSINESS

According to a 2004 survey by the Center for Work-Life Policy, three-quarters of women who "off-ramp" out of the workforce to become Stay-at-Home moms, but later want to return to work, do find a job. However, the "on-ramp" they take to get there is typically not commensurate with their training and past level of achievement.

The hardest jobs to find are the kind that moms returning to the workforce need most, which are those allowing real part-time work (as opposed to thirty-five-hours-a-week "part-time" work) or flexible schedules. Least successful at finding suitable employment are women who have been out of the workforce for more than ten years, are looking to change fields, or who live in a different geographic area from where they formerly worked. On the plus side, in an article by work-family blogger Leslie Morgan Steiner, the editor of the anthology *Mommy Wars,* a managing director at Lehman Brothers is quoted as saying, "Well-educated Stay-at-Home moms have experience, judgment, and maturity that our companies need." That's reassuring to hear, although Steiner does note that returnees do suffer a salary penalty.

Survey respondent Krishna, a software marketing executive, has been home for more than four years with her two preschoolers. She's considering going back to work. "It does worry me somewhat," she says about how she'll be received. "But I've also heard a lot about how your time at home can have a positive outcome. You go back to working with a whole new perspective and, to some level, added confidence." (Note to Krishna: Apply to Lehman Brothers!)

I very much agree that the Stay-at-Home mom experience can turn a woman into a stronger employee. I truly believe I'm a better, more efficient, and more confident, writer, editor, manager, and overall person after six years as a Stay-at-Home mother than I was during my more than fifteen years on the job in New York. I believe my enhanced abilities in part stem from no longer having any tolerance for bullshit, bullying or incompetence. Busy moms don't have time for wasteful power plays, indecisiveness and dilly-dallying.

Motherhood, and especially Stay-at-Home motherhood, is a great training ground for working productively under chaotic, rushed circumstances. So much about being a successful Stay-at-Home mom runs contrary to the stereotype that an employer takes a risk when hiring a woman with children. Just as many people in the workforce are, to be blunt, idiots, many Stay-at-Home mothers are superb managers, and those with career-oriented backgrounds and education are typically superconscientious. It's as inaccurate to assume a person is intelligent and exceptionally competent because he or she is in the workforce and has an impressive title as it is to assume dimwittedness for someone who's not. Stay-at-Home mothers are capable women with valuable, marketable skills. The title of journalist Ann Crittenden's 2004 book says it all: *If You've Raised Kids, You Can Manage Anything.*

Rachel, a graphic designer now at home in Manhattan with her three children, is an example of Stay-at-Home mom efficiency and confidence. "I do small design projects here and there, and it's enormously restorative," she says. "Clients and their immediate issues create little to no stress for me now. I have found that when I agree to take on a project, I am extremely organized and proficient in my process. I just don't have time to dawdle."

REDEFINING WORK

Most of the survey respondents who said they want to go back to work someday were also very clear about wanting to work in a *different* way than they had before having children. Needing family-friendly schedules, they either have chosen—or will choose—

to make their comeback via lower-level positions that enable them to work without the demands of a true rat-race job.

"Financially, I should go back in September, when my son goes to kindergarten," says Erin Z., a former Wall Street trader. "But mentally, I don't know if I'm ready to go to an office. I like being here for my kids. Ideally, I want to find something from home, but I have been researching that angle for months, and it seems unlikely. I will definitely not go back into finance. I would like to work for a nonprofit."

Management, executive-level, and fast-paced in-the-moment jobs often require face time, long hours, and extensive interaction with staff and supervisors, and as such are not so easily done part-time or offsite. But some jobs and careers are more mom-friendly than others, because the hours are regular, the work can be done alone or from home, and because the responsibilities lend themselves more readily to job shares, part-time, or even extremely part-time work.

Interestingly, three lucrative fields that can be mom-friendly are medicine, dentistry, and law. I know several female dentists and physicians who worked part-time, even one or two days a week, when their kids were small. I've also met female attorneys who go into an office or work from home for a set number of hours, creating and reviewing legal documents such as briefs, contracts, wills, depositions, or other court filings. Such limited working hours bring in a significantly reduced income and prohibit, for the moment, having a high-powered, high-profile career or practice. (Hence no front-page trials or history-making surgeries.) But these women keep their licenses valid, their skills current, their résumés updated, and their contacts fresh in anticipation of someday returning to the full-time workforce.

My orthodontist worked one day a week in someone else's office when her three children were young. With her kids now in high school and college, she leads a highly successful, female-run office that operates on a four-day work week. Stacey, a full-time Stay-at-Home mom for nine years, anticipates an easy return to the nursing career she had put on hold. "I have a great education and a flexible career choice, so problems about reentering the workforce don't concern me at all," she says.

Survey respondent Debbie, a mother of three, finds that substitute teaching has provided her with a manageable way of transitioning back into the workforce. "I only applied to my children's school district for now, so I can be close to where they are," says Debbie. "I feel that everything worked out great: I taught for a while before I had children, then I stayed home with them while they were young, and now that they're all in school, it's the right time for me to return to work. I plan on living to about ninety, so having taken nine years off from work to have children is just a drop in the bucket."

Other women plan to use their comeback to make a career change. Lisa, an MBA and former project manager, says "I would like to start my own company and be my own boss." After more than a decade at home raising three girls, Nancy, once an analyst at the Federal Reserve, is pursuing a master's degree in social work. "I think after getting my MSW I should be able to combine my knowledge of statistics and math with social work research," she says.

"I get excited thinking about it. I also think it's good for my daughters to see that their mom can start a new career doing something she loves to do."

Robin, who before having children served in the U.S. Air Force and later worked as an analyst with the Department of Defense, looks to her own mom for inspiration in being able to have a long career after Stay-at-Home motherhood. "My mother started working when I was in high school, but she was still there when we came home from school," recalls Robin. "Those afternoons are some of my favorite childhood memories. My mother has been working in the same place now for about twenty years."

For Dixie, whose two now-young-adult children are living away from home, the post hands-on mom years are a time of endless possibilities. "The things I want to do now don't involve a nine-to-five job," she says. "I hope I'll never need a job. I'd love to do things I haven't done yet, and to do them for fun: open an antiques shop, get a master's in American decorative arts, join the Jefferson Society, help raise grandchildren, learn to speak Italian."

ONE HOT MAMA

Sometimes a comeback is a crowning achievement.

A week after I moved to Maryland, my doorbell rang. It was late morning. I had just succeeded in taking a shower, which was hard to do in an unpacked house while home alone with a four-year-old and seven-month-old twins. I had even managed to get dressed. With the twins in my arms, I opened the front door.

There, towering above me, was a buxom blonde straight out of the St. Pauli Girl beer ads. She was holding a painted mailbox (a gift for me) and cheering, "Welcome to the neighborhood! I'm Ginny Meerman. I live across the street."

Now I have long blonde hair, somewhat similar to Ginny's, but during this encounter, my hair was sopping wet and wrapped in a drooping towel. At that moment, I was also barefoot, which exposed me at my true 5'2" self. Ginny, who is 5'8", had on sandals with three-inch-high wedges. She was wearing micromini white shorts and a cleavage-boosting white shirt with an elastic neckline (hence the St. Pauli Girl beer-wench imagery). Diamond studs flashed from her ears, and a big rock twinkled on her left hand. To make matters worse, the living Barbie doll in my doorway was my age (thirty-eight at the time) and a mother of *four!* I felt like such a schlump.

But beneath Ginny's perfectly bouncy mane of blonde hair is a sharp mind. And behind those bursting boobs is a huge heart. As we became friends, I learned that when Ginny was seventeen, she was a new high school grad about to give birth to her first child. Within four years she was a divorced, homeless mother of two who worked at a nursing home while her toddlers attended daycare. At night, the family of three slept in her car. By the time I met Ginny, she had been married for many years to a man she adores: He owns a successful business, and she spent most of her twenties and thirties at home with four children—her first two, and two boys they had together.

When Ginny appeared at my front door, she was at the tail-end of her hands-on childrearing. With older children, she had time to keep her house and yard in immaculate condition. She ran neighborhood committees and, by her own admission, shopped a lot.

Having herself grown up in an abusive home, and having experienced great poverty, Ginny worked tirelessly as a volunteer fundraiser for a food pantry benefiting poor families, as well as a volunteer Court Appointed Special Advocate (CASA) working on behalf of abused and neglected children who need representation in family court. It was from our attendance at a CASA benefit that Ginny happened upon her post Stay-at-Home mom career.

Seated at our table that night was a similarly stunning blonde, who was introduced to us as Mrs. Annapolis. Turns out, there is a huge beauty pageant circuit specializing in married women.

I whispered to Ginny, "You could be Mrs. Annapolis."

"Absolutely, *if* I lived in Annapolis," she answered. "But I *can* be Mrs. Maryland."

Months after that evening, I jokingly sent Ginny a newspaper clipping about a pageant seeking married contestants. She competed in that pageant, coming in third. She was quickly invited to participate in another pageant, and then others, until she was ultimately crowned Mrs. Maryland 2007.

Ginny has used her beauty-queen platform and the exposure it brings to accelerate her work as a fundraiser, activist, and spokesperson for various aid organizations, advocacy groups, and disease-research foundations. She also started a national, nonprofit organization called HopeLink, which works to connect people in crisis to resources that can help. Although Ginny doesn't have a paid job, she is an active member of the local Rotary, a social-service club whose members are typically business owners. This woman, who never got to go to college, who worked but never had a professional career, who spent her young adulthood as a financially struggling parent, is now, having raised four children, enjoying an active mid-life career as an influential fundraiser and advocate. True, Ginny's husband has an income that allows her to be extremely charitable with her time and money and not have to work for pay, but she's a lively example of one of the many positive paths a woman can take after having had a career as a Stay-at-Home mom.

As Ginny says, "I became a beauty queen at age forty-one. How amazing is that!" (And the following year, she became a grandmother.)

KEEPING YOUR BIG TOE IN THE DOOR

You may already know that, someday, you'll return to the workforce. Or perhaps you're so sleep deprived right now you can't even think beyond the next hour. Either way, it's important to not shut the doors or burn the bridges behind you.

Tory Johnson is the head of Women for Hire, a company that plans high-level recruiting events for women. She's also a contributor to television's *Good Morning America*, on which she said to Stay-at-Home moms hoping to someday get back into the workforce: "You have to keep your big toe in the professional arena, even when you're home with your kids." Following are ways to do just that:

Volunteer strategically: Your volunteer work can be listed on your résumé if it shows that you made a commitment to a significant task and played an important role in its success. So instead of (or in addition to) selling cupcakes at the school fair, become the PTO president. (Remember Andrea in "Money Matters"? Her years of high-level volunteer work filled a résumé that landed her a much-need post-divorce job.) As discussed in Chapter Eleven—"Get Me Out of Here!"—many mom-filled volunteer positions are major undertakings for which people in the business world are well paid. Stay-at-Home women are the backbone of fundraising auctions, not-for-profit boards, and event committees. Volunteers with professional skills are needed to write newsletters, manage children's sports leagues, keep the books for social-service clubs. (Come to think of it, I was the secretary/treasurer of a 900-household homeowner's association with more than a million dollars in annual revenues and expenditures. I should put that on my résumé!)

Stay in touch with your working friends: Stay-at-Home moms tend to hang out with other Stay-at-Home moms, which as we all know is essential to one's domestic survival. But when it comes to getting back into the workforce, it's your former colleagues and employed friends who will know about jobs and can help you make new connections. Says survey respondent Pilar, who used to work in sales: "I'm staying in touch with former colleagues, not only because I always had a good relationship with them, but because they'll be my references for a future job."

Keep current: You should absolutely keep your skills and, if applicable, licenses current. But during that *Good Morning America* segment advising Stay-at-Home moms, Johnson instructed women to also, "Do one thing a week to keep updated with the trends in your field." This can involve subscribing to an industry journal, or checking a particular website. It's important to have an awareness of who the current players are in your field and, said Johnson, occasionally "nourish the professional side of your brain." I'll add that another keeping-current tactic is to be familiar with new technology and terminology. For instance, you don't need to have a Blackberry or an iPhone to know what one is. You don't have to use MySpace or YouTube to know what both are about. You don't have to write a blog or text message your BFF (Best Friend Forever) to be familiar with the lingo.

MOTHERHOOD AS A CAREER

For some women, motherhood and homemaking is both a new and future career, one that won't end just because she has survived the Stay-at-Home, little-kid years. Running a home, caring for a family, and managing the upkeep of a house is a *job*, and an important one at that. And after several years of being hands-on with babies and toddlers who need *everything* done for them, it can be so nice to do the work of a Stay-at-Home mom without having to do everything at once. (Example: Pay bills while you cook dinner, wipe up after a toddler, fold laundry, and carry a baby.) It can be very satisfying to work at a job that involves children with whom you can have conversations, do projects, and easily go on outings. It can be very fulfilling to be able to watch over and guide a young person as he or she grows into an independent, productive adult. Not that the work will be a cake walk. Needy babies become somewhat independent children who become (good, bad, or both) teenagers!

"My job isn't over just because my children are school age," says Sandra about having a twelve- and ten-year-old (the elder of whom she homeschools). "It's very apparent I'm going to need to be the most available during the teenage years. My children are real people with real interests, independent of me signing them up for something I choose for them. Because they can't drive themselves, I'm indispensable to them pursuing their interests, to an extent they would not be able to do if there were no one to drive them in different directions at what seems to be the same time."

Like many moms currently home with small children, Heather fantasizes about the freedom of having time to herself during the day. "I enjoy staying home," she says. "So I can imagine how much better it will be when the kids are in elementary school and I can run errands and clean the house while they're at school, and then have time to just be with them and help them with homework when they come home."

A few years ago, after seven years of at-home parenting, all three of Nora's children were finally in school full day. And Nora, a former mortgage banker, quickly grew tired of people asking when she would return to work. She says she won't, unless a time comes that she has to for financial reasons. The only slight negative she sees in her decision is that her children don't know her as anything other than a Stay-at-Home mom, and because of that, they don't fully understand that women can go to work and earn money just like dads do. "They have a hard time accepting that I once had a paid career, or actually ever could," she explains.

Although she's chosen not to "get a job," Nora absolutely considers motherhood her career and work. "I look at the six hours a day my kids are at school as my catch-up time for the seven years I didn't have *any* time to myself," she told me. "My workday now starts when my children get home from school and need my help with homework and getting to and from sports and activities. Besides, in many ways, it's just as important for me to be home with them now, and later when they're teenagers, as it was when they were babies."

On Nora's last point, many parents strongly agree. In our fast-paced, and at times more dangerous society, lots of couples don't feel it's judicious for both parents to be in the full-time workforce until the last of the kids has left for a college. As every generation laments, accurately or not, life just isn't like it used to be. Back in the 1970s, my siblings and I walked to and from school by ourselves or with the kids on our street. When my divorced mother went back to work by necessity, the three of us, who ranged in age from high school down to elementary school, unlocked the house with our own keys and remained unattended until her dinnertime return.

Parents today don't have that same confidence (or naivete) about the safety and welfare of unsupervised children. Fearful of sexual predators roaming the streets and the Internet, many parents don't trust leaving their children to fend for themselves. Safety concerns, the potential for teens to get involved in really bad things, and—due to suburban sprawl—the need to have a car to get around, are reasons some women remain home even when their children are in school full time. In fact, concerns about the trouble that can find or be found by an older child or teenager lead many employed parents to keep paying for a nanny, or at least an afternoon caregiver, long after their kids need constant babysitting.

While most Stay-at-Home women consider parenting to be a *more than* full-time job, Diane D., who is quoted earlier in this chapter, says, quite boldly: "Mothering is a part-time job." Although she left a lucrative Silicon Valley career to stay home with her first born, Diane D. still devotes three hours every morning to futures trading on her personal accounts. Now pregnant, she plans to hire a full-time nanny when her second arrives in order to meet the demands of two children while continuing her investment efforts. When I asked Diane D. to explain how mothering can be a part-time job for a woman who *doesn't* have a nanny, she responded: "Yes, I can imagine my view is contrary from most, but what it might be is just a longer-term view of my role as a parent. For me, part-time refers to the fact that while children are in preschool and school, they are being cared for by other adults. Since parents aren't parenting during that time, they have time to do other things. If I, as a person and a mother, haven't done anything to develop myself further, when my children leave the nest, I will have become, hopefully, a very good parent, perhaps a good housekeeper, but I will most likely have fallen back in areas of my career, my education, the bigger things in life."

Although Diane D. makes some good points (i.e., you need to do for yourself as well as for your kids), very few Stay-at-Home moms—or, for that matter, very few people—can afford a full-time nanny, and very few can earn a significant income while working from home just a few hours a day. Moms who have a child in pre-school for less than three hours a day, three days a week, don't have enough time to get involved in significant non-parenting or non-housekeeping pursuits. (Especially if they also have younger children to care for.) Even when children are in school all day, few women are lucky enough to be able to find work that allows the flexibility to be home when the kids are home.

Anne, another highly educated Northern California mom with a toddler at home and babe on the way, is also thinking about the future, but she has come to a slightly different conclusion from Diane D's. "I have a dream of a career outside the home, but I also have a dream of a well-cared-for family and home and children," explains Anne. "This dream of a happy hearth does not go away when the kids go to school. Schoolchildren do not suddenly stop needing care and attention."

In thinking about my own past, present, and future, I often wonder how I can help my two daughters and my son prepare for a life in which they can pursue a career and care for a family without giving short shrift to either. The traditional answer has been: "Get a wife." I'm hopeful their generation will have a better solution.

Proud Mamas:
Taking Pride in What We Do

I n the last chapter, we talked about what our futures may or may not hold. But I'm guessing that if you're reading this book, you are deep in the trenches of Stay-at-Home motherhood, or you're jumping in, or you're *thinking* about whether or not to jump in. One way of dealing with any conflicting desires—"I want to be home with my kids" *and* "I want a paid job"—is to look at your situation in a "best of both worlds" capacity. And also to tell yourself, *I can have it all* (whatever that means), *just not all at the same time.*

So, to use another cliché, instead of looking at how your glass is half empty ("I don't earn a paycheck," "I just take care of kids"), you can, and should, look at how full the glass is: "I don't *have* to earn a paycheck, and I *get* to take care of my kids." It's important, and entirely deserved, to take pride in the job you do. And instead of feeling that the world is passing you by, as I know for sure I have at times, it's essential to look at how important you are to the immediate world in which you live.

When an employed person leaves a job, he or she is replaced (and sometimes not even missed very much). If you or I were to disappear or walk out on our job, it's likely our entire household would fall apart—due to both heartache and to not knowing how to manage the important minutiae of family life. It's important to take a step back and look at Stay-at-Home motherhood as being a position of strength rather than weakness.

"At times I feel very powerful, because when it comes right down to it, I control the show here," says Ginny, whose story we learned in the previous chapter. "If not for me, there would be no clean clothes, no clean toilets, no groceries in the cupboards, and no dinner on the table. I pay the bills each month, so I'm also in control of the household finances."

It's also worth remembering that many people in the paid workforce don't receive the praise or compensation they deserve. In fact, for many if not most people, work is work, and not an exciting, esteem-building, or particularly rewarding or enjoyable way to spend the day. Conversely, a Stay-at-Home mom literally experiences the fruits of her labor. Many a Stay-at-Home mom receives the sincere praise and gratitude of her spouse: "My husband is so supportive and appreciates what I do," says Deb, a former pediatric physical therapist with three children. "He often admits that he could never be a Stay-at-Home dad and that he admires my work." A Stay-at-Home mom can also be showered with "all the hugs and kisses any human being has a right to enjoy," as mother of two Gerri notes in this book's opening chapter.

During my first few years as a Stay-at-Home mom, I felt guilty about having left my career. I felt bad for letting down the bosses and colleagues who had invested in me over the years. I felt bad for not being able to keep up the juggling act. I felt bad for the added pressure and responsibility I had placed on my husband by making him the sole breadwinner, although it was a role he was glad to take. Choosing home over work is often viewed as a cop-out, as a huge step backward into drudgery and dependency.

More recently, I've come to realize that leaving my career to care for my kids was an enormous gift to my husband and our children. While I'm lucky we can afford for me to stay home, they are also lucky that I chose to take on the job. I had other options, such as not having children, or keeping my career going by hiring a live-in nanny and having a commuter marriage. I've also come to realize that any man who wants children, and who has a partner who puts aside other options to be the full-time caregiver of his children, should be immensely grateful.

Looking at my situation this way has made me realize I'm not a burden. I'm an enormous benefit. Without me, my husband couldn't have the career he has and the children and family life he very much wanted. The path I originally imagined and pursued for myself as a young woman is very different than the one I'm on today. I love my husband and our children and what we have together, but I did put ambitions and a part of myself aside for us to have what we have.

Lyn, a former lawyer, did the same for her husband and three children. She's glad she did, and she says her friendships with women who didn't have comparable options have gone "a long way to change my attitude about my life as a Stay-at-Home mom. Knowing women who have to work makes me understand how fortunate we all are in my family that I am willing and able to stay home."

Granted, the good fortune can land in many ways. There are Stay-at-Home women who are lucky to have found a spouse to support them and their dream to be at-home moms. There are women who are fortunate to be Stay-at-Home moms because they aren't particularly well suited to being in the workforce, or who expect to be financed and pampered. (Mind you, there are men like this too, guys who marry rich or whose dads pull strings to get them into good colleges or jobs, or bankroll their businesses.) Every occupation includes a mix of skilled professionals and folks who should be looking for a different career path. And like in any occupation, within motherhood there are women who are very good at some aspects of the job, but weak in other areas. While one woman may bring great organizational skills to the job of Stay-at-Home mom, another seemingly scatterbrained gal can be equipped with an amazing capacity to nurture and love.

Kanoko, who before having her son was a student and self-described "Stay-at-Home wife," reports "I've never worked in my life." However, she takes great pride in being the hands-on caregiver of her child. "I remind myself that not many people can do what I do," she says.

SEEING THE BIG PICTURE

One challenge about being a Stay-at-Home mom can be the lack of positive feedback, but even on the days I feel as if I'm nothing more than a personal assistant and household domestic, the praise is there when I open my eyes enough to see it. My husband always thanks me for making dinner. Despite our constant companionship, my daughters don't tire of me; one invites me to cuddle every evening, and the other saves me a seat next to her at meals. My son wants to spend time with me and tell me about events at school and things he learned. The people I now work for more than full time don't pay me, or effusively compliment my efforts, but they love me and want to be with me. I'm sure the people in your home feel the same way about you. That's something to be proud of.

Although I know my husband is glad that I'm home with our children, I can't expect the kids to fully understand the work-family issues women struggle with, and as such be thankful to have a mom who's at home instead of a mom who goes to a job. While I suspect my children are glad to have the former, I don't know if they'll ever look back with gratitude for my choice. However, I do get some motivation from gracious comments made to me by other people about their own moms. When I notified the staff at *People* about my resignation, and my need to be home and more available to my then three-year-old son, a young writer sent me an email describing how thankful she was to have had her own mom at home when she was growing up. "I know my mother gave up a lot to be a Stay-at-Home mom," this twentysomething gal told me. "Someday your son will appreciate what you're doing for him."

My other twentysomething cheerleader is a young man named Nanda, who is a midshipman at the U.S. Naval Academy. As my husband and I live near Annapolis, we volunteered to be a Naval Academy "sponsor family," which essentially means we are a home away from home, a refuge from the rigors of military life, for the midshipmen assigned to us. (Five, thus far.) While discussing this book with Nanda, he talked about how his own mom, who has a degree in economics, left her information technology career at Intel because he and his sister hated attending daycare. ("We were the first ones there and the last to leave," he recalled.) When her children were in high school, Nanda's mother began studying to become a teacher. Today, she teaches second grade, and Nanda speaks with both love and gratitude about her choice to stay home when he was little. I'd be thrilled for my own son to someday speak the same way about me.

DISPATCHES FROM THE FRONTLINES

Part of being proud of the job you do is not letting other people's misconceptions, assumptions, or attitudes undermine you. Although full-time, long-term Stay-at-Home motherhood was once the norm rather than the exception, we're fortunate to live in a time when women can make many different choices about their lives. Because of that, it can sometimes feel as if everyone and her brother has an opinion about motherhood. It's good to know how to handle the backhanded compliment or (intentional or not) put-down.

Staying home is not boring: The following story was related to me by a Stay-at-Home mom friend about a mutual acquaintance, whom we'll call Paula. My friend was at a gathering in which Paula reported that her sister was considering quitting her job to stay home with her kids.

"I said to her, 'Don't do it!'" declared Paula. "I told her she's too smart for that. She'll be bored out of her skull." The Stay-at-Home mom to whom Paula was speaking smiled politely so as not to make a scene. But she vowed to give Paula what for if she ever told that story again. Here was an employed mom, who had never stayed home to care for her children, telling a woman who was staying home that, in essence, women who are home full time as hands-on moms are a bit simpler than other women, perhaps lazy, and can be satisfied with the less intellectual pursuits of childrearing and a life of spousal dependence. Of course we experience boredom staying home, as people do in any job. But by Paula's reasoning, staying home to care for children is the province of dumb women.

I've never been able to figure out if Paula herself is just dumb, and she has no idea that what she said is insulting, or whether she knew exactly what she was doing, and made such pointed statements (that wasn't the only one) in order to feel better about her own choices. I tend to think she's just ignorant about anything she hasn't experienced herself.

Survey respondent Sandra, a former attorney, had a Paula-like experience with a former colleague. "She asked me if I was bored at home with kids," recalls Sandra. "I finessed the question. While I didn't point out that I had often been bored in meetings with her and people from, say, the insurance industry, I did explain how I presided over meals with kids between the ages of four and six, discussing things like how infinity is not actually a number, but rather a concept—and they all understood it. Those kids were a lot smarter than a good number of the people at the meetings I used to go to. So who's bored?"

If you find yourself in a tug-of-war with an oh-so-subtle critic, it can be useful to follow the lead of Jennifer, who, with an infant son, is new to both motherhood and staying home. "There isn't just one way to be a good mother," she wrote in her survey questionnaire.

"We're the best mothers when we are most fulfilled. If we don't give to ourselves, we will have nothing to give to our children. For me, I am most fulfilled being at home. But I have friends who are most fulfilled working during the week and being at home at night and on weekends. And they are wonderful mothers. I think their children would suffer if these women *didn't* work, because the moms would start to resent the children on some level and be unhappy more days than not. We don't all have to do the same thing." Tell the know-it-all *that*.

Staying home doesn't make kids needy: Diane A. was at a children's birthday party when she got into a conversation with a guest. While they were talking, the woman boldly declared, "You must be a Stay-at-Home mom, because your daughter is so clingy." *Whoa!* The same can be said of the clinginess exhibited by the offspring of employed moms. Children are clingy whether they've been with their moms all day or not. The arguments for and against parental attention, and how much is too little or too much, can make you dizzy: "Children with Stay-at-Home moms who do everything for them can't do anything for themselves." "Children left in daycare or with sitters are more aggressive because they're always competing for attention and love." "Moms who are always available to their children raise spoiled kids who never grow up." "Parents who work compensate for their absence by indulging their children, which leads to spoiled, entitled, and materialistic kids."

The arguments are both on target and way off base, depending on the parenting involved. Yes, children of Stay-at-Home moms can become unappreciative and dependent upon mom doing everything, but so can children who are raised in a two-income household with lots of money and hired help. After all, a family that hires out for *everything*—housekeeping, yard maintenance, tutoring, home repair, childcare—doesn't provide a child with do-it-yourself skills.

"I do sometimes think that by always being there for my kids, I discouraged their independence and resourcefulness," says Dixie, whose two twentysomething children still aren't totally out and on their own. Raising needy kids is something I worry about, as does Liz R., who is home caring for three boys. "I often wonder if I am coddling my children by trying to make their day and routine easier," she says. "Because if I was working, I don't see how I would be able to have the 'stuff' they need taken care of and worked out. There are so many phone calls and scheduling and dropping off and picking up of things for them."

But as parents, it's our job to train our children to survive on their own. And Stay-at-Home moms can and do teach their children to fend for themselves. Instead of mom feeding the dog, a child can have that assignment on his job chart. When my husband and I refuse to get out of bed at six o'clock in the morning on a Saturday, our three children fend for themselves until we're up and moving. My son, who's in fourth grade, will make himself oatmeal or even a scrambled egg in the microwave. The twins can serve themselves cereal and milk. It's a daily battle, but I work very hard at getting my kids to be responsible for themselves, their stuff and their spaces.

Sandra, who has two preteens, reinforced the "Mom is *not* a maid" lesson while she was busy answering the questionnaire for this book.

"I have to work constantly at getting people in my household to take responsibility for themselves," Sandra wrote. "Right this instant is an example. I'm typing, and my twelve-year-old just came in and told me that he's hungry. 'That's nice,' I said. This is a child who has cooked dinner for the family, but he would be perfectly happy for me to drop what I'm doing right now to make him a sandwich. I would never let someone push me around like that in an office, so I'm not going to let it happen here. You know, now that he's in the kitchen, I'm going to ask him to bring me a glass of water!"

The bottom line is, children will grow up to be incompetent and entitled if that's what they see in the adults around them, or if they're so spoiled and catered to that they have little choice but to become incompetent and entitled. Whether a mom works outside the home or not is only one influence, and perhaps not the most important one.

You can take the heat: It can be hard to spend a day home alone with one child, or many. But you can do it. You do it every day. Some parents actually don't spend much time solely in charge of their kids. And there are parents who don't know *how* to spend time solely in charge of their kids. "I know that it's not a choice for some," says survey respondent Laura, a mother of two. "But I think staying home is a great sacrifice, and some people aren't willing to make the sacrifices needed."

Erin Z., a former Wall Street trader, makes a similar observation: "Some women work because they have to, and some work because they want to. I used to think the latter were just self-centered and greedy, but I've realized that many women really can't handle caring for their kids."

Saying as much is an observation, not necessarily a judgment. It's hard to spend a day caring for children, and doing so well is not an innate, nor gender-specific, skill. Yet women are always assumed to either have the necessary skills or the ability to develop them. Men are still allowed to be all thumbs when it comes to caring for their kids. (Imagine a mother admitting to not knowing how to change a diaper.) In many ways, women who work outside the home are just following the accepted male model of parenting: Have the baby, provide for the baby, love the baby, hand the baby to someone else to care for on a daily basis.

Although women are often criticized for stepping into "men's shoes," a father who can actually care for his children on his own for an entire day is practically awarded a blue ribbon. Last year, when I went away for two nights with my book group, my husband took our three kids to a fall festival—and got his picture in the paper! People we know who saw the newspaper photograph of Brian and the kids (both human and goat, as they were at the petting zoo exhibit) were mightily impressed that he took three children out on his own and cared for them alone while I was away. Countless women care for children by themselves and go out on their own everyday with multiple kids in tow. We just don't get a pat on the back for it, and certainly not our picture in the newspaper.

Brian was applauded for his weekend domesticity, which shouldn't be such a surprising sight for people that it warrants the praise it did. Parents should be at ease caring for their children. It is odd, and even sad, to see men or women who are so uncomfortable being with their own kids that they'll do whatever they can to avoid any stints of solo hands-on parenting. And it can be irritating to be around people whose family time always has to involve other families, because the parents are terrified of having any extended time alone with their children.

It is an accomplishment to be able to navigate a child (or children) through a single day, and then weeks and months and years. Women who stay at home to care for and raise their children need to take pride in themselves, even if society at large occasionally doesn't. As Erin Z. points out: "Some women just aren't cut out for staying at home. It's a very tough business, and only the strong survive."

OUR HOPES FOR OUR DAUGHTERS

Knowing what we know now, how would we advise our daughters (real or potential) about balancing or choosing between work and family? Many women who answered *The Guide*'s survey talked about making smart choices and having options.

"I hope my daughters pick occupations that provide more part-time opportunities than my field did," says Diane A., who was a media supervisor at an advertising agency. Adds Mary, a corporate brand manager, "I would advise my daughter to do something flexible so she can work part time, like physical therapy or consulting."

Erin Z., who worked on Wall Street, makes a similar point. "I'm very envious of women who have careers that allow them to work part time, or from home, or take a leave," she says. "My industry was very male driven and structured, with no flexibility. I was the only woman on my trading desk, and I got a lot of flack about phone calls from my nanny, or for having to take my daughter to the doctor, or for staying home when she was sick. I would advise my daughter to plan for a time when she can be flexible about what her career is." Career specifics aside, Sarah B. says, "I hope that when my daughter is in a position to choose whether or not she will stay home with her children, she will find support and encouragement from other women."

Molly, who has a master's degree and worked as a corporate project manager, says she'd advise her daughter to do as she did. "I would tell her to put herself first for a while and reach some professional and personal goals before marriage and children. I think this path has made me a better parent, and it has made me a more confident person outside of motherhood. I don't pine for another life wondering if I could have done XYZ at work. There will be many more years to work outside the home once my kids are grown."

Do we want our daughters to be Stay-at-Home moms? That's a question Andrea had to consider even before answering *The Guide*'s survey. "The funny thing is, my daughter tells me she wants to be a mom when she grows up," says Andrea. "My knee-jerk reaction is, 'Why are you selling yourself so short?' And yet I have tremendous pride in the job I've done. What do you suppose that means?"

I'll answer my own question, in case my daughters ever choose to read this book. My advice to my girls would be to do as I did, up to a point.

I would absolutely recommend that they get their degrees, travel the world, pursue their careers, and experience success. My shortsightedness was that as a young woman, I never believed I'd ever actually get married and have children. Once I did envision children in my future, I never thought I'd stay home with them full time. Because I didn't perceive myself in the role, I didn't plan as well as I could have.

After several years of working at Time Inc., I was asked to choose between the paths of becoming an editor or a writer. I told my boss I wanted to do both. When he said I had to pick one or the other, I chose editor. I liked the idea of office-based, managerial-level work, and I like editing. (You skip that "writer's block" step in the process.) However, being a writer is often more suitable for part-time or work-from-home employment. While, thanks to this book (and more recent work from home technology), I am now writing as well as editing, if I had chosen the writer route more than a decade ago, I might not have had to disappear from the workforce for as many years as I did. For me, being a top-level editor at a major magazine was not conducive to having a family-flexible career. I hope my daughters never have to leave the workforce entirely, unless they absolutely want to, in order to be a mom.

My other two bits of advice for my daughters, and all girls: First, if you have children, try to live near where you might work. When I moved to the suburbs, one of my bosses, a woman with two children, explained that she and her husband stayed in a Manhattan rental because she didn't want to work far away from her children. In an emergency, she could be home in fifteen minutes. On a typical day, I needed more than an hour to get back to my house from work. On 9/11, countless commuting parents like me couldn't get out of Manhattan and home to their children. By chance, I had taken that day off, but my long commute is one of the reasons I chose to leave my job. My second bit of wisdom: When you're earning money, save as much as you can, since your future may include years of earning little or no income. Related to that point, always be in charge of your money and, ideally, your household's finances. Both the working world and husbands can be unpredictable. You can be a Stay-at-Home mom, or variation thereof, without becoming a powerless, dependent person.

Hmm. This section has got me thinking. Perhaps *The Stay-at-Home Survival Guide* should be given to young women long before they even consider having children. Maybe I'll give each of my girls an autographed (strategically censored) copy of *The Guide* on their sixteenth birthdays. ("Uhh, gee. Thanks a lot, Mom.") They might not appreciate the gift right then, but someday they will.

Women who have chosen to or, for myriad reasons, been required to leave the workforce to raise their kids need to keep the following realities in mind.

BEING A MOTHER IS HARD WORK

It's not a sign of failure or weakness when you don't enjoy the job you have to do. The idealized version of motherhood tells you that children are blessings, nothing is more pure than a mother's love, that motherhood is instinctual . . .

But you know what? Every mother has times when she is so tired, so overwhelmed, so desperate for freedom that she feels somewhat less than *blessed* to be surrounded by little beings every minute of the day. When this happens, a woman (and any short-sighted folks around her) may begin to question her worthiness as a mother: *A good mother wouldn't want to get away from her children. A good mother would enjoy doing puzzles for hours on end with her three-year-old. A good mother would love pushing her toddler on a park swing everyday. A good mother is constantly enthralled by her children.* That mom sure would be a good mother. In fact, she'd be a great mother. But by such standards of perfection, I'd hazard to say that there are no great mothers. We're good, perhaps even great—but no one is *that* great.

WE NEED TO STOP ROMANTICIZING MOTHERHOOD

And for that matter marriage. Being a spouse is much more important than being a bride or a groom, but we focus our energy on the wedding. Being a parent is so much more important than the excitement of pregnancy and the arrival of a newborn, but many young women fixate on the sugarcoated fantasy of having a baby to cuddle and dress up. Lately, many young men seem more interested in siring a child (or many) than *fathering* one.

As the oldest of three children, I had to help care for my siblings. I was also a regular babysitter for my neighbor's kids. Both experiences contributed to my having my first child at age thirty-three, even though my husband and I have been together since I was nineteen and he was twenty. Since my preteen years, I'd been fully aware of the demands and sacrifices involved in caring for children. The only surprise I experienced when my son was born was the extent to which I fell totally in love with him. But I have friends, female and male, who never cared for a baby until they held their own and who so idealized parenthood that they were caught off guard when the real thing arrived. As a result, some limited themselves to having one child, or reduced their dream family of four or five kids to just two.

YOU'RE A PERSON WHO IS ALSO A MOTHER

Men go through life as the men they are, whether or not they have children. Men with children aren't questioned for working outside the home, or for having lives and interests separate from their roles as fathers. Women, regrettably, are still judged by their childbearing. Women who don't have children are often considered curiosities. Those of us who do become moms are subject to all sorts of nattering—from family, friends, neighbors, employers, clergy, politicians, perfect strangers—about what's best for us and for our children, about whether or not we're good mothers.

All women with children need to feel secure in the choices they've made, for themselves and their families. Employed moms aren't bad moms. And Stay-at-Home moms needn't be burdened by pundits who label them sell-outs for leaving the workforce. Nor should we be so exalted as mothers that we're expected to forfeit every ounce of ourselves for our young.

CHILDREN ARE LITTLE FOR A VERY SHORT TIME

With her three children now grown, Pulitzer Prize–winning writer Anna Quindlen looked back on her life as a parent for a 2007 Mother's Day column in *Newsweek* and captured a truism that should be heard by all parents. Quindlen writes:

> The biggest mistake I made is the one that most of us make while doing this. I did not live in the moment enough. This is particularly clear now that the moment is gone, captured only in photographs. There is one picture of the three of them, sitting in the grass on a quilt in the shadow of the swing set on a summer day, ages 6, 4 and 1. And I wish I could remember what we ate, and what we talked about, and how they sounded, and how they looked when they slept that night. I wish I had not been in such a hurry to get

on to the next thing: dinner, bath, book, bed. I wish I had treasured the doing a little more and the getting it done a little less.

Now that this book is finished, and there will be a little less I have to get done, I will work at treasuring more of the doing. I hope you survived reading *The Stay-at-Home Survival Guide,* and that you found it helpful and enjoyable. (By the way, if it took you years to finish the book because it's long and you have no time to read, congratulations on raising your children to adulthood!) Seriously, thank you for devoting some of your precious time to flipping through these pages. I appreciate it. If you'd like to get in touch with me, I can be reached at sah_survivalguide@yahoo.com or via the book's website, www.stayathomesurvivalguide.com.

—*Melissa Stanton*

Final Words of Wisdom from the Experts

"The key to being a successful Stay-at-Home mom is to find friends who are experiencing similar things that you are, and who make a point to hang out together. Find a little time to yourself (to exercise, read, take up a hobby), and don't get so bogged down in domestic chores that you forget to have fun with your kids."

—Deb

"Once you make the decision to stay at home, don't second-guess your decision. If you're feeling guilty the whole time you're home, like you should (or would rather) be somewhere else, your kids will sense that. Enjoy it while it lasts, and don't look back."

—Amy

"Don't be too shy to offer and ask for help. We often feel we should be able to do everything on our own. I think most moms would be happy to have help and to give help."

—Heather

"Be proud of what you are doing, and realize that your children are the true beneficiaries of your willingness to stay home."

—Stacey

"A danger of being a Stay-at-Home mom is that we tend to do way too much for our kids long after they've stopped needing the assistance, and it's not good for them. In the end, all we do is infantilize them. Keep your eye on the big picture: Your job is to guide your child into adulthood, not to teach him or her that being a mom means being a slave."

—Sandra

"Get used to going out with the kids to all kinds of places. If you let yourself get stuck at home, you'll be miserable, and your children won't learn about the world around them, or how to socialize in it. Teach your kids the proper way to behave in various settings. It'll be good for all of you."

—Megan

"Have fun with your kids. Get down on the ground to see the world through their eyes. You'll appreciate everything around you a little bit more. You've never known the joy of finding a worm under a rock until you hear your two-year-old squeal with joy (and fright) over his discovery."

—Elizabeth

"Seek advice from other moms who are going through the same child-development stage you are. And keep in touch with old friends. They keep you grounded."

—Nancy

"Not every woman thinks her husband is capable of, say, changing a diaper as well as she is. My advice to new moms: Let your spouse do these things. If you give the hint that you're better at the childcare tasks than he is, you'll end up doing all of them long into the future. I know moms who have to manage the feeding/bathing/homework at the end of the day prior to getting out in the evening themselves because they made it clear, long ago, that this was their terrain, and so it has remained."

—Pat

"I've learned that children are different people at different times of the day. Three-year-olds get cranky at dinnertime. There's no sense in trying to reason with them then. At those times I tried to have even more patience than usual, but sometimes the best thing to do is to walk into another room for a few minutes."

—Debbie

"Some of the best advice I've ever gotten is that the most well-rounded kids come from homes that are not run perfectly, because they learn to adjust, cope, and manage better. I live on that inspiration, a lot!"

—Andrea

The Moms You Met

The following women responded in detail to the forty-question survey distributed for *The Guide* in the spring of 2007. Some names have been changed by request. Most children's ages are rounded to their next closest birthday. A woman's years as a Stay-at-Home mom are also rounded to the nearest whole and may include the time from a child's birth to the present—or combined periods during which she moved out of and back into the workforce. An asterisk (*) indicates the woman has returned to the workforce either full or part time after being a Stay-at-Home mom.

NAME	AGE	FORMER OCCUPATION	CHILD(REN)'S AGE(S)	YEARS AS A SAHM
Amy	34	book editor	4, 1	4
Andrea	35	administrative assistant	9, 8	9*
Annabel	36	executive recruiter	3, 3, 3 months	2
Anne	33	biologist	2 (+ expecting)	2
Aoife	38	magazine editor	3, 10 months	2
Barbara	38	finance manager	9, 6	4*
Beth	34	pension fund manager	2, 1	1
Cindy	42	attorney	7, 4	7
Colleen	36	sales coordinator	11, 8, 7, 2 (+ expecting)	10
Deb	38	pediatric physical therapist	7, 4, 16 months	7
Debbie	36	teacher	9, 7, 5	9*
Denise	37	bank management	6, 3, 2	6
Diane A.	39	ad agency supervisor	4, 2	4
Diane D.	38	business consultant	14 months (+ expecting)	1
Dixie	59	biostatistician	25, 19	20+
Elizabeth	30	Navy intelligence analyst	3, 14 months	3
Emily	31	financial operations specialist	4, 2 (+ expecting)	3
Erin S.	32	corporate trainer	4, 1	4
Erin Z.	41	bond trader	8, 5	5
Florida	40	accounting manager	9, 8, 8	4*
Gerri	35	human resources director	4, 2	4
Ginny	42	business manager/model	24, 22, 18, 14	16
Heather	30	preschool teacher/nanny	6, 4, 2	6
Jen	32	attorney	3, 1	3

NAME	AGE	FORMER OCCUPATION	CHILD(REN)'S AGE(S)	YEARS AS A SAHM
Jennifer	30	office manager	13 weeks	13 weeks
Jennifer D.	35	accounting manager	10 months	10 months
Jill	43	corporate vice president	4, 2	4
Johanna	47	bookkeeper	28, 28, 14	7
Joni	31	Internet sales strategist	4, 2	4
Julie C.	38	public relations executive	4, 4	2
Julie F.	38	bond trader	3, 2, 8 months	3
Kanoko	32	student	2	2
Kara	31	hotel sales manager	4, 2	4
Kellie	36	sports agency assistant	6, 16 months	6
Krishna	35	software marketer	4, 2	4
Laura	37	editor/military linguist	5, 2	5
Laura P.	37	social worker	6, 3	6
Linda	39	systems consultant	7, 5, 3, 1	7
Lisa	37	project manager	8 months	8 months
Liz H.	38	training and development	3, 1	3
Liz R.	40	sales and marketing	10, 8, 5	9
Lyn	42	attorney	12, 10, 8	11
Mary	34	brand manager	4, 1	4
Maura	38	teacher	13, 11, 9, 6, 5	13
Megan	28	writer/editor	4, 1	4
Molly	33	project manager	2	2
Nancy	42	admin assistant/analyst	15, 13, 8	12
Nicki	33	marketing coordinator	6, 3, 10 months	6

NAME	AGE	FORMER OCCUPATION	CHILD(REN)'S AGE(S)	YEARS AS A SAHM
Pat	40	social worker	11, 7	11
Pilar	35	sales representative	3	3
Rachel	38	graphic designer	7, 4, 1	7
Robin	34	defense analyst	4, 6 weeks	4
Samantha	36	retail buyer, muralist	8, 6, 2	8
Sandra	50	trial lawyer	12, 10	12
Sarah B.	30	fundraiser	4, 2 (+ expecting)	4
Sarah G.	42	museum retail director	10, 8	5
Sheriene	41	business consultant	3, 1	3
Sherry	30	office manager	3, 1	3
Stacey	40	registered nurse	10, 8	9
Tina	34	sales representative	5, 3	3
Tracy	41	accounting manager	2 (+ expecting)	2
Whitney	39	museum educator	3, 2 months	3

ACKNOWLEDGMENTS

W ords cannot express how thankful I am that Brooke Warner, then the acquisitions editor of Seal Press, didn't throw my proposal in the trash back in the fall of 2006, when I sent her an unsolicited submission for a book I called *The MotherHood: What It's Really Like to Leave a Career to Stay Home with Your Kids.* For reasons I don't know, Brooke chose to work with me, by email, over the course of several months to shape my query into a full-fledged book proposal. Alas, in the end, Seal chose to pass on the project. More than a dozen other publishing houses and agents passed as well. They liked the writing. They liked my credentials. They just weren't into producing another motherhood book, especially one so specifically targeted to Stay-at-Home moms.

A couple of months after Seal rejected my pitch, Brooke contacted me to say that she and Seal's managing editor had been brainstorming about ways to make a Stay-at-Home motherhood book work, and she wondered if I'd take a stab at the idea. Using a page of notes Brooke sent me, along with my original *MotherHood* pitch, I spent a weekend crafting a revised proposal. Having been turned down repeatedly before, I didn't want to devote more than that one weekend to working on something that would never come to pass. A few weeks later, my proposal was resoundingly accepted by Seal's editorial board.

The Seal Press managing editor who championed and came up with the idea for *The Stay-at-Home Survival Guide* is a former Stay-at-Home mom who made her career comeback after being at home with her two young daughters. I believe that Laura Mazer, having been a Stay-at-Home mother, was able to understand the need for such women to be supported—and most of all *heard*. It is because of her that *The Stay-at-Home Survival Guide* has become a reality.

When Laura left Seal to freelance, she shared the final editing on the book with Leslie Miller, a former Seal editor and current mother of two small boys, and the cofounder of Girl Friday Productions, an editorial consulting firm. Leslie and I spent a sleepless weekend together—she was in Seattle, where she lives, I was home in Maryland—fine-tuning the manuscript for production. Both Laura and Leslie (neither of whom I have ever met or spoken with at length, as we worked together entirely by email) provided wonderful comments, guidance, and solutions. I am so appreciative of their time, wisdom, insight, and support.

More personal thanks go out to my friends, relatives, acquaintances, and former colleagues who passed along my call for Stay-at-Home mom survey respondents. And I am beholden to every woman who completed the at times very personal forty-question survey on which so much of this book is based. It took a lot of trust for them to put those responses into an email and send them to a person most don't know. Similarly trusting were the women I *do* know who shared with me details about their own lives. (When one gal asked if she could see her friend's survey responses, I refused, and that's still the rule.) I am thankful to my many Stay-at-Home mom friends, both near and far, for letting me be part of their lives and for being part of mine.

Closer to home, I thank my mother and especially my sister, Jennifer, for helping with my children so I could squeeze in extra writing time. I am grateful to both of my talented parents for passing down to me the creative, organizational, and literary genes that helped me be able to actually write a nearly 400-page book part time while caring for three young children full time. I absolutely thank my husband, Brian, for taking charge of the threesome at night and on the weekends so I could run off with my laptop. And if it weren't for the overwhelming love I have for our first born, Jack, I might never have pursued a career as a Stay-at-Home mom—well, at least not until his twin sisters, Ava and Corinne, put me on the path. In every way, if it weren't for Brian and our three children, I couldn't have written this book.

Stanton and her
young trio in 2003.

About the Author

Prior to leaving her Manhattan-based magazine career and becoming a Stay-at-Home mom, Melissa Stanton was a senior editor at *People* magazine. Previously, she spent a decade at *LIFE* magazine, where she rose from the reporter ranks to become a senior editor for the magazine and editor-in-chief of assorted books and special issues. Stanton's articles have appeared in *The New York Times*, *Glamour*, *Parenting*, *Redbook*, *Chesapeake Family*, and *Organize*, among other publications. A New York native, she has a bachelor's degree from Fordham University and a master's in public health from Hunter College. Stanton lives with her husband and three children in a rural suburb of Washington, D.C.

SELECTED TITLES FROM SEAL PRESS

How to Fit a Car Seat on a Camel: And Other Misadventures Traveling with Kids edited by Sarah Franklin. $15.95, 1-58005-242-8. This anthology of outrageous and funny stories captures the mayhem that accompanies traveling with children.

I Wanna Be Sedated: 30 Writers on Parenting Teenagers edited by Faith Conlon and Gail Hudson. $15.95, 1-58005-127-8. With hilarious and heartfelt essays, this anthology will reassure parents of teenagers that they are not alone.

Dirty Sugar Cookies: Culinary Observations, Questionable Taste by Ayun Halliday. $14.95, 1-58005-150-2. Ayun Halliday is back with comical and unpredictable essays about her disastrous track record in the kitchen and her culinary observations.

Confessions of a Naughty Mommy: How I Found My Lost Libido by Heidi Raykeil. $14.95, 1-58005-157-X. The Naughty Mommy shares her bedroom woes and woo-hoos with other mamas who are rediscovering their sex lives after baby and are ready to think about it, talk about it, and DO it.

The Truth Behind the Mommy Wars: Who Decides What Makes a Good Mother? by Miriam Peskowitz. $15.95, 1-58005-129-4. A groundbreaking book that reveals the truth behind the "wars" between working mothers and Stay-at-Home moms.

Women in Overdrive: Find Balance and Overcome Burn Out at Any Age by Nora Isaacs. $14.95, 1-58005-161-8. For women who take on more than they can handle, this book highlights how women of different age sets are affected by overdrive and what they can do to avoid burnout.